Tomashi Jackson
The Land Claim

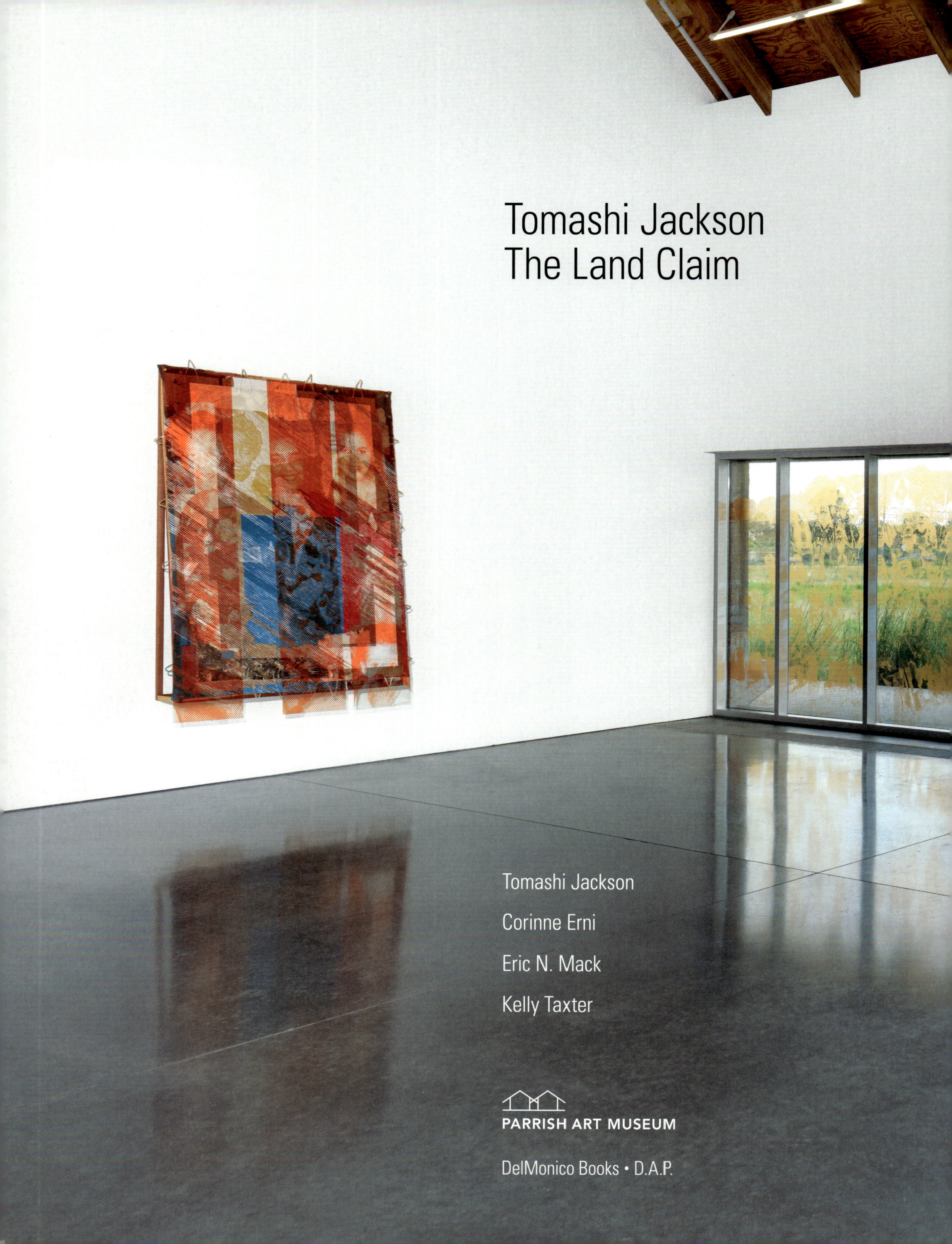

Tomashi Jackson
The Land Claim

Tomashi Jackson

Corinne Erni

Eric N. Mack

Kelly Taxter

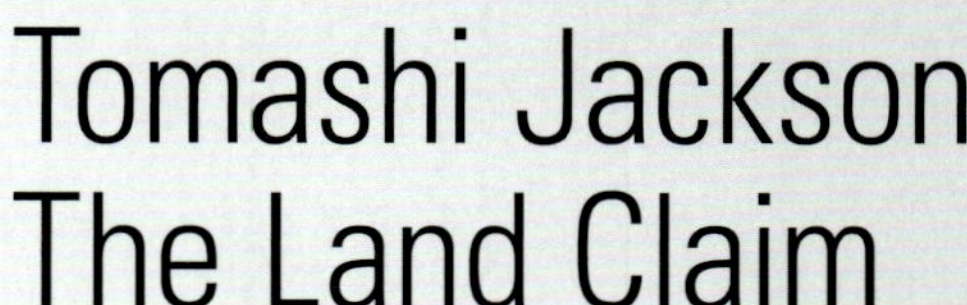

DelMonico Books • D.A.P.

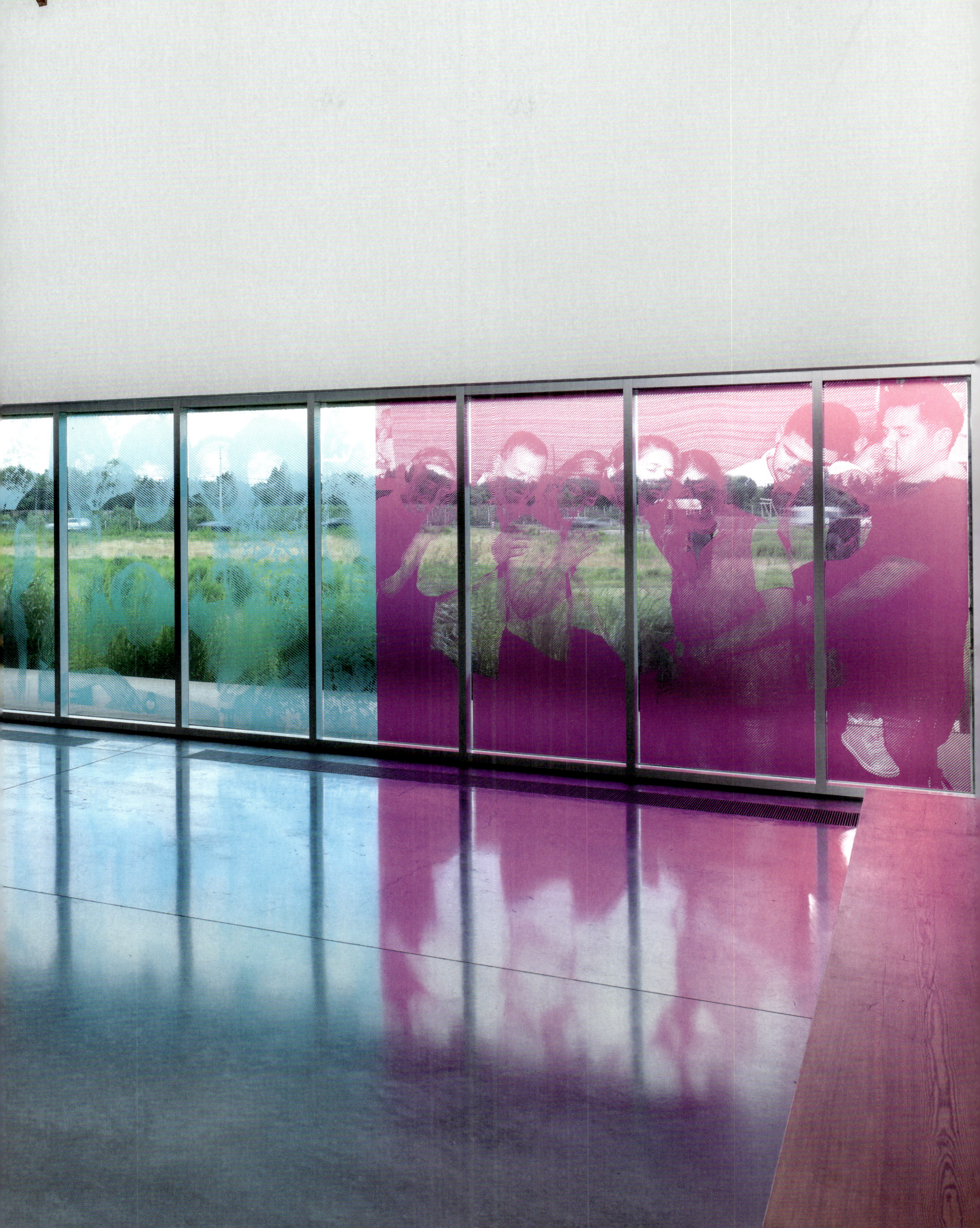

Published in conjunction with the exhibition:

Tomashi Jackson: The Land Claim

July 11–November 7, 2021

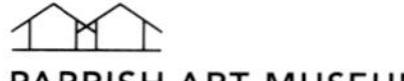

PARRISH ART MUSEUM

279 Montauk Highway
Water Mill, New York 11976

First published in 2021 by the
Parrish Art Museum

Parrish Art Museum
279 Montauk Highway
Water Mill, New York 11976
parrishart.org

Library of Congress Control Number: 2021914904

ISBN 978-1-63681-033-1

Designer: Eileen Boxer, boxerdesign.com

Cover designed by Tomashi Jackson

Managing Editor: Corinne Erni

Printer: Trifolio SRL, Verona, Italy

Cover: Tomashi Jackson, *Among Heirs (Niamuck and
Azurest)*, 2021. Detail. Photo © Dario Lasagni

Inside front cover: Tomashi Jackson, *Among Harvests
(Aserrin de colores)*, 2021. Detail. Photo © Dario Lasagni

Inside back cover: Tomashi Jackson, *Among Protectors
(Hawthorne Road and the Pell Case)*, 2021. Detail. Photo
© Dario Lasagni

Previous spread: *Tomashi Jackson: The Land Claim*, 2021.
Installation view. Parrish Art Museum, Water Mill, NY.
Photo © Dario Lasagni

Following spread: Still from projection of video collage
Self Portrait: Tale of Two Michaels (2014) onto Parrish Art
Museum, 2020. Photo © Philippe Cheng

Plates pp. 65–95: All photos © Dario Lasagni

Tomashi Jackson: The Land Claim is made possible, in
part, thanks to the generous support of The Andy Warhol
Foundation for the Visual Arts; National Endowment
for the Arts; The Bandier Family Foundation; The Mr.
and Mrs. Raymond J. Horowitz Fund for Publications;
The Dorothy Lichtenstein ArtsReach Fund, established
by Agnes Gund; Connie Tilton; The Lumpkin-Boccuzzi
Family; The Deborah Buck Foundation; Miyoung Lee
and Neil Simpkins; Sandy and Stephen Perlbinder; The
Speyer Family Foundation; and Nina Yankowitz. We are
also grateful to Night Gallery, Los Angeles, and Tilton
Gallery, New York, for their in-kind support.

We are pleased to partner with The Watermill Center in
support of Tomashi Jackson's project and acknowledge
their generous partnership through their Inga Maren
Otto Fellowship.

The Museum's programs are made possible, in part, by
the New York State Council on the Arts, with the support
of Governor Andrew M. Cuomo and the New York State
Legislature, and by the property taxpayers from the
Southampton School District and the Tuckahoe Common
School District.

Contents

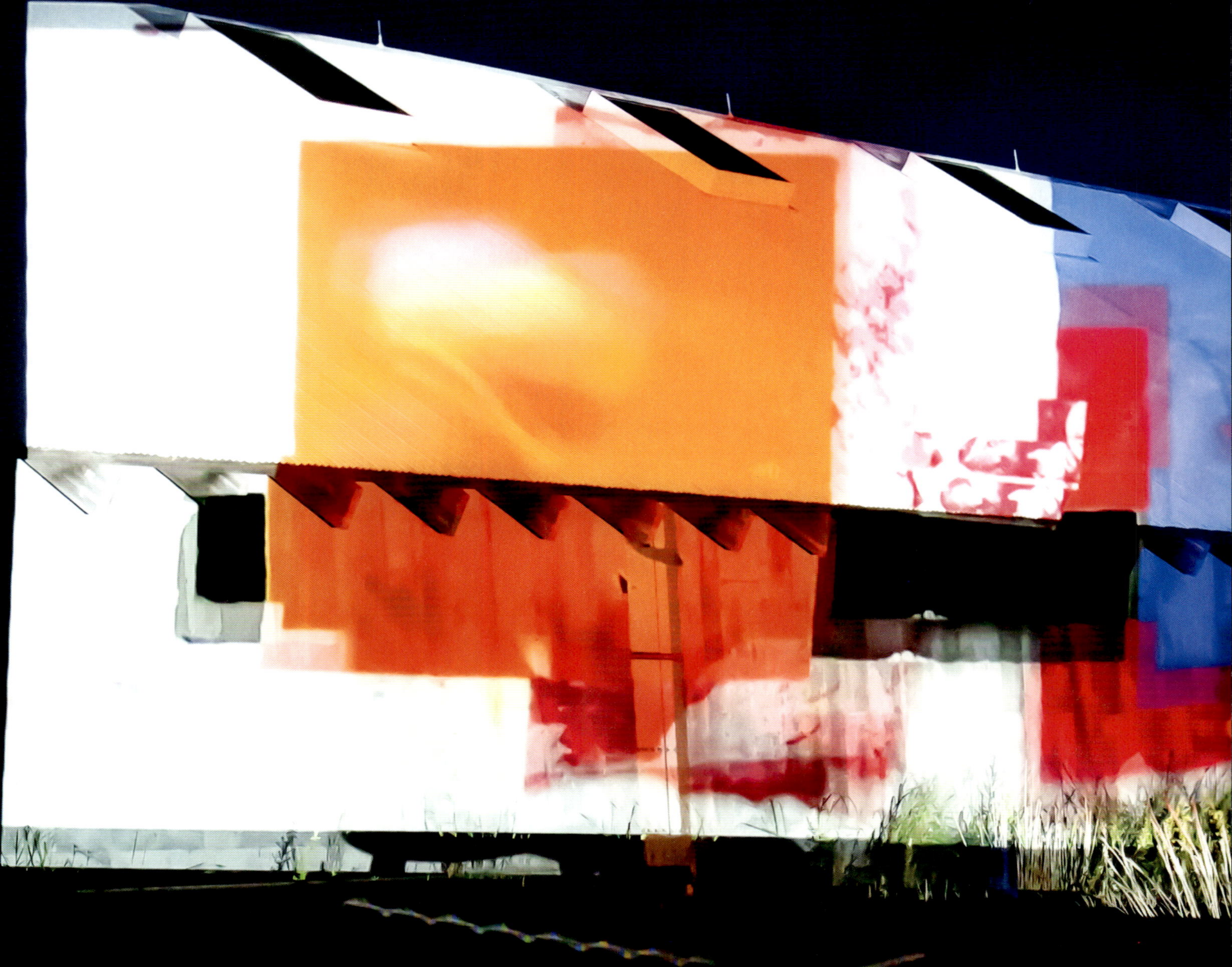

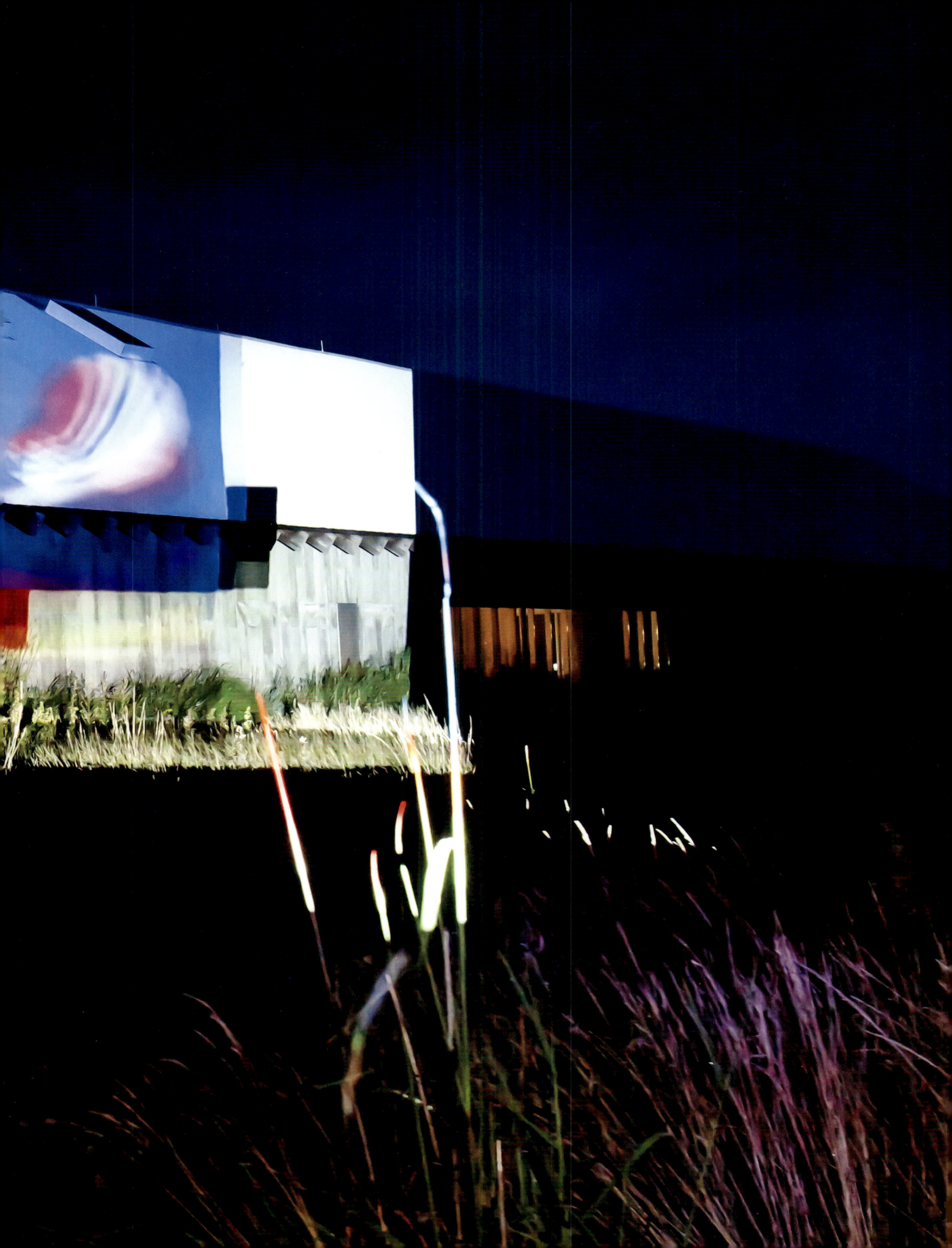

Tomashi Jackson's intricately layered and boldly composed work reveals an unrelenting interrogation of form and meaning. She elicits an interplay between recognizable objects and abstract gestures, density and lightness, opaqueness and transparency. Jackson visually entices and at the same time provokes an urgent discourse around systemic racism and the perpetual disenfranchisement and displacement of BIPOC (Black, Indigenous, and people of color) communities.

Tomashi Jackson: The Land Claim is an exhibition of work newly created for the Parrish Art Museum that addresses the historical and present-day experiences of BIPOC communities on the East End of Long Island. It arose from Jackson's yearlong engagement with members of the area's Indigenous, Black, and Latinx families, who are linked by concerns around housing, transportation, livelihood, migration, and agriculture. Over time, the Hamptons has morphed from a predominantly farming and fishing culture to an artists' haven, to an elite enclave for the very wealthy—an evolution that has systematically erased certain cultures and histories. *The Land Claim* tells a local story, yet it is also a quintessentially American story.

Jackson's exhibition is an opportunity to foster a deeper understanding of who we are and what we have been as a community and a culture, both locally and nationally. Art and artists not only reflect our time but also have the power to change it. Through their work, artists help us move forward together with empathy, equity, and optimism.

As the newly appointed Director of the Parrish, I am grateful to host *The Land Claim* at this moment of national reckoning with white supremacy. The Museum is proud to offer itself as a platform for critical discourse, connection, and discovery.

Organized by Corinne Erni, Senior Curator of ArtsReach and Special Projects, *Tomashi Jackson: The Land Claim* is supported by the Dorothy Lichtenstein ArtsReach Fund, established by Agnes Gund in 2017. The ArtsReach Fund recognizes that the Parrish serves a year-round community profoundly affected by social injustices; it reinforces our efforts to examine and address inequity through artists' voices, and affirms the power of art to transform lives and challenge the status quo. Initiatives backed by ArtsReach bring focused, meaningful programming to the Parrish, and foster community in the broadest sense to transcend geographic, racial, and socioeconomic barriers.

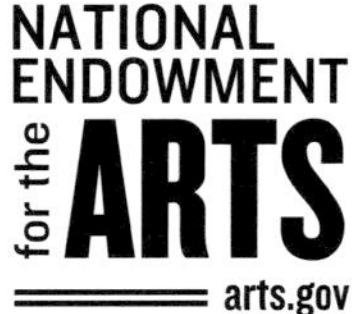

Acknowledgments

Tomashi Jackson: The Land Claim could not have been realized without the dedication of many individuals. We are deeply grateful for the generous exhibition and publication support provided by The Andy Warhol Foundation for the Visual Arts; National Endowment for the Arts; The Bandier Family Foundation; The Mr. and Mrs. Raymond J. Horowitz Fund for Publications; The Dorothy Lichtenstein ArtsReach Fund, established by Agnes Gund; Connie Tilton; The Lumpkin-Boccuzzi Family; The Deborah Buck Foundation; Miyoung Lee and Neil Simpkins; Sandy and Stephen Perlbinder; The Speyer Family Foundation; and Nina Yankowitz.

We are also grateful to Night Gallery, Los Angeles, and Tilton Gallery, New York, for their in-kind support.

We are pleased to partner with The Watermill Center in support of Tomashi Jackson's project, and we acknowledge the Center's generous partnership through the Inga Maren Otto Fellowship.

The Museum's programs are made possible, in part, by the New York State Council on the Arts, with the support of Governor Andrew M. Cuomo and the New York State Legislature, and by the property taxpayers from the Southampton School District and the Tuckahoe Common School District.

We are immensely thankful to the artist Tomashi Jackson for her luminous enthusiasm, determination, and commitment. Her work honors communities of color in the Hamptons by shining light on their untold stories. Jackson's research was nurtured by many friends and partners on the East End, including Donnamarie Barnes, Curator and Archivist at Sylvester Manor Educational Farm and Co-Director and Chair, Plain Sight Project; Bonnie Cannon, Executive Director, Bridgehampton Child Care & Recreational Center; Dr. Georgette Grier-Key, Executive Director, Eastville Community Historical Society of Sag Harbor; Minerva Perez, Executive Director, OLA of Eastern Long Island (Organización Latino-Americana); and Richard "Juni" Wingfield, former community liaison for Southampton School District; and members of the Shinnecock Indian Nation, in particular Kelly Dennis, Esq., Secretary, Shinnecock Indian Nation Council of Trustees, and Coordinator, Residency & Public Programs at The Watermill Center; Jeremy Dennis, fine art photographer; Tela Loretta Troge, attorney and counselor at law; and Shane Weeks, artist, dancer, drummer, educator, hunter, and fisherman. We thank photographer Steven Molina Contreras for the poignant portraits of his family; Martha Schnee for the exquisite drawings; and K. Anthony Jones and Rachel Vogel for editing the interviews. Thanks as well to Bryan Downey; Odell Ferebee; Durell Godfrey; Christopher Patrick; Hope Sandrow; Dana Shaw, Photo Editor of the Express News Group; and Zachary Taylor, Curator and Registrar of the Southampton Historical Society, for archival material and stories. We recognize our friends from the press, David Rattray, Editor of *The East Hampton Star* and cofounder of Plain Sight Project; Joe Shaw, Executive Editor at Express News Group; and Dana Shaw, Photo Editor at Express News Group, for their devotion to unearthing the truth.

We thank Corinne Erni, Senior Curator of ArtsReach and Special Projects, who invited Tomashi Jackson and worked closely with her. They were assisted by Curatorial Fellow Lauren Ruiz, who engaged in critical research. Thanks to composer Michael J. Schumacher for bringing the voices of the interviewees to life. We are grateful to Eric N. Mack for contributing an essay to this catalog and appreciate his unique insight into his longtime friend's work. Finally, we thank Connie Tilton, Meagan Bartsch, and Jacob Billiar of Tilton Gallery, who played an invaluable part in this project, as well as Davida Nemeroff of Night Gallery.

At the Parrish Art Museum, staff worked diligently to bring this endeavor to fruition. Chris Siefert, Deputy Director; Cara Conklin-Wingfield, Education Director, who introduced us to those advocating for their communities; Alicia Longwell, Lewis B. and Dorothy Cullman Chief Curator, Art and Education; Registrar Chris McNamara; Preparator Robin Klopfer; Curatorial Assistant Savannah Petrick; Director of Communications Susan Galardi; Grants Manager Eliza Rand; and Administrative Assistant Barbara Jansson were all indispensable in realizing *Tomashi Jackson: The Land Claim*. We fondly remember Chief Financial Officer Janet Fernandez for her judicious guidance until her passing in March 2021; and we are indebted to Terrie Sultan, former Parrish Director, for championing this project early on.

We are fortunate in our ongoing partnership with our friends at The Watermill Center, Director Elka Rifkin and Director of Institutional Advancement Micah Bozeman. Thanks to Eileen Boxer for her creative approach to the design and production of this book and Mary DelMonico, Publisher, DelMonico•D.A.P., for its distribution;; Anna Jardine, Lauren DiGiulio, and Hilary Becker for their copyediting; Miko McGinty for the exhibition graphics; Ruben Palencia for the frames; José Vargas and Jeff Harris from Duggal Visual Solutions, New York, for their prints; Dario Lasagni for the installation photography; Philippe Cheng for capturing the projections; and Rachel Judlowe of Judlowe, LLC, for communications advice.

We are especially grateful to the Parrish Art Museum Board of Trustees, and to the intrepid leadership of our Co-Chairs, President Mary E. Frank and Mark Renton. This ambitious project was fueled by their unyielding support and encouragement.

Kelly Taxter
Director,
Parrish Art Museum

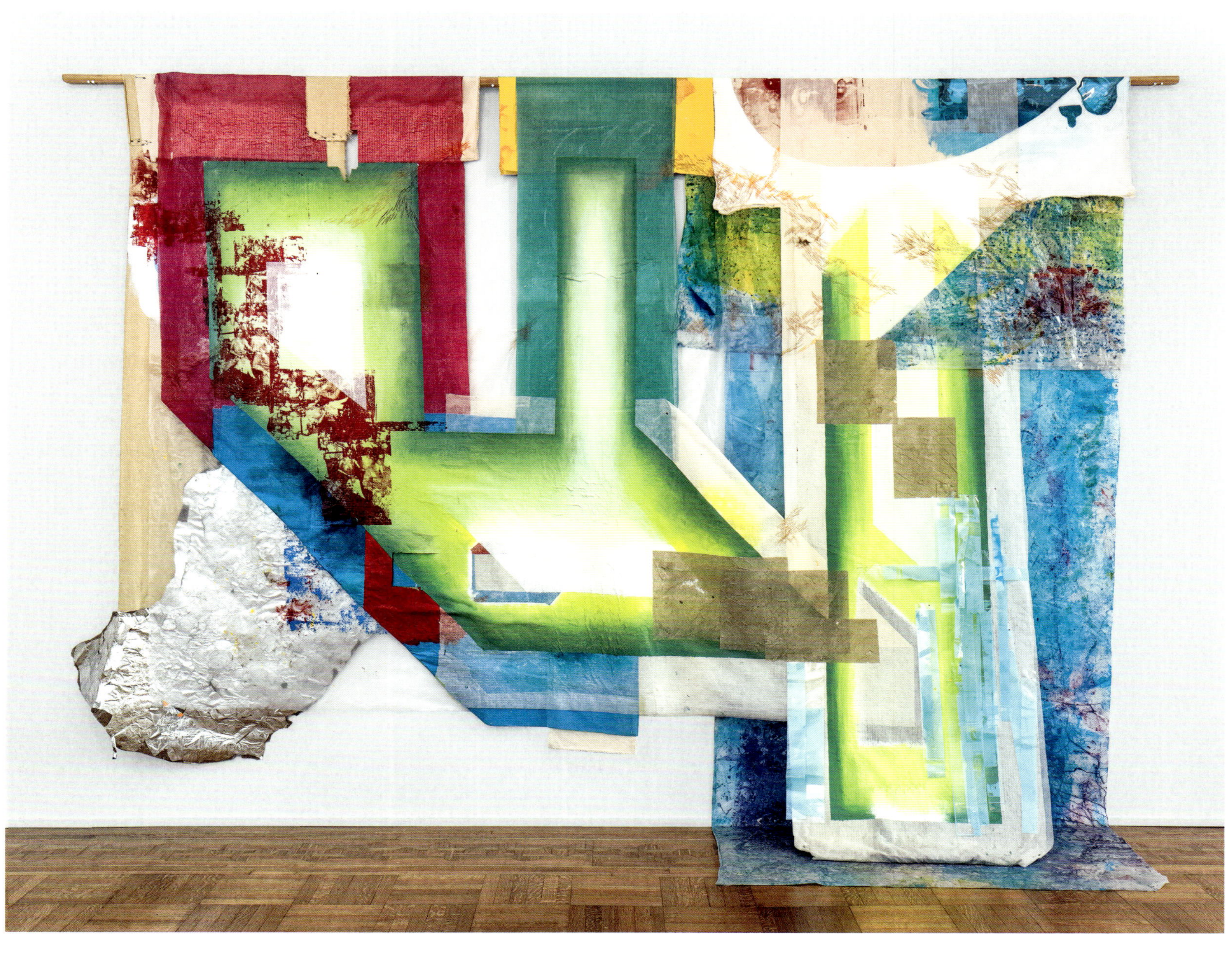

Corinne Erni

Tomashi Jackson: The Land Claim

A Sublime Encounter
Tilton Gallery, January 7, 2017

I first met Tomashi Jackson during a snowstorm, on the last day of her second solo exhibition, *The Subliminal is Now*. I had journeyed into New York City from Water Mill, Long Island, determined to catch this show by a young artist who had piqued my interest. Upon entering the gallery, I felt a warm embrace, paired with something echoing the cosmic force outside. Bursts of colors, shapes, and materials had been gathered, layered, collaged, draped, and suspended in a dexterous choreography. The paintings were born of large but controlled gestures, rendered with reflected and assured precision in various media. The sculptures were made of tubular knits draped over wood structures and paralleled the colors of the paintings in stronger, condensed tones. The video collages—poetic celebrations of lives interrupted—felt like extensions of both. I was captivated by the energy and aesthetics of the works and intrigued by their titles referencing landmark Civil Rights–Era legal cases concerning education and more recent examples of police brutality targeting Black children (fig. 1). Meeting Jackson was fortuitous, and our conversations led to this exhibition at the Parrish Art Museum.

Jackson told me that the work in *The Subliminal is Now* was inspired by a 2014 Boston City Council hearing on school transportation for Boston Public Schools. She had documented that with video and photography while supporting the efforts of various organizations to preserve school bus service. She realized how little she understood about the 1954 case of *Brown v. Board of Education of Topeka*, which was mentioned by community members, advocates, and city councillors testifying at the hearing. Months later, as a first-year graduate candidate at the Yale School of Art, Jackson began reading the history of *Brown*—transcripts of the preliminary cases and the Supreme Court case, argued by Thurgood Marshall and the National Association for the Advancement of Colored People Legal Defense and Educational Fund. At the same time, while studying color, she was reintroduced to Josef Albers's 1963 text *Interaction of Color* and found similarities between the language describing color perception in visual art in Albers's book and the language used in legal transcripts concerning segregation in education. She realized that both Marshall and Albers had arrived at the conclusion that color perception is not static and that the values of colors are defined by their boundaries.

Avocado Seed Soup (Davis, et. al. v. County School Board of Prince Edward County) (Brown, et. al. v. Board of Education of Topeka) (Sweatt v. Painter), from 2016 (fig. 2), was a particularly imposing work—a multilayered wall hanging approximately fourteen feet wide and nine feet high. Constructed of painted geometric forms, screen prints, rawhide, foil, sand, screen-printed mylar, and embroidery, which were painted, pinned, or sewn onto layers of gauze and plastic sheeting, the work embodied visual beauty and thoughtfully suggestive narrative. Making it was a challenge. "I was guided by music and research about school segregation, on a mission to make things that didn't exist already," Jackson told me. She wanted to better understand her intuitive relationship with geometry, not just inside the square of a painting, but by making the actual shape of the painting. Moved by the song title "Avocado Seed

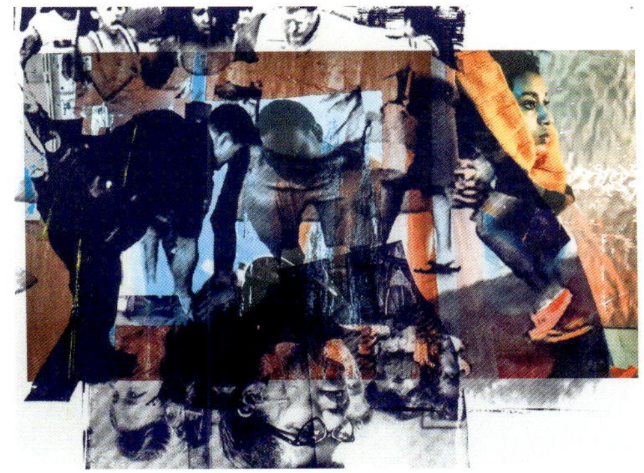

Fig. 1
The Essence of Innocence: Texas Pool Party, 2016
Mixed media on paper
22 × 30 inches
26¼ × 34¼ inches (framed)
Courtesy the artist and Tilton Gallery, New York

Fig. 2
Avocado Seed Soup (Davis, et. al. v. County School Board of Prince Edward County) (Brown, et. al. v. Board of Education of Topeka) (Sweatt v. Painter), 2016
Mixed media on gauze, canvas, rawhide and wood
111 × 168 × 32¾ inches
Courtesy the artist and Tilton Gallery, New York
Collection of the Museum of Contemporary Art, Los Angeles

Soup Symphony," by Slim Gaillard and Leo Watson, she created a pouch at the bottom right corner of the painting, filled with avocado seeds, that serves as a foot gently pulling the painted layers of gauze away from the wall and anchors the piece to the ground.

Jackson's attraction to color and soft fabrics that contrast rigid structural frames is a recurring element in her work. Her knitted-fiber works serve multiple functions: as singular wall-bound framed works, as sculptures stretched around freestanding or leaning wooden forms (fig. 3), and as multicolored wrapping to merge human forms into specific paintings and landscapes for her time-based video collage works.

In the 2014 video collage *Self Portrait: Tale of Two Michaels*, Jackson pairs herself with artist Alteronce Gumby (fig. 4) to explore the narratives of two Michaels raised in Ferguson, Missouri: the late Michael Brown, Jr., and the singer Michael McDonald. In the video, Jackson and Gumby are both covered with knitted color studies, as they sway and lip-sync to the sound of "It Keeps You Runnin'," from the 1976 album *Takin' It to the Streets* by the Doobie Brothers, of whom McDonald was a member. The knitted color studies join the figures with the color field painting behind them, and meld with video footage from Al Jazeera America's "Ferguson: City Under Siege," which documents demonstrations responding to the murder of eighteen-year-old Michael Brown; the absence of formal consequences for his killer, Darren Wilson; and the militarized response of local police.

Jackson titled her exhibition *The Subliminal is Now* as a historic nod to "The Sublime Is Now," the 1948 essay by Abstract Expressionist painter Barnett Newman. Newman posited that the awe-inspiring in art could be accessed without the figure, that the sublime should be sought through the production of painting itself, and that abstraction was a vehicle for intellectual content. Jackson's replacement of "sublime" with "subliminal" added a layer to Newman's assertion by looking to color interaction as an interrogative lens for viewing societal color perception and its subconscious impact on the value of human life in public space.

This and later exhibitions recall a process that Jackson once described to me in a public talk. While studying experimental sculpture with artist Michael Queenland, she was given the word "vehicle" to consider deeply. From that she formed the following questions regarding existing and potential operations of color: "Can color function as a vehicle for sound? Can sound function as a vehicle for complex narrative? Can complex narrative function as vehicle for emotion? Can emotion function as a vehicle for color?"

Rising Waters of Truth
Whitney Museum of American Art, September 15, 2019

As a participating artist in the 2019 Whitney Biennial, Jackson facilitated a panel discussion titled "From Seneca Village to Brooklyn: A Conversation with Tomashi Jackson." Her work in the Biennial was part of a series based on two cases of displacement of Black communities in New York City, 150 years apart. In 2018, Jackson began following investigative journalism in the online periodical *Kings County Politics* that chronicled the City of New York's use of the Third Party Transfer Program to seize properties owned by Black and Latinx families across rapidly gentrifying boroughs. The stories bore a startling resemblance to the historic 1857 displacement of the community of primarily Black-owned properties known as Seneca Village.

Panelists at the Whitney included archaeologists who had excavated and preserved the site of the village, which was razed to

Fig. 3

Color Study (Mayor Doubles Down) (Same Old, Same Old), 2019

Acrylic fiber, digital prints on vinyl on wood

55¼ × 47 × 8 inches

Courtesy the artist and Tilton Gallery, New York

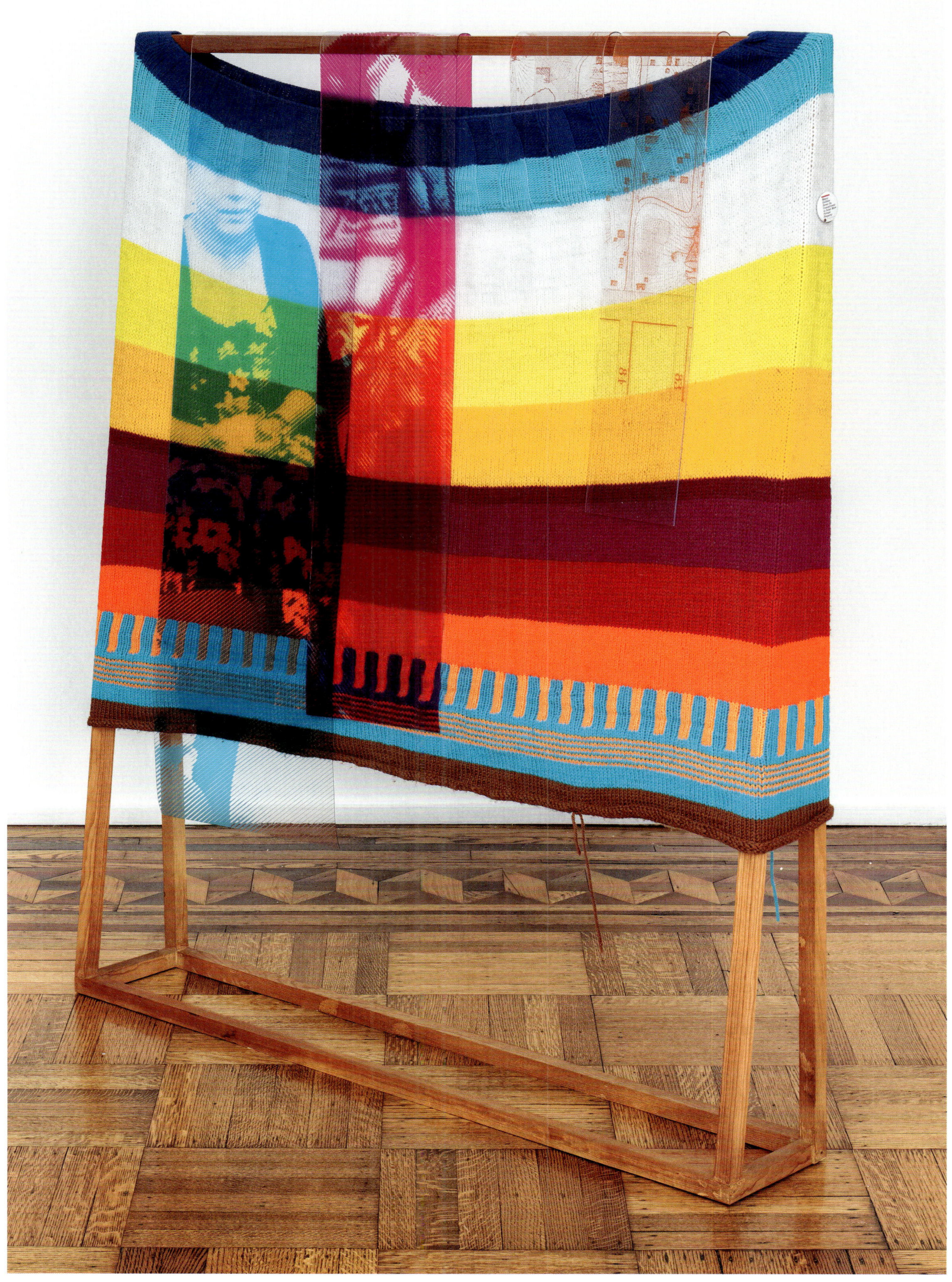

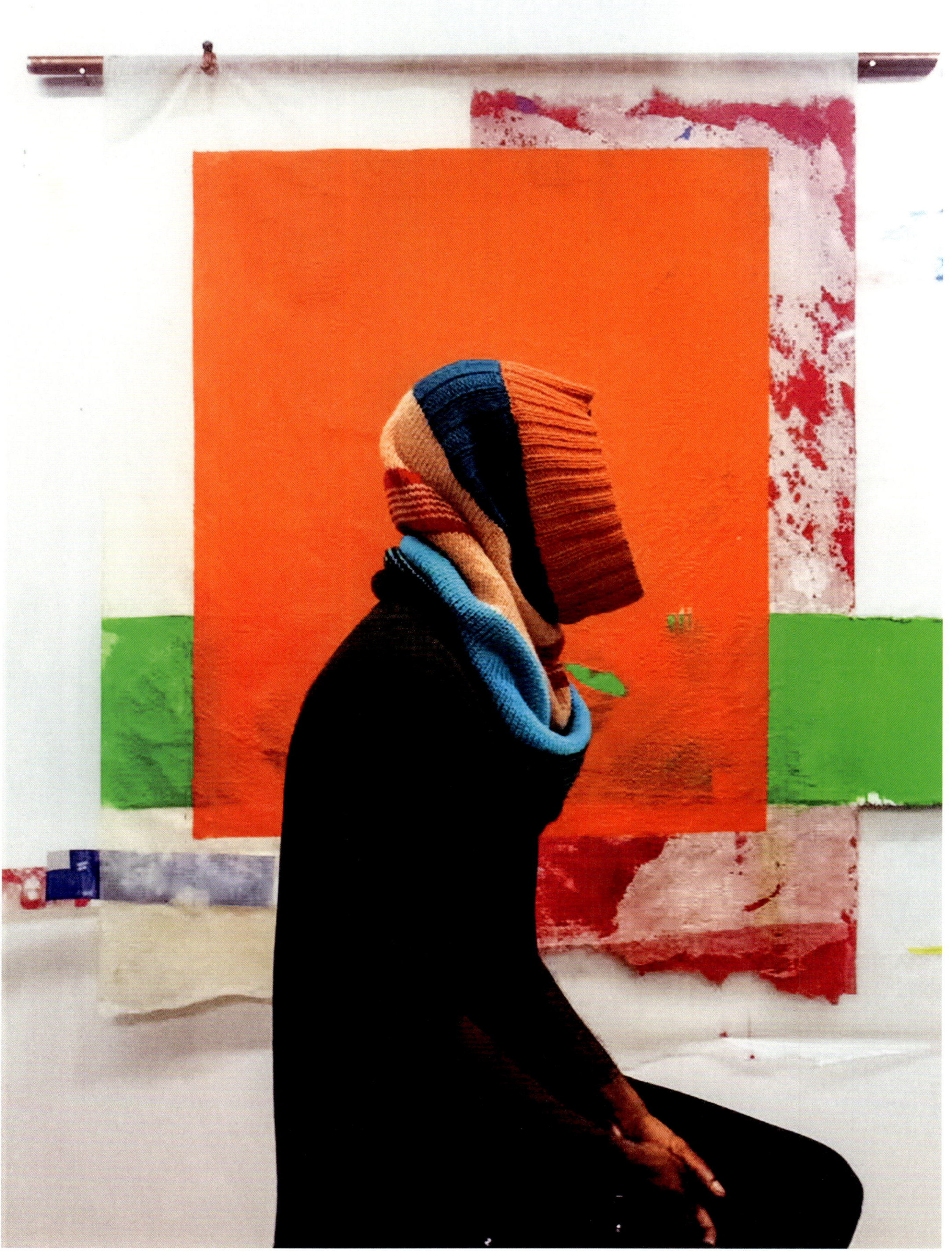

Fig. 4
Alteronce in Hannah, 2014
C-print
41¼ × 32½ inches
Courtesy the artist
and Tilton Gallery,
New York

construct Central Park; a representative of the Central Park Conservancy; a legal scholar and attorney specializing in foreclosure law; three New York City journalists who had covered mass foreclosures of Black and Latinx properties; and an artist and filmmaker who visualized the life of a Black trans woman in Seneca Village.

Jackson described the experience of learning from the panelists' visual and narrative timeline of Black home ownership, suffrage, and dispossession as "standing together in rising waters of truth." Their presentations illustrated pieces of a historic puzzle, which informed her processes of research and production to create her work for the Biennial. To me it was an extraordinary moment: an artist invoking experts in such varied fields who would normally never meet all at once. Her deep understanding of the many layers of truths and myriad ways of telling a story—through articles, photographs, and archives; color, material, and medium; sound, rhythm, and human emotion—was riveting. The panel lasted for two hours, and given the significant engagement among audience members, it could have continued for much longer.

During our many conversations, I was always struck by Jackson's profound desire to tell the heartbreaking stories of racial injustice, discrimination, suppression, and exclusion through art that was aesthetically gratifying. Using both intuition and intention, she continuously challenges herself to refine an artistic vocabulary that charms the viewer into a dialogue.

Jackson's three works in the 2019 Whitney Biennial marked the introduction of large-scale prints of halftone photographic images interacting with her painted surfaces. Drawing and printmaking, always essential to her work, were now visibly integrated into paintings such as *Hometown Buffet Two Blues (Mr. Ronald Callender's building, Seneca Villagers Limited Value Exercise) (Still Thinking of Renisha)*, from 2019 (fig. 5). Perhaps a continuation of the formal quest of *Avocado Seed Soup*, it appears more condensed and charged, featuring laminated paper bags and buttons the artist emblazoned with news headlines about the Third Party Transfer Program scandal, an 1800s New York City demolition map for Seneca Village, a plan drawing for what would become Central Park, and portraits of activists Harriet Tubman, Arturo Schomburg, and Thurgood Marshall.

Make Two Black Property Owners Look Like One (Limited Value Exercise) (Mr. Lyons & Mr. Dorce), a work from the same series and year, is one of Jackson's most explicitly photographic works (fig. 6). Shown in *Time Out of Mind*, her 2019 solo exhibition at Tilton Gallery, it captures how past and current histories of displacement are connected and repeat themselves. Again inspired by Albers, Jackson uses two subtly different reds that intersect in two halftone images, creating the illusion of a mirror image or reflection—uniting two men from two different eras, Albro Lyons and McConnell Dorce, into a single image.

After a residency in its birthplace, Athens, in 2019, Jackson began a deeper investigation into democracy in America. She created two bodies of paintings focused on Black American experiences participating in electoral processes. In *Love Rollercoaster*, shown at the Wexner Center for the Arts, Columbus, Ohio, in September 2020, five paintings collapse images of people lined up to cast ballots in front of the Antioch Baptist Church, at an unidentified location, and in two Ohio counties in 2012 and 2016 with images of Lyndon B. Johnson signing the Voting Rights Act in 1965 in Washington, D.C. (fig. 7). The paintings' surfaces are embedded with ephemera from elections before 2020 in Georgia, Florida, Ohio, and Virginia, as well as Pentelic marble dust collected from the Greek quarry that supplies stone for the restoration of monuments on the Acropolis, including the Parthenon (after which the U.S. Supreme Court is fashioned),

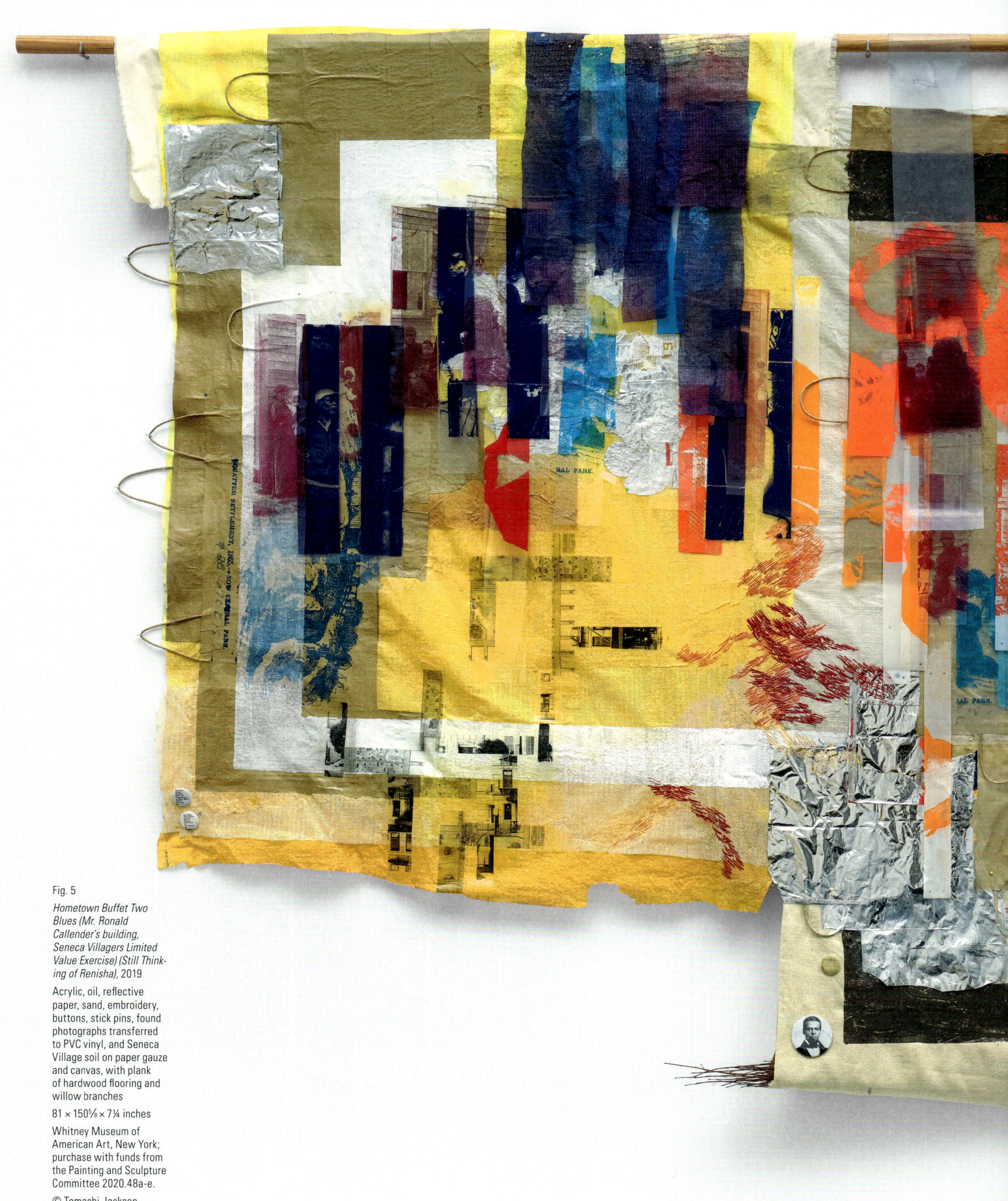

Fig. 5

Hometown Buffet Two Blues (Mr. Ronald Callender's building, Seneca Villagers Limited Value Exercise) (Still Thinking of Renisha), 2019

Acrylic, oil, reflective paper, sand, embroidery, buttons, stick pins, found photographs transferred to PVC vinyl, and Seneca Village soil on paper gauze and canvas, with plank of hardwood flooring and willow branches

81 × 150⅝ × 7¼ inches

Whitney Museum of American Art, New York; purchase with funds from the Painting and Sculpture Committee 2020.48a-e.

© Tomashi Jackson, courtesy Tilton Gallery, New York

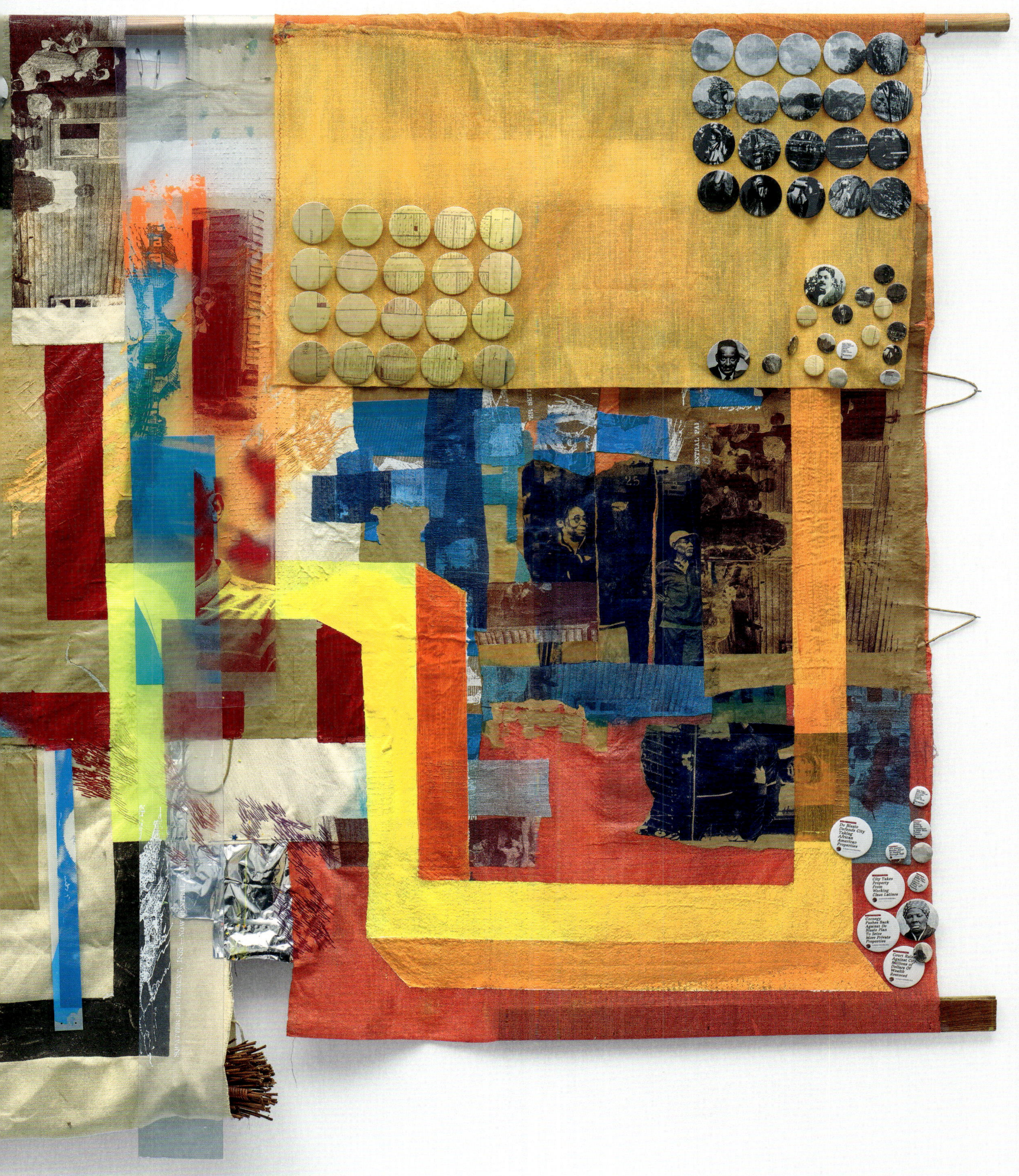

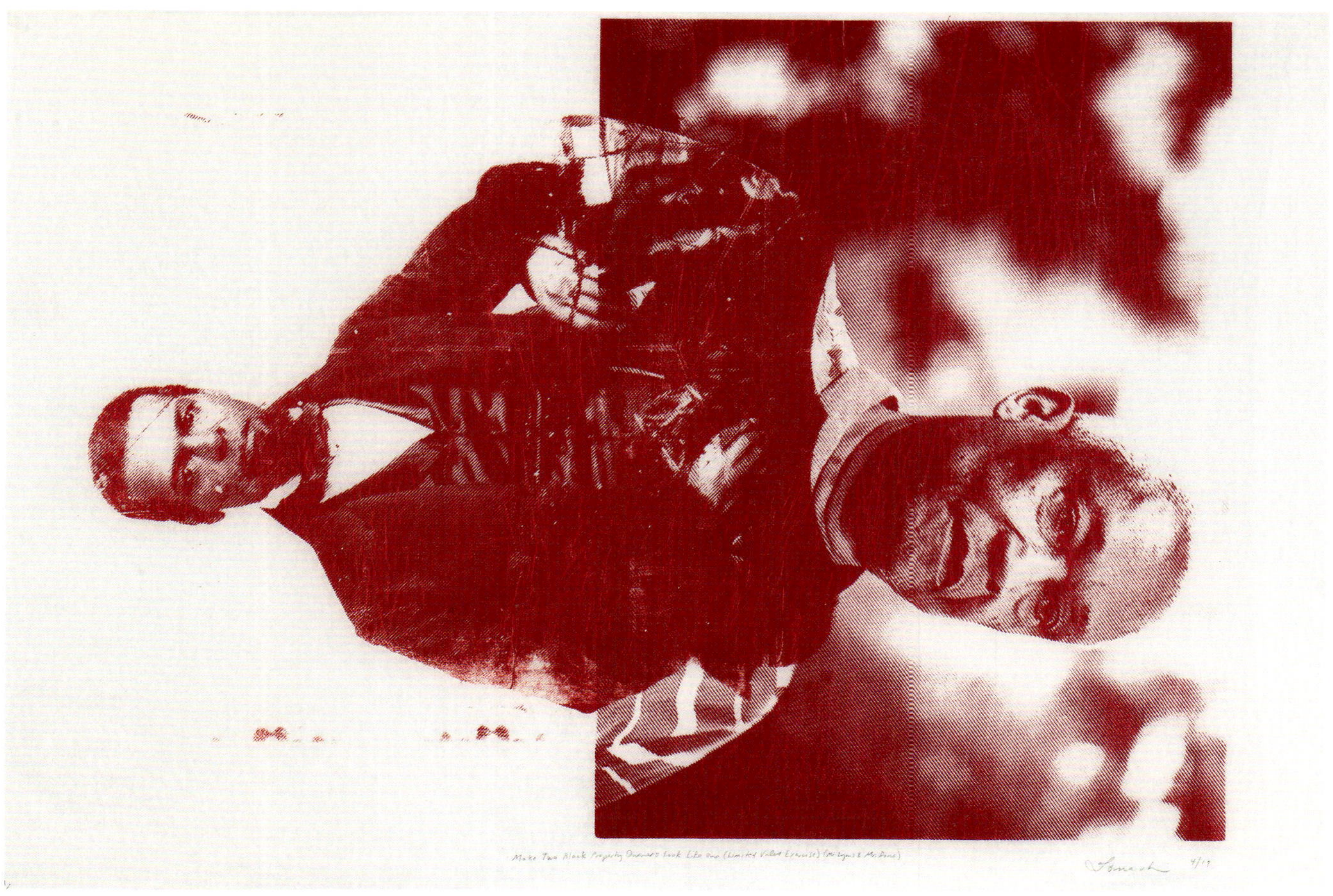

and soil from the Underground Railroad site preserved at Lucy Depp Park in Powell, Ohio.

The frames project from the walls in vertical right triangles inspired by the shape of storefront awnings, allowing the halftone lined colors printed on the vinyl strips that hang from the armature to be cast onto the walls beneath the frames. The lines of color printed on the overlaid vinyl strips interact in a complementary way with the colors painted onto the stretched surface of the work. The layering of material and meaning, the interaction of translucency and color, the collapsing of images from past and current struggles, and the optical illusions they generate allude to the complex and often delusional democratic process in America.

What's Going On in the Hamptons?
Water Mill, New York, January 31, 2020

Jackson visited the Hamptons only a few weeks before the country entered the COVID-19 pandemic lockdown. When we first began discussing a project for the Parrish, she asked me, "What's going on in the Hamptons among Indigenous, Black, and Latinx communities?" As always, understanding the patterns of experience for people of color in public space was important to her. I mentioned the infrastructural segregation of Long Island's East End—the lack of affordable housing and public transportation; displacement of Black and Indigenous communities for development; Immigration and Customs Enforcement checkpoints and raids to uncover undocumented immigrants from Latin America.

To assist in her immersion in the area, I arranged for meetings with advocates, historians, and members of Indigenous, Black, and Latinx communities, many of whom the Parrish partners with on a regular basis: OLA (Organización Latino-Americana) of Eastern Long Island, Eastville Community Historical Society of Sag Harbor, Bridgehampton

Fig. 6
Make Two Black Property Owners Look Like One (Limited Value Exercise) (Mr. Lyons & Mr. Dorce), 2019
Silkscreen on paper
24 × 35¾ inches
Courtesy the artist and Tilton Gallery, New York

Child Care & Recreational Center, and the Shinnecock Indian Nation in Southampton. The conversations were focused and intense, and Jackson's copious handwritten notes would nourish her for months to come. During these conversations, she found common concerns of migration, labor, housing, and mobility among these communities. Despite the fact that these experiences are mostly hidden from visitors to the Hamptons, as Jackson points out, certain policies affect all of us as a society even when some of us are not consciously aware of their presence.

Summer of Loss
Water Mill, New York, August 7, 2020

Jackson's exhibition at the Parrish, originally scheduled for July 2020, was postponed because of the COVID-19 pandemic. To mark her presence at the Museum, which seemed necessary during a summer when the entire world erupted in protests after the murder of George Floyd, Jackson and I decided to project five of her video collages on the south façade of the Museum. One of the selections was *Self Portrait: Tale of Two Michaels*, which I had seen in 2017. It was a sad constancy that this work made in 2014, during what seemed to Jackson "an endless epidemic of blatantly racist violence against people of color without recourse," gained a renewed urgency as Black people across the United States were being killed at a breathtaking rate and with unfathomable impunity.

Reminiscent of Jackson's early practice as a muralist and public artist, the video projections were visible from Montauk Highway both as a drive-by and up-close experience, which meant also listening to

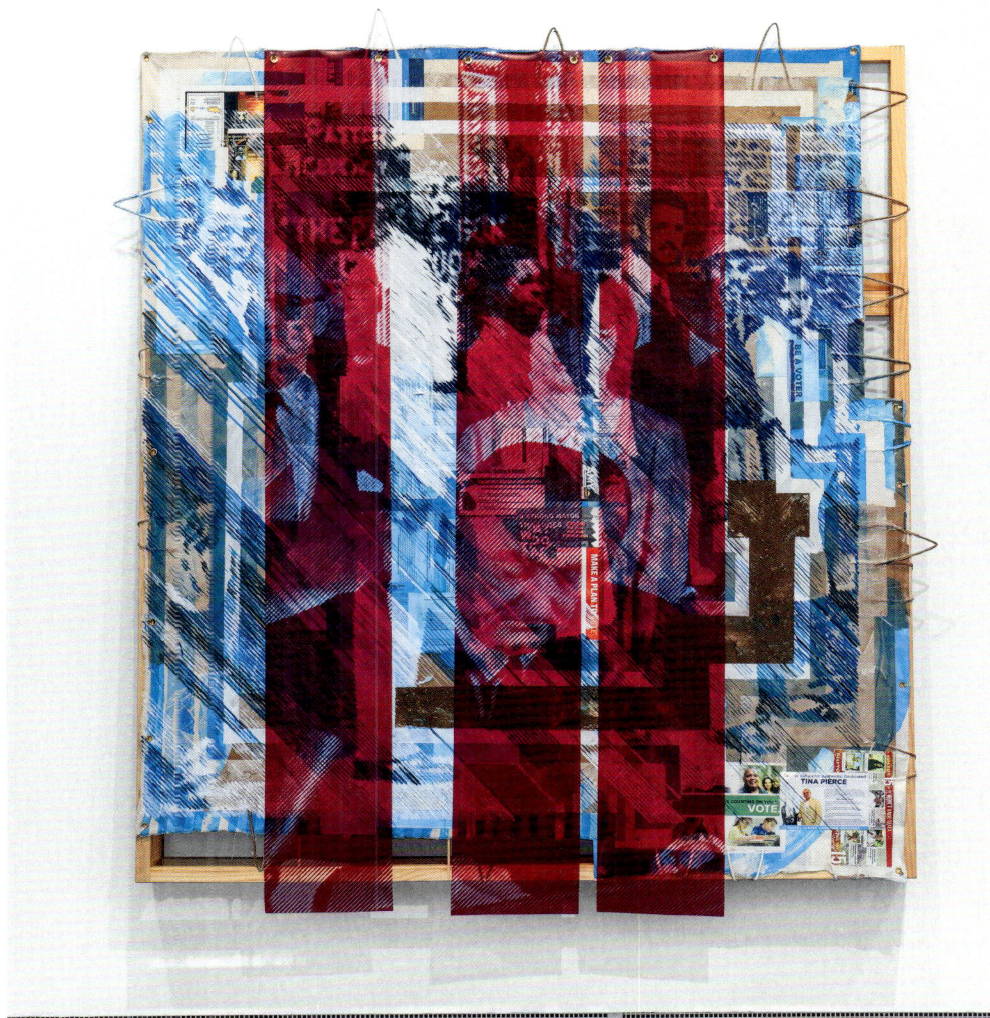

Fig. 7
Time and Space (1948 End of Voter Registration Line) (1965 LBJ Signs the Voting Rights Act), 2020

Acrylic, Pentelic marble, Ohio Underground Railroad site soil, American electoral ephemera, and paper bags on canvas and fabric

89⅜ × 83¾ × 8 inches

Courtesy the artist and Tilton Gallery, New York

Commissioned by the Wexner Center for the Arts at The Ohio State University their sound. The audio component remains important: the video collages employ sound as a vehicle for the complex emotion of mourning. Music and rhythm are a means to release emotions, their call and response reflecting the patterns of human communication. Two of the artist's recent exhibitions—*Forever My Lady*, at Night Gallery, Los Angeles (fig. 8), and *Love Rollercoaster* at the Wexner—took their titles from rhythm-and-blues and funk love songs performed by Jodeci and the Ohio Players. Experiencing Jackson's rhythmic images on the Parrish façade and hearing the songs of her videos during a period when we were all grappling with painful losses while forbidden to be close together was immensely cathartic.

The Land Claim
Water Mill, New York, July 2021

Over the course of 2020, Jackson continued her research and dialogue with the people she had met earlier, and many others, in the Hamptons. They all contribute to the puzzle of the Hamptons' history. One conversation with a member of the Shinnecock Indian Nation brought her to understand that the story of the Hamptons is inextricably connected to land appropriation, and thus she has titled this exhibition *The Land Claim*. Excerpts of the interviews are in the middle section of this publication, and full versions are available online. Jackson was in residence at The Watermill Center as an Inga Maren Otto Fellow from May 12 to June 11, 2021, to complete her new work for this exhibition—paintings, window prints, and a sound installation. Perhaps it is not a coincidence that the untold histories of the Hamptons are revealed by an artist in a place like the Parrish that comes to life through the interaction of light, space, and the people of this place. And none could reveal them better than Tomashi Jackson.

Fig. 8

Ecology of Fear (Abrams for Governor of Georgia) (Negro Women wait to congratulate LBJ), 2020

Archival prints on PVC marine vinyl, Pentelic marble dust, acrylic paint, American election flyers, Greek ballot papers, paper bags, muslin

84 × 60 inches

Courtesy the artist and Night Gallery, Los Angeles

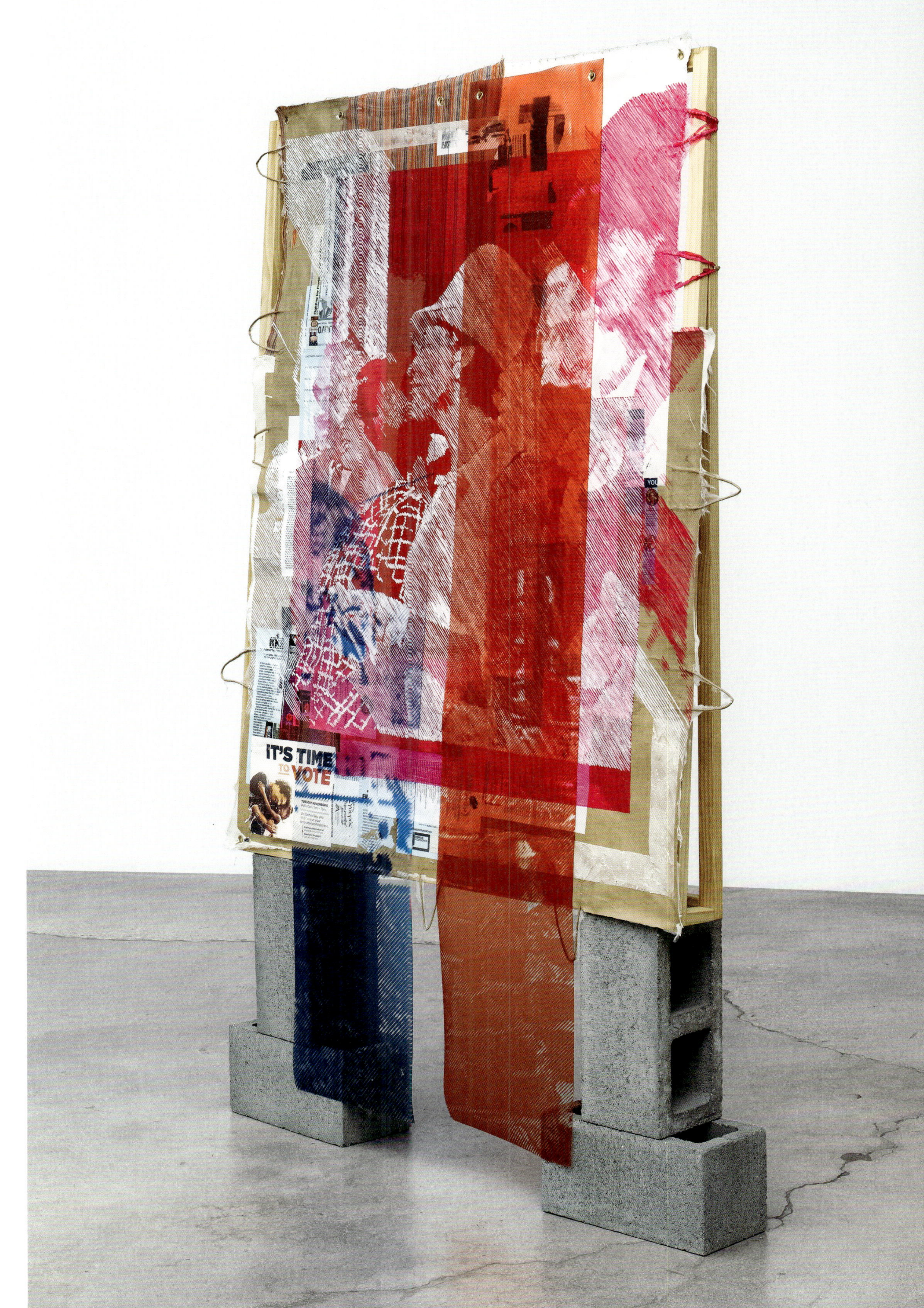
IT'S TIME
TO VOTE

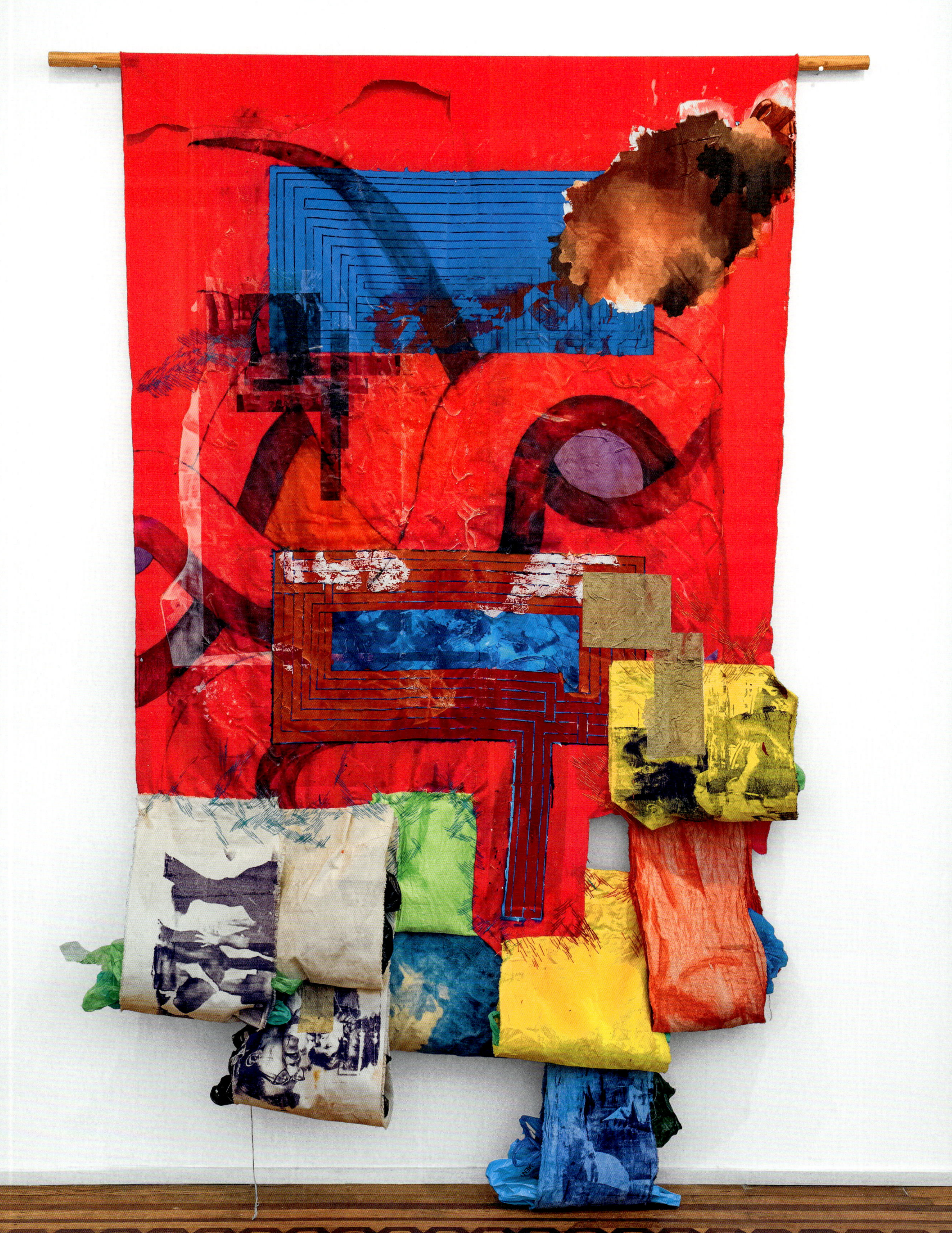

Eric N. Mack
For The Land Claim: A Radical Archive

The possibility of art to commemorate loss is tremendously useful at this moment—a shrine for life and images that reconstitute memory. In observing the work of my friend Tomashi Jackson, I know the task: that art must have a conviction. This task involves great patience and agility, to do justice to her layered work, becoming rewarding and jubilant in its effect. Ideas within the work address voter suppression in Ohio and Georgia; making visible the results of gentrification in New York; critical interpretations from *Interaction of Color* by Josef Albers; innovative methods of process painting from principles of modernism, as well as a legacy of murals from Los Angeles. All made evident in her last three solo exhibitions, *The Subliminal is Now* at Tilton Gallery in New York, *Forever My Lady* at Night Gallery in Los Angeles (fig. 1), and *Love Rollercoaster* at the Wexner Center for the Arts in Columbus, Ohio.

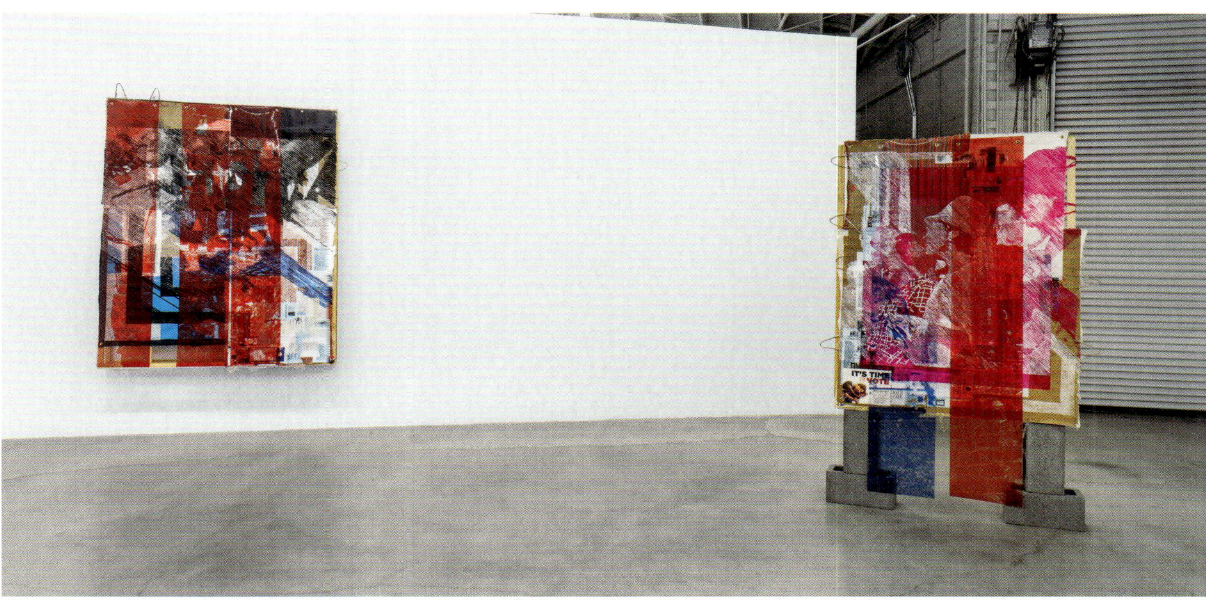

Fig. 1

Forever My Lady,
Installation view
at Night Gallery,
Los Angeles, 2020

Courtesy the artist
and Night Gallery,
Los Angeles

Fig. 2

*Dajerria All Alone
(Bolling v. Sharpe
(District of Columbia))
(McKinney Pool Party)*,
2016

Mixed media on cotton
and canvas

101 × 72⅜ inches

Courtesy the artist
and Tilton Gallery,
New York

My objective is to provide support for the vital abstraction in Jackson's practice, how her conceptions make tangible histories of humanism and civil rights bound to the American landscape. Her practice is grounded in research into public policy and anticipates entering the world with a legible address. I want to reroute literalisms that could compromise the practice's focus on chromatic dynamism—heat and cool, transparent and opaque properties emit varying degrees of light.

Dajerria All Alone (Bolling v. Sharpe (District of Columbia)) (McKinney Pool Party), from 2016 (fig. 2), attaches to the wall with a wooden dowel that passes through the top of the textile. It leans on two nails hammered to the wall in integral support. The mostly quinacridone red canvas drapes, and such chromatic saturation has been absorbed to the surface. Fields of contrasting color remain, as the work billows to the floor, weighted at the bottom and fortified by a patchwork of textiles, which conceal plastic bags as soft, yet robust support. These fields of color read as concentric mazes in contrasting blue chroma.

There is a simple rectangle that enters a brown cloudlike presence that creates a rupture for the center connection of the maze—this is a pictorial rupture. The second concentric maze, below, expresses itself as a boundary where the chromatic blue is contained at its center

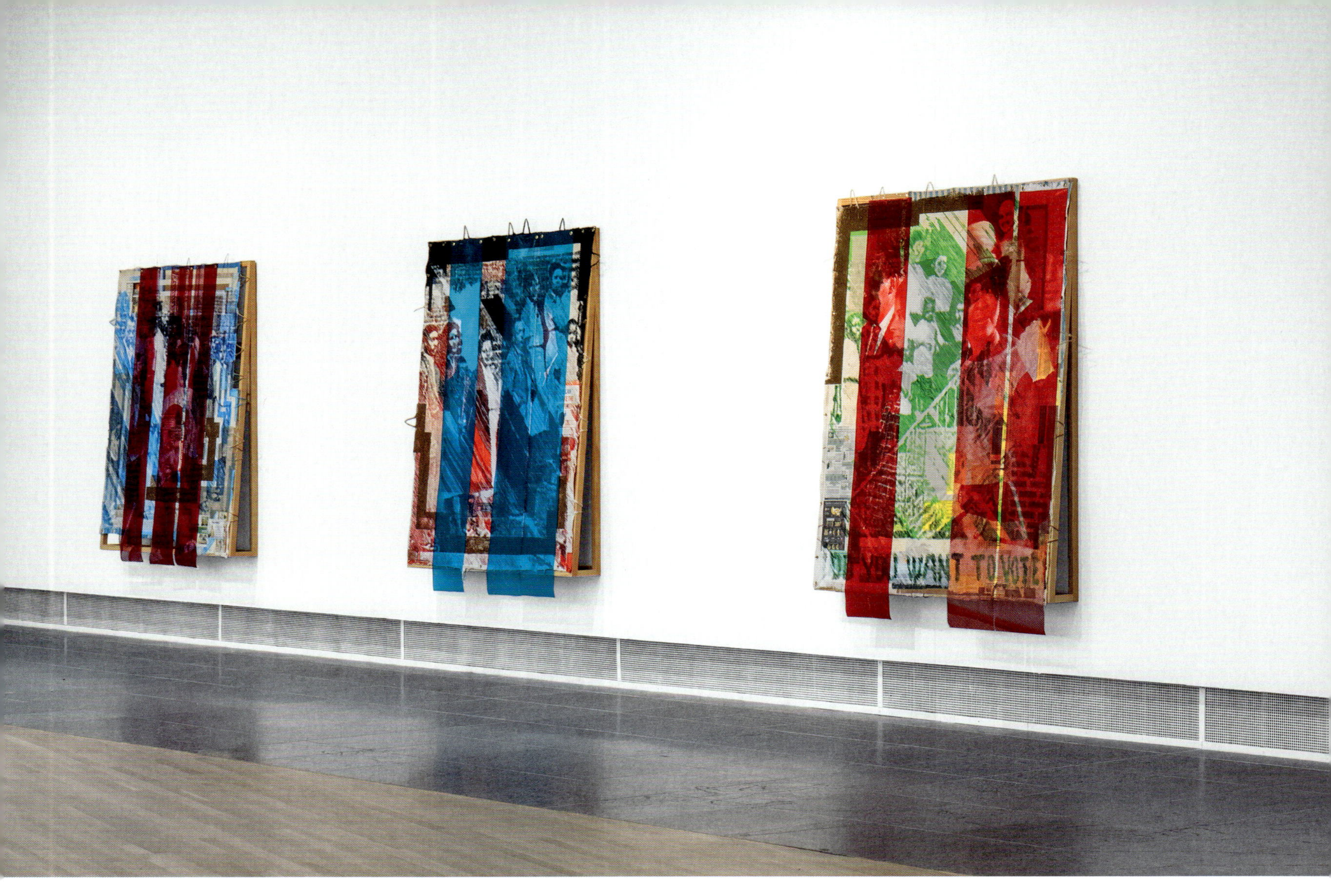

and variants of red build a kind of fortress. This boundary line extends down a strip of fabric, as if depicting a corridor or hallway, acknowledging these spaces as a kind of expressive blueprint, a stand-in for architecture or aerial landscape.

Enter Dajerria Becton: a fifteen-year-old Black girl who was slammed to the ground, physically restrained, and violently detained by a white police officer while in her bathing suit at a pool party in McKinney, Texas—a predominantly white suburb of Dallas—in 2015. Indeed, Dajerria was alone and vulnerable, as the title of this work suggests. Her portrait is rendered on the painting's surface as an embellishment; she is overlaid where the concentric blue rectangle and red meet. Dajerria glances off the surface with shock and confusion, undoubtedly addressing the viewer: indeed, Jackson imposed her image transfer at the viewer's height. Dajerria is fractured within two fields of color. We know that her nightmare is not an isolated incident. The use of excessive force by the police has resulted in national tragedies with the deaths of Sandra Bland, George Floyd, Breonna Taylor, and numerous other Black citizens, deaths for which the police are seldom held accountable.

The structure of the work is congruent to a post-and-lintel scaffold, an ancient construction known for its utility and ease. Jackson's investment in foundational histories maps onto the current status of policy, with questions about perception and truth. Parenthetically cited is *Bolling v. Sharpe*, referring to the impactful Supreme Court case centered on school desegregation in the nation's capital. A case like this one documents a desire for educational equity in American schools by acknowledging the practice of segregation as unconstitutional. *Bolling*

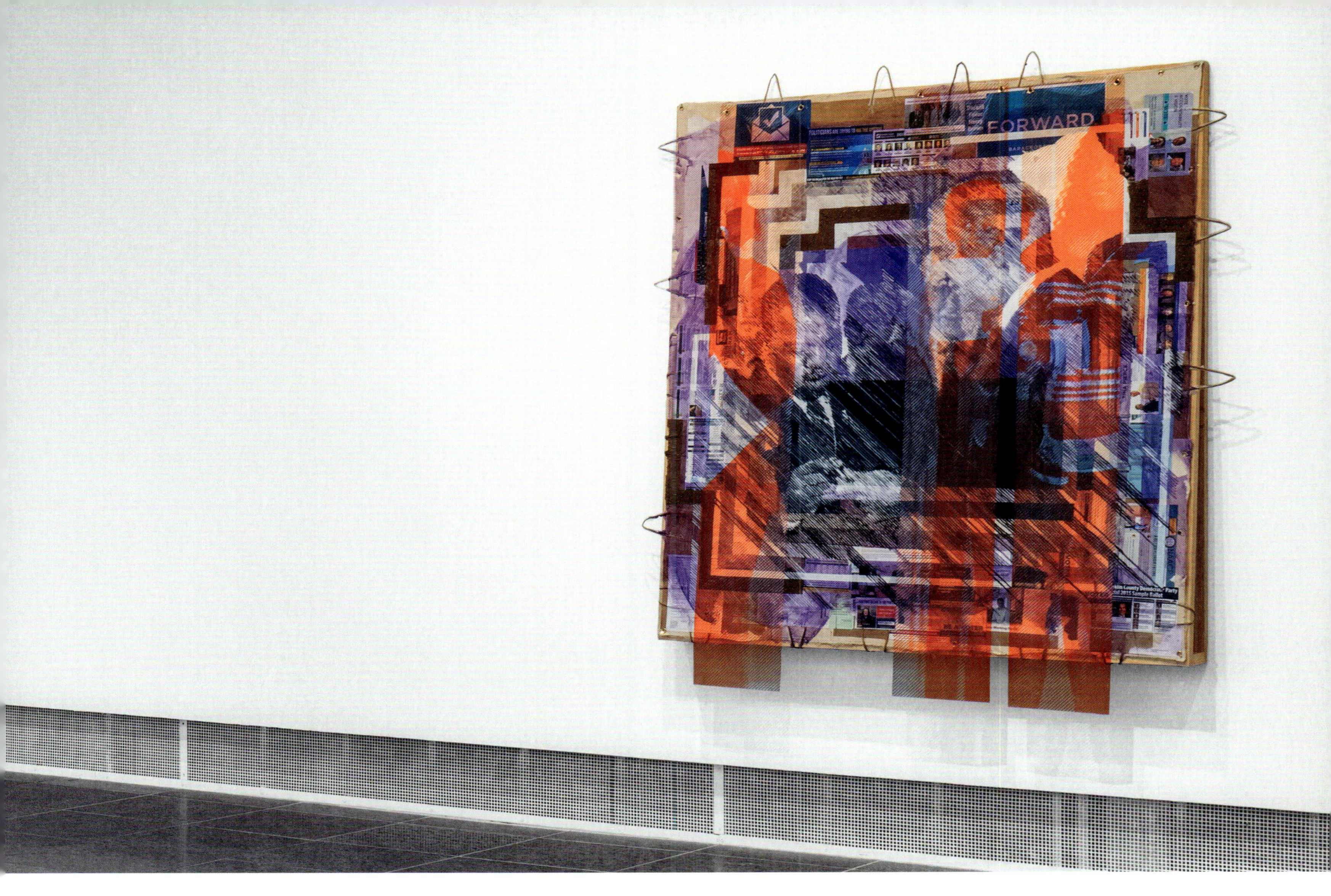

documents a pivotal struggle for equity, especially considering the subject of this work, Dajerria Becton, a then fifteen-year-old high school student. Jackson's work responds formally through material investigations that literally ground the work. What draws me to her practice has always been the depth of her inquiry.

The urgency of the present wraps around the spaces and emerges from the walls as symbolic structures for home, domestic economies, and statehood. *Love Rollercoaster* at the Wexner Center for the Arts (fig. 3) included five new paintings centered on themes of voter disenfranchisement and suppression in Ohio's Black community. It uses the soundtrack of the Ohio Players' 1975 hit song "Love Rollercoaster" and multiple songs from the musicians' catalogue is interspersed with conversations with Black Ohioans.

A wood awning is the support for many works and allows for the surface to project from the wall. The awning cantilevers off the wall, reaching out above the floor. As Jackson's work attaches to the gallery wall, the depth of the painting juts out, pointing toward the viewer. *Ecology of Fear (Gillum for Governor of Florida) (Freedom Riders bus bombed by KKK)*, from 2020 (fig. 4), is currently on view at the Solomon R. Guggenheim Museum. This work was first shown at Night Gallery in Los Angeles in the exhibition titled after Jodeci's 1991 hit single, "Forever My Lady."

An election sign is lodged within a crease as if it had become a ballot and the painting itself doubled as a voting apparatus. In origin, this makes sense, as the canvas is made of striped cotton from Greece. It is folded conceptually within the artwork as a reference to the birthplace of democracy. The striped field yields at the center to horizontal stripes that meet vertical ones to create an optically active space. Dark and light, and chromatic red/blue play with the radiance, the incandescent quality, of this work. What shines through is the multilayered media. The surface projects primarily blue; perceptively, Jackson creates these harmonies using simultaneous contrast with a mixture of other chromas.

The textured reality of the surface mixes acrylic paint and Pentelic marble dust from an ancient Greek quarry; this gives grit and resistance to the halftone line that makes up an image of President Lyndon B. Johnson signing the Voting Rights Act of 1965, which prohibits racial discrimination in voting. The halftone lines are made by hand and are a gestural and seismic tool, accumulating image through redaction and underscore. The line is continuous with the formal language of the stripes, and the Pentelic dust creates an ancient organic ground.

The waterproof marine plastic hangs off the canvas like vertical blinds. Ruptures serve as a contrary set of lines, as wayward as they are lyrical. The perimeter of the picture plane is mended with brown paper bags fortified by adhesives. The shopping bags are transient and of the masses, used by shopworkers' hands and blue-collar consumers. These reminders of life are woven in, often with paint radiating around the border of the canvas in markings of integration and harmony. Jackson paints within the decorative stripes to identify depth in flatness. Formal strategies move the eye around the picture plane for the viewer to be captivated by a signal from the outside world—the historical world near and far.

The works from this series are open from the side, structurally exposed. The wooden profile of the structure is nearly prismatic; the space behind the work constructs chromatic projection and a container at large. The use of the awning serves as a vessel for lost memory of neighborhoods, fragile economies. It acknowledges that these too function in the framework of the built environment. In this series, everyday life is enmeshed within the surface of the painting in a process of corresponding with the quotidian. Affirmation of gridded space is woven to make a newly textured surface connected to the awning as support.

I have written a portion of this essay while sitting under a protective awning of aluminum and shaped plastic, a recent addition to a Harlem coffee shop's outdoor dining area, in response to COVID-19 protocols. The space has a constructed overhang, claiming the sidewalk as habitable, complete with a table and chairs for communal dining. The objective of such an area is open ventilation, to allow air to circulate and reduce airborne transmission of disease. I mention these everyday constructions because they represent a real architectural negotiation of space seen in Jackson's work. Public policy is evident throughout. Consequently, the forms are reiterated as readymade painting structures, enforcing vernacular architecture that physically takes root in the gallery space.

For her upcoming show *Tomashi Jackson: The Land Claim*, at the Parrish Art Museum on Long Island, Jackson has employed systems of research and questioning that yield a better understanding of the identity of the East End and its townspeople. The research allows for collaborative content in the ways of public address. Social justice and a refined language of abstraction that speaks visual practice into existence often sign together in an intricate latticework.

My questions are: How do these works change the exhibition space in being together? And what is the philosophy of the exhibition?

In *The Land Claim*, the process of Jackson's practice and the collaged nature of the work draw from an archive of lively materiality, inspired by the surrounding community. This research has come from a series of interviews conducted on Zoom in 2020 with historians and

Fig. 4

Ecology of Fear (Gillum for Governor of Florida) (Freedom Riders bus bombed by KKK), 2020

Archival prints on PVC marine vinyl, acrylic paint, American campaign materials, Greek ballot papers, Andrew Gillum campaign sign, paper bags, Greek canvas, Pentelic marble dust

91 × 100 × 12 inches

Courtesy the artist and Night Gallery, Los Angeles

Collection of Solomon R. Guggenheim Museum, New York

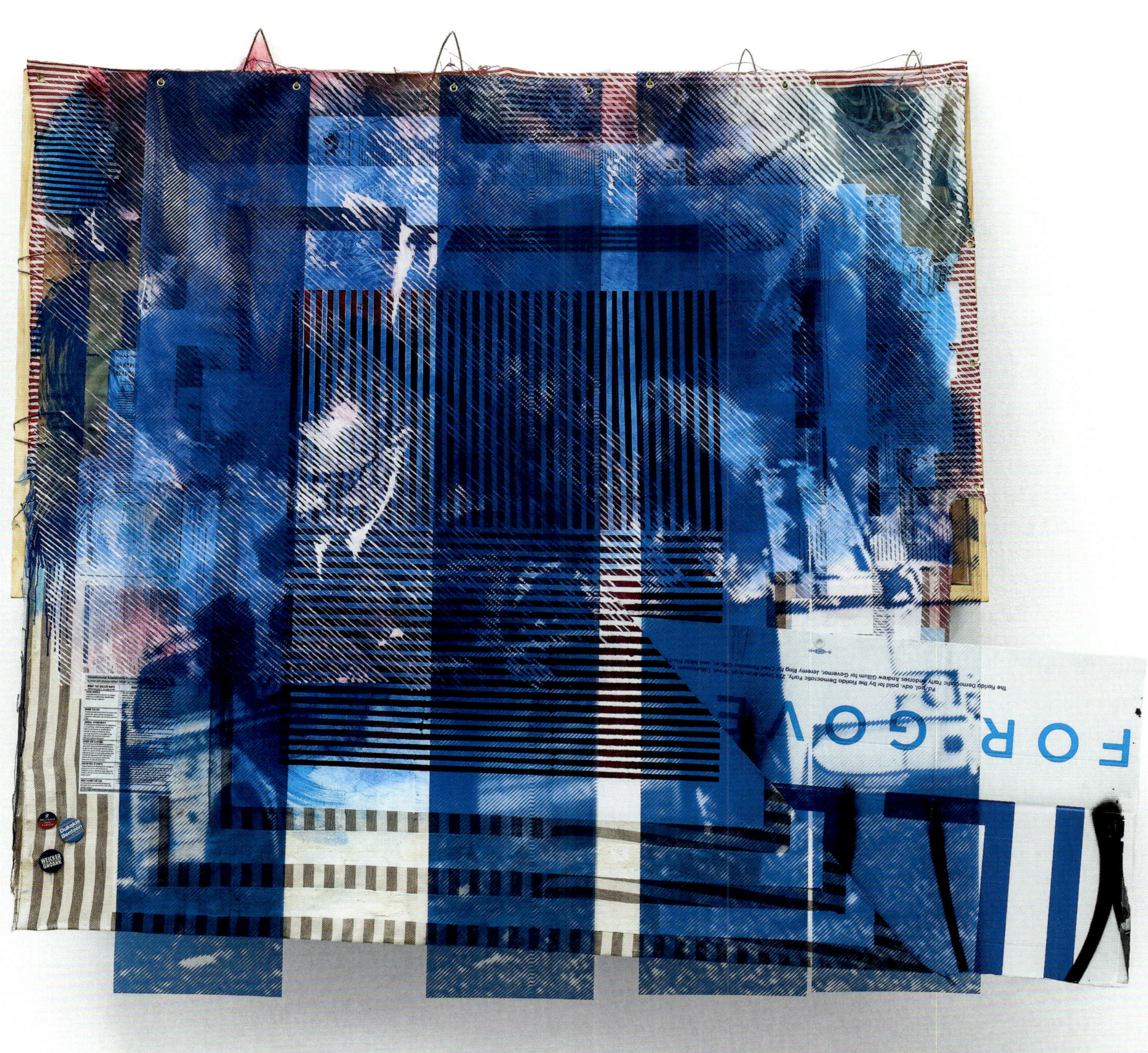
FOR GOV

community organizers such as Donnamarie Barnes, Georgette Grier-Key, Kelly Dennis, Bonnie Cannon, Jeremy Dennis, Minerva Perez, and Richard "Juni" Wingfield—all citizens of Long Island's East End. Each interview highlighted the dynamism of each community centering experiences of indigenous Shinnecock peoples, descendants of West African slaves by way of Barbados, European settlers, and a vibrant Latinx community. Drawings of each discussant were made by the artist Martha Schnee as Jackson directed the inquiries.

The thematics for *The Land Claim* divide into various concerns of the local community: housing, agriculture, transportation, and labor. Shelter Island, Sag Harbor, East Hampton, and Southampton are among the sites of inquiry. According to interviewee Georgette Grier-Key, executive director and chief curator of Eastville Community Historical Society of Sag Harbor, Sylvester Manor was one of thirteen manors built through a land grant from King George. The manor served as a provisioning plantation to replenish resources for sugarcane harvested by enslaved Nigerian people in Barbados. An essential part of the triangular trade, the manor helped sustain production of sugarcane that ended up as refined sugar and molasses destined for Britain. The photographer and curator of Sylvester Manor, Donnamarie Barnes, expands on the site of migration for enslaved peoples brought to Shelter Island from Barbados after the plantations in the Caribbean closed. Barnes, a descendant of this migration, introduces the first Black published poet in North America, Jupiter Hammond, who was born into slavery at Lloyd Manor, the child of enslaved parents from Nigeria, by way of Barbados.

Shelter Island is ancestral land for the indigenous Shinnecock tribes and existed as a place where largely three cultures came together to live and work. The land has space for agriculture as well as burial. The memories are not just in the buildings: they are earthen and in the soil. The process is orchestration, as a container for word of mouth and the use of a growing archive. The works in the exhibition reflect the community surrounding the Parrish Art Museum. Jackson anticipates the viewership by including its members as part of the exhibition's content, thereby claiming the museum as public space and allowing for that to be reflected in this expansive body of work.

Eric N. Mack (b. 1987, Columbia, Maryland) lives and works in New York City. A recipient of the 2021–2022 Rome Prize and the 2017 inaugural BALTIC Artists' Award, he has held residencies at the Rauschenberg Foundation and the Delfina Foundation, London. Institutional solo exhibitions include *In austerity, stripped from its support and worn as a sarong*, The Power Station, Dallas; *Dye Lens*, Scrap Metal Gallery, Toronto; and *Lemme walk across the room*, Brooklyn Museum (all 2019); *BALTIC Artists' Award 2017*, BALTIC Centre for Contemporary Art, Gateshead, England; and *Eric Mack: Vogue Fabrics*, Albright-Knox Art Gallery, Buffalo (2017). Major group exhibitions include the Whitney Biennial 2019, Whitney Museum of American Art, New York; *Grace Wales Bonner: A Time for New Dreams*, Serpentine Gallery, London (2018); *Ungestalt*, Kunsthalle Basel; *In the Abstract*, Massachusetts Museum of Contemporary Art; and *Blue Black*, Pulitzer Arts Foundation, St. Louis (all three 2017); *Making & Unmaking*, Camden Arts Centre, London (2016); and *Greater New York 2015*, MoMA PS1, Long Island City, New York. Mack's work is in the permanent collections of the Albright-Knox Art Gallery, Brooklyn Museum, Hood Museum of Art, Studio Museum in Harlem, and Whitney Museum of American Art. He received his BFA from The Cooper Union and his MFA from Yale University.

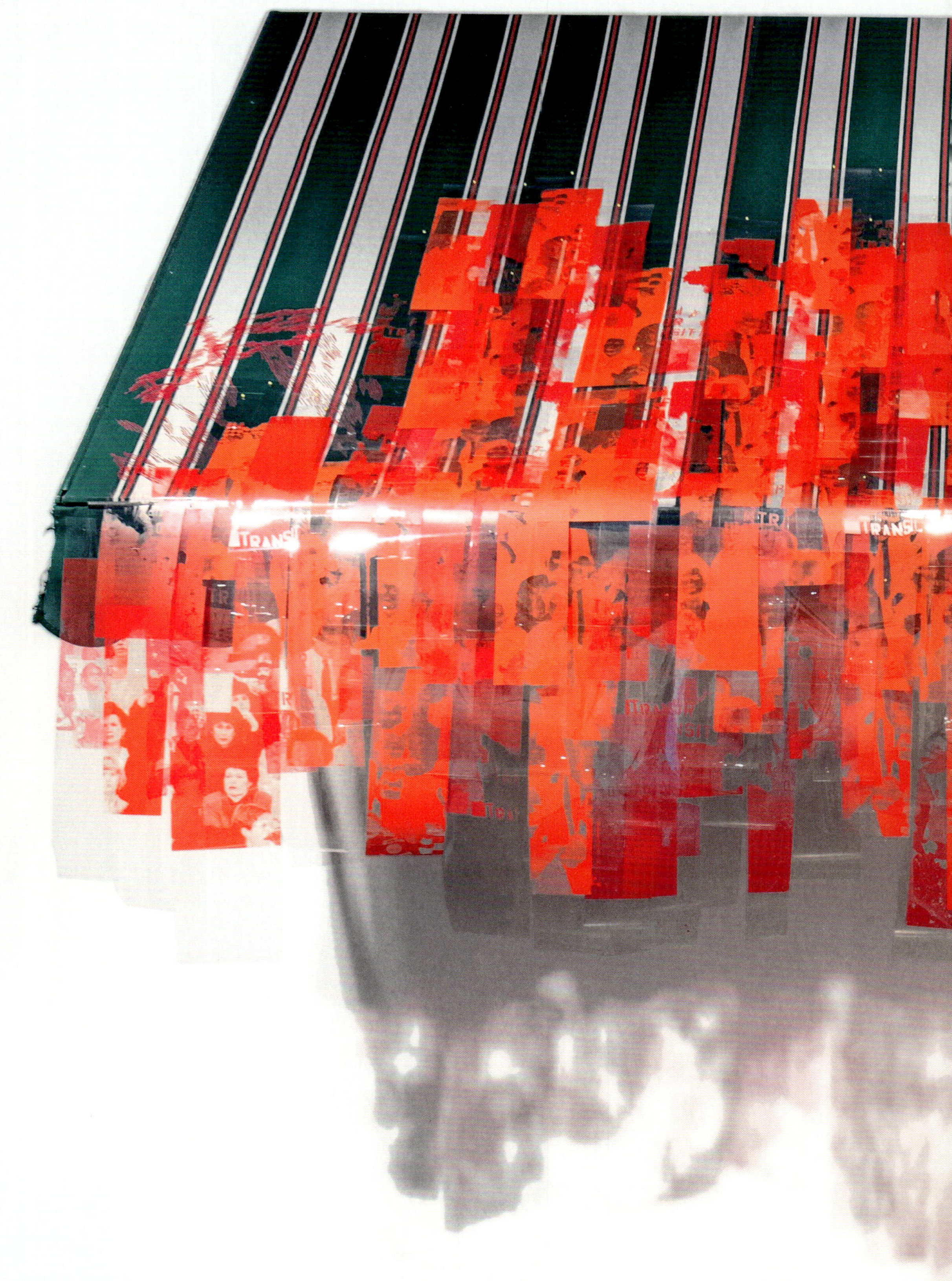

Fig. 5

Interstate Love Song (Friends of Clayton County Transit) (Pitts Road Station Opposition), 2018

Mixed media

40¼ × 111½ × 42¼ inches

Courtesy the artist and Tilton Gallery, New York

Photo: Fredrik Brauer

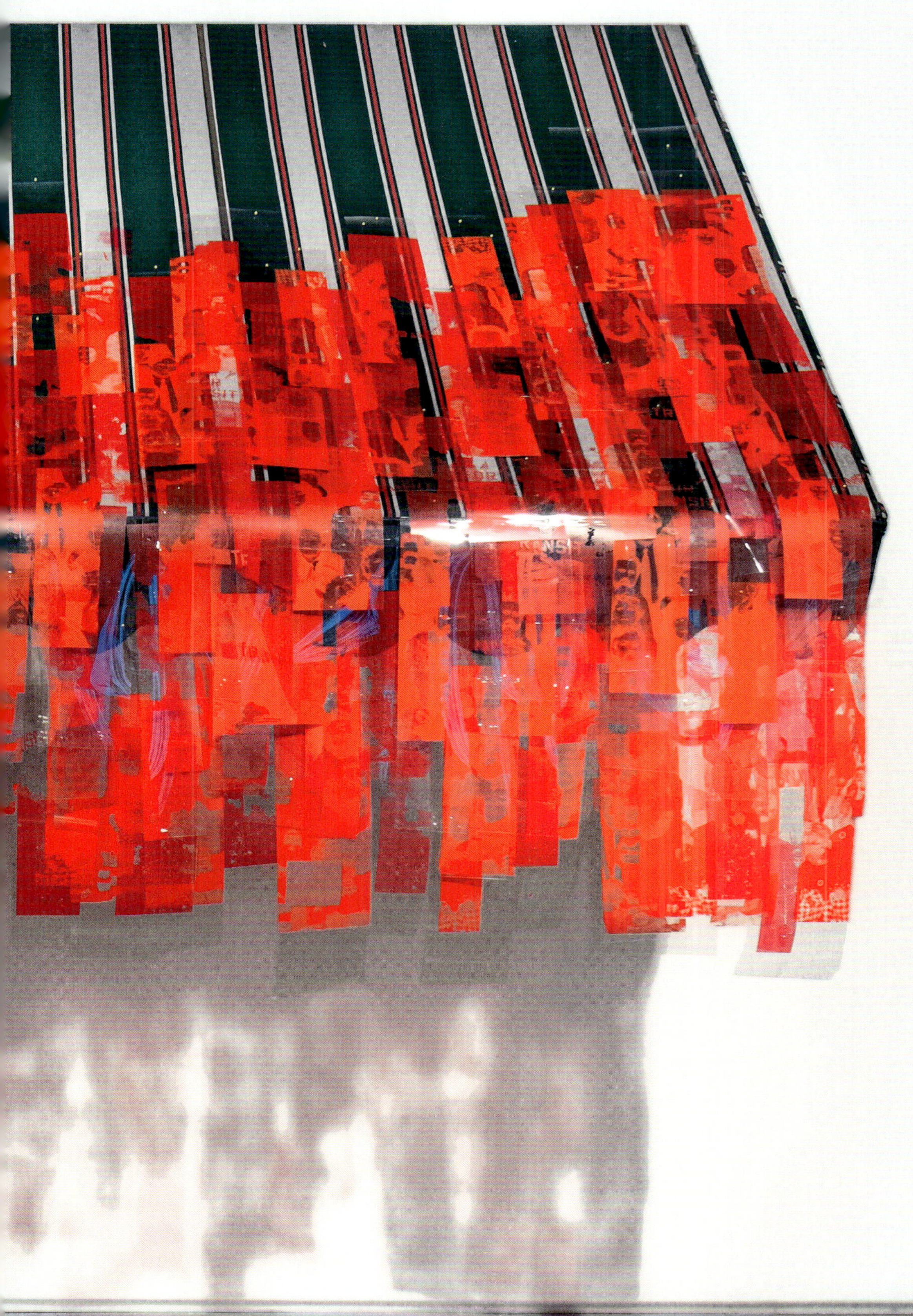

31

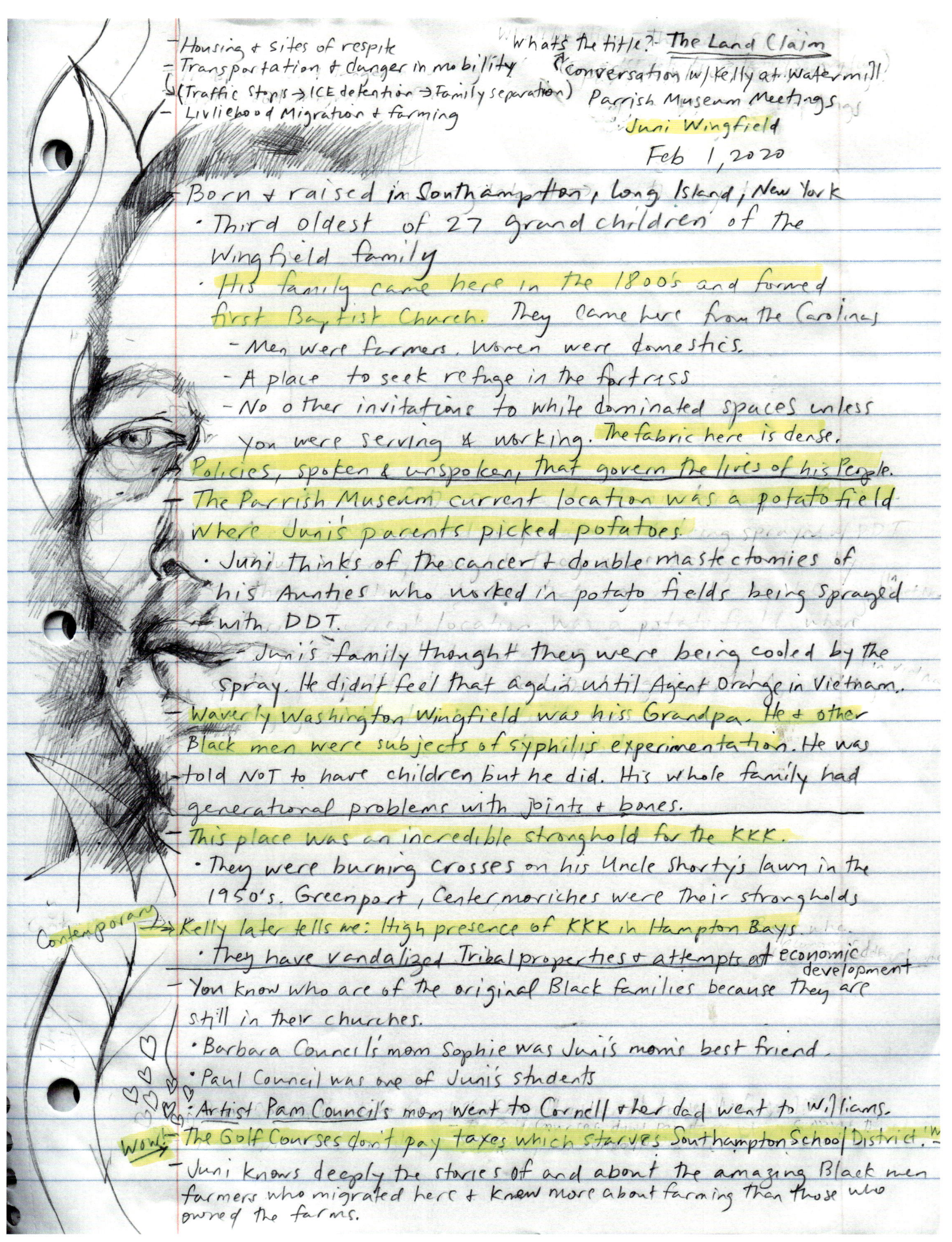

1.
Notes from the first in-person interviews for *The Land Claim*, January 31, and February 1, 2020.
Courtesy Tomashi Jackson.

The Three Sisters

The following eight interview excerpts are transcripts of recorded video conversations, which took place between January 2020 and May of 2021. They have been condensed and edited for clarity. Each transcript presents history as each speaker remembers it and as is true to the context of their lived experience.

In 2017, I asked Parrish Art Museum curator Corinne Erni what was happening among communities of color in the East End of Long Island. She told me about how the Latinx community often faced discrimination through frequent traffic stops that led to Immigration and Customs Enforcement (ICE) detention and ultimately family separation, even as there is an unquenchable thirst for their labor. I visited Southampton in January 2020 as a working artist to begin learning about the lived experiences of Black, Indigenous, and Latinx people of the East End. I met with five community members in person (Bonnie Cannon, Kelly Dennis, Georgette Grier-Key, Minerva Perez, Richard Wingfield), as well as staff members at the Parrish and The Watermill Center. My initial questions were focused on issues of transportation, livelihood migration, and labor. Soon after, the COVID-19 pandemic prevented me from returning to the East End for more than a year.

While sheltering in place in Massachusetts, I worked with a team of Harvard graduate and professional students at the Radcliffe Institute for Advanced Study. Though we remained in physical isolation, we discovered ways to continue our project that focused on topics surrounding educational equity after the *Brown v. Board of Education II* Supreme Court decision of 1955. Our methodology centered on meaningful generosity and the creation of multiple accessible archives from recorded and transcribed conversations. This information served as my source material to produce new visual artworks, a publication, a body of interview drawings and notes, a selection of archival images, a music playlist, and designs for ongoing museum programming and curricular materials for displaced learners. We identified the publication as an important tangible outcome that, during our yearlong process of collection and analysis, we came to regard as the work itself, the work of prioritizing underrecognized narratives in public spaces.

This practice of creating research-driven multimedia works inspired by video-recorded and transcribed interviews began in 2011 with my graduate thesis work at the School of Architecture and Planning at the Massachusetts Institute of Technology. While interrogating the realities of infrastructure and labor in the built environment, I asked my mother, Aver M. Burroughs, questions about our family's history of informal domestic labor in Texas and California, and this led to the creation of projects informed by our recorded interactions. The methodology reemerged out of necessity with fresh life and purpose in 2020 as we employed it for the *Brown II* project at Harvard Radcliffe and then in preparation for my exhibition at the Parrish called *The Land Claim*, where it has transformed again.

Over a number of months, I've worked closely with artist and Parrish curatorial fellow Lauren Ruiz and with artist and educator Martha Schnee to facilitate eight videoconference interviews with people of the Indigenous, Black, and

2.
Interview for
The Land Claim,
February 22, 2021

(Clockwise from top left) Martha Schnee, Lauren Ruiz, Georgette Grier-Key, and Tomashi Jackson

Courtesy Tomashi Jackson

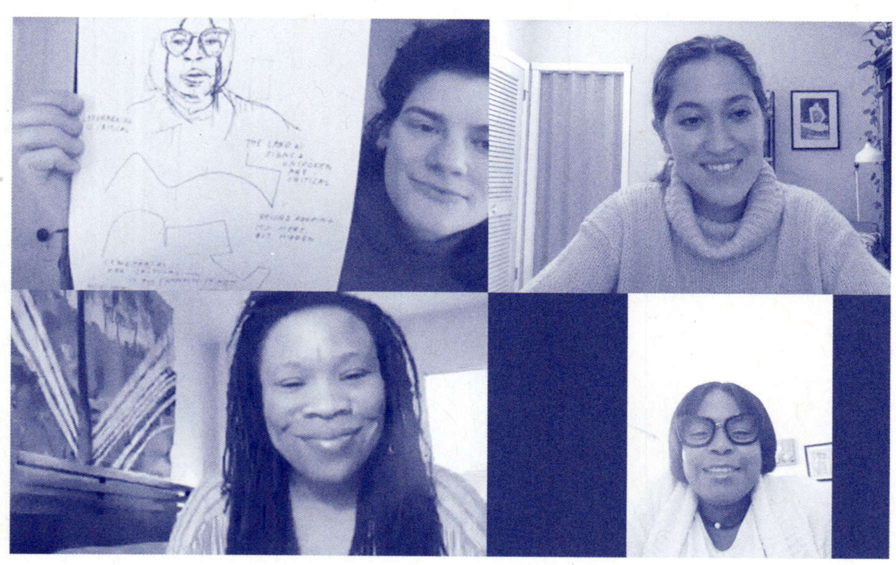

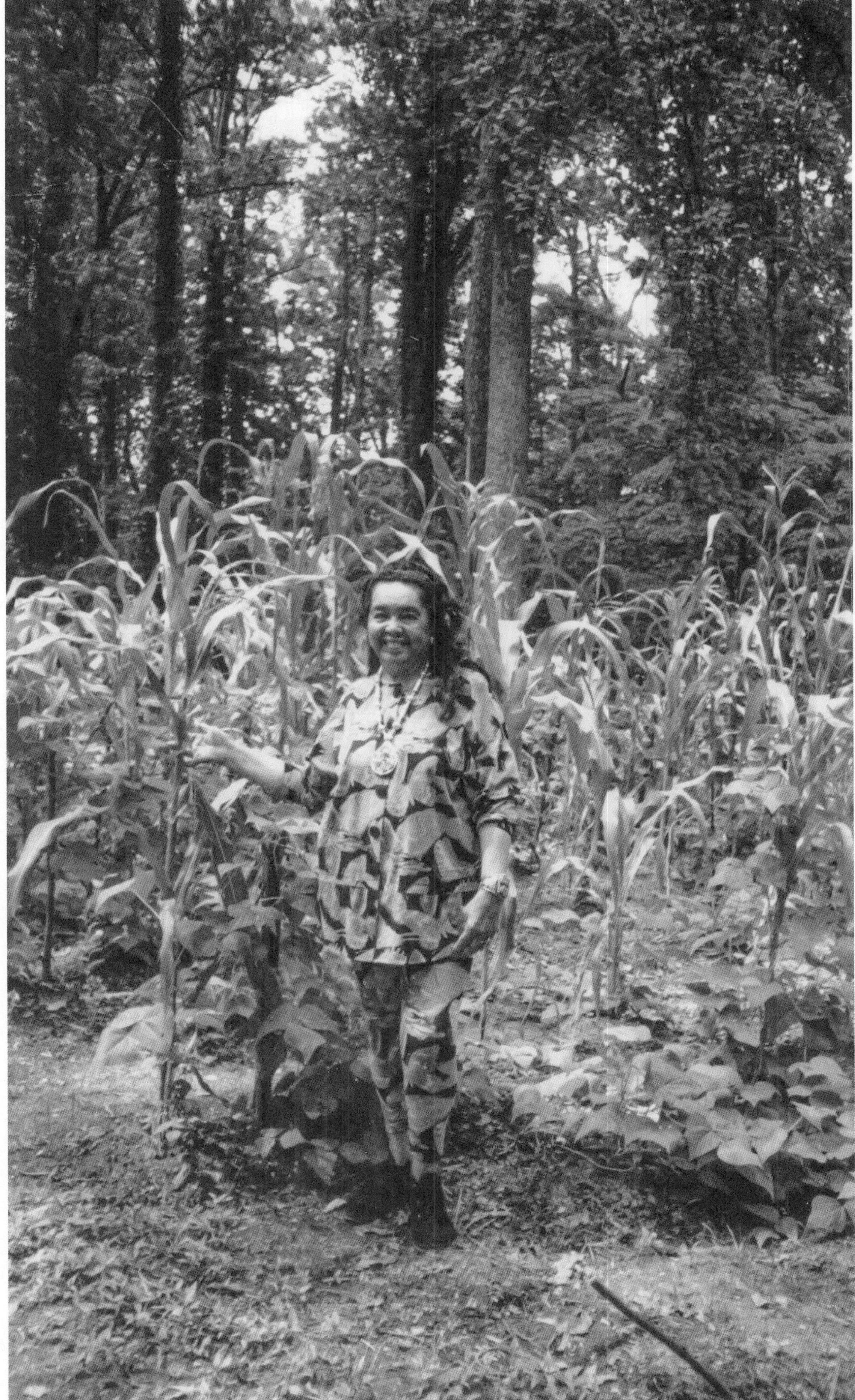

3.
Loretta "Princess Arrow" Silva at a farm in Virginia during a family vacation. Princess Arrow stands in a Three Sisters intercropped garden of corn, squash, and beans, ca. 1997

Courtesy Jeremy Dennis

Latin American communities on the East End. We returned to some of the community members I met in early 2020 and included four additional interviewees for a total of eight recordings. During each conversation Martha drew portraits of our discussants as all three of us took notes. Joined by research scholar K. Anthony Jones, we later returned to the archive of Martha's drawings to guide us in processing and analyzing information for this manuscript. In studying the drawings and notes we found an echo of common emphasis among these distinct and interrelated communities. Each one of the interview participants spoke about their communities being held together by the work of women, the sacredness of the land, and meaningful generational experiences of labor. This narrative pattern forms the structure for the following interview excerpts called "The Three Sisters."

The Three Sisters refers to the North American Indigenous farming intercropping method of planting corn, squash, and beans together in mounds in which each life form helps the others to grow and thrive as they have for centuries. Matriarchy, sacred relationships with the land, and the meaning of labor have arisen from this effort as similarly interrelated and intertwined among the three distinct communities centered in this inquiry. These interview excerpts and the related collection of archival photographs inform the seven new paintings in *The Land Claim* exhibition. For this project, there is no one without the other. The encompassing work explores illuminating, understanding, and affirming the shapes of things, and the intersecting nature of lives in historic realms of public and private spaces. This would have not been possible without the extraordinary contributions of the participants and the research team, to whom I am immensely grateful.

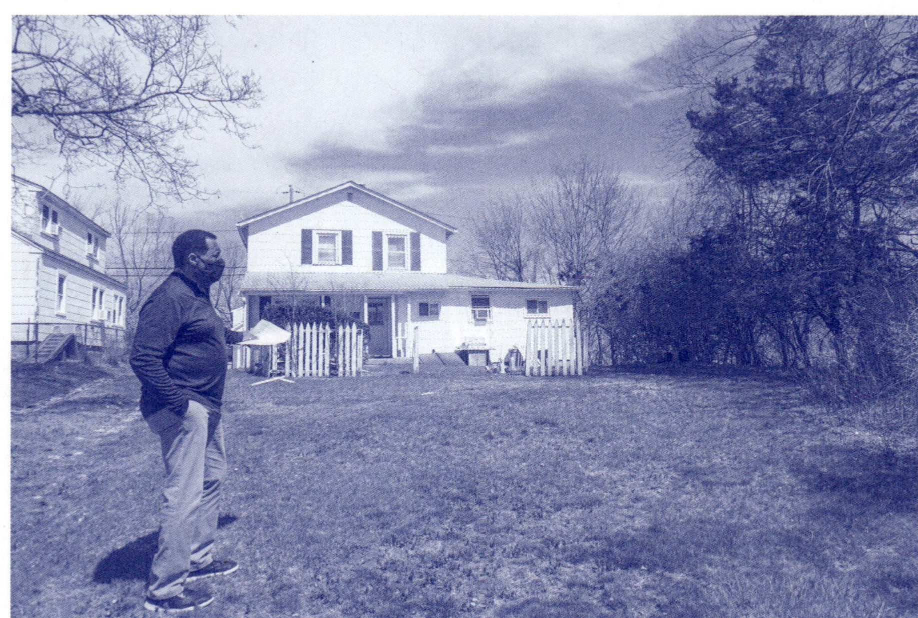

4.
Richard "Juni" Wingfield with what remains of a garden on Hillcrest Avenue in Southampton, NY, 2021

Courtesy Lauren Ruiz

5.
Puerto Rican immigrants working on a potato farm, ca.1950

Courtesy the Migration Division Collection at the Archives of the Puerto Rican Diaspora, Center for Puerto Rican Studies, Hunter College, City University of New York

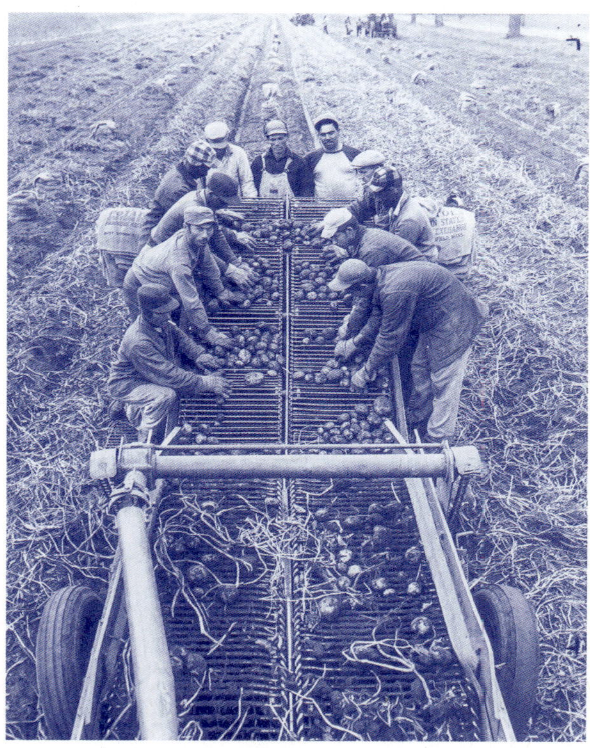

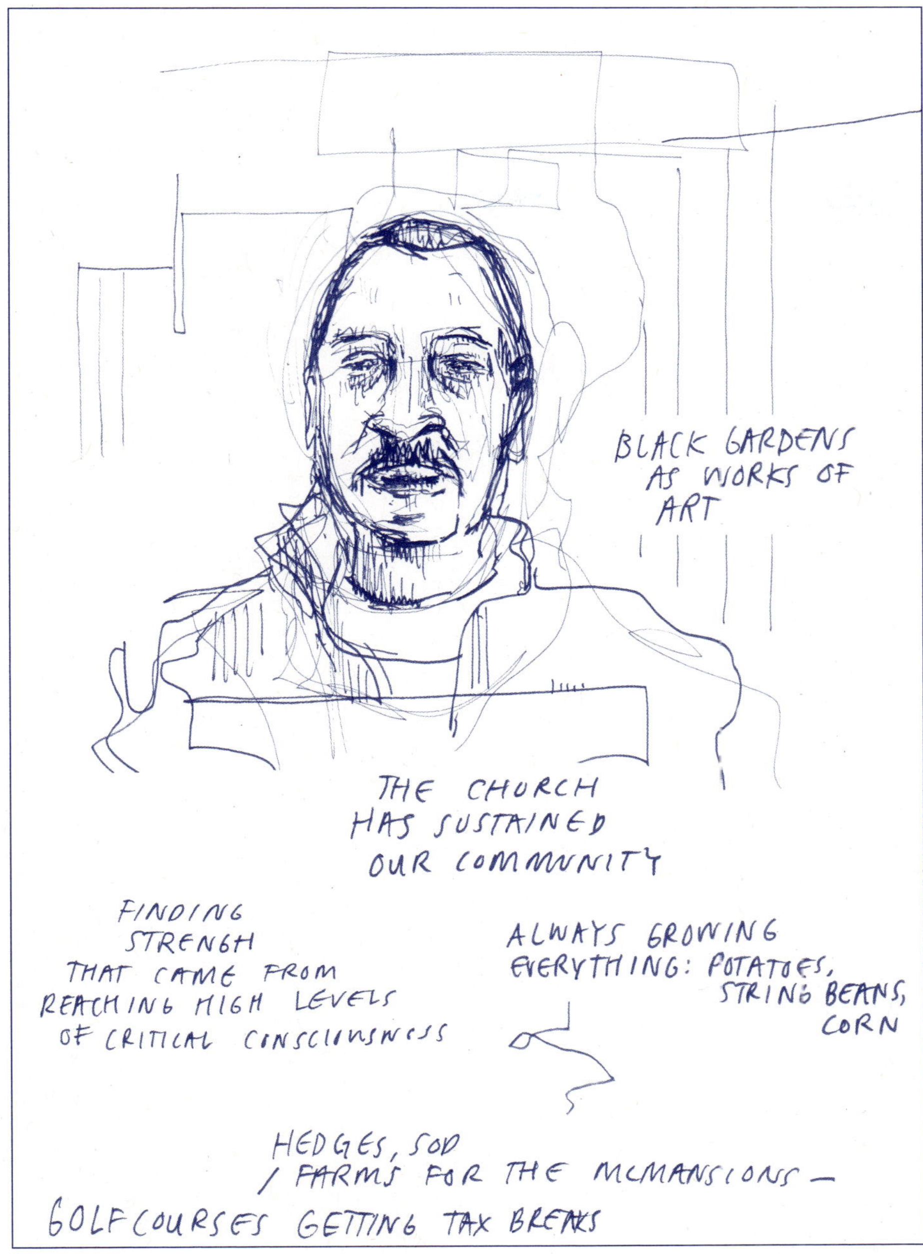

Martha Schnee
*"Black gardens
as works of art"*
*— Richard "Juni"
Wingfield on
strength and
sustenance,* 2021

Richard "Juni" Wingfield
To Make a Life

Richard "Juni" Wingfield served as community liaison and athletics coach at Southampton school district for thirty-five years. He continues to coach three sports and codirect the S.T.A.R. (Social Thinking and Reasoning) youth program. A lifelong resident of Southampton, New York, he fills a critical role in the community today.

In our discussion, Juni shares the history of his family's migration to the East End of Long Island in the 1920s and explains how the strength of women sustained the community, especially through gardening and farming.

At one point on this one little place called Hillcrest ("The Hill") my grandmother's four daughters all got plots themselves and built houses around her. Those daughters stayed right up underneath Mom. So here I am now. I was growing up in the most incredible, powerful way you can imagine. Who was the most important influence in my life? The women. They were the ones—they were free. They were strong, and giving strength, and they were so important to so much of the development of what happened, and to so much of the community. Like on the Shinnecock Reservation. It's the women there who contributed so much of the powerful work in that community.

So again, Juni is here, and I start to realize that this is an incredible dynamic. Charm and challenge, I call it. That's when I began to see all the charm and challenge of growing up in Southampton. I was at the Parrish Art Museum and people were talking about the outside sculptures. They have these pillars as part of the project [Theaster Gates's *Monument in Waiting*]. They encourage people to stand up on it and take their pictures. They said, "Who would you put up there?" I said, "I'd put my grandma up there."

I told them the story: the land that the Parrish Art Museum is built on is the same land that my grandma and her daughters were picking potatoes in. The pesticides were so strong and no one was controlling the DDT. It was not a coincidence that later my same lovely aunts came down with breast cancer. Charm and challenge. Everyone talked about how charming it is in terms of landmass here. But there was so much challenge. It was great that the people who were working that land were fortunate enough to get something to build on. But sometimes they got sick because no one was controlling the pesticides then. They were trying to kill the Golden Nematode, better known as the potato bug, just to get that potato to market. And people literally were getting sick.

To Create a Community

Ceal was this incredible, wonderful woman who was a part of the Havemeyer estate, and the Havemeyers also happen to own one of the largest collections of art. She decided that it was important for the kids within that Hillcrest community to come in and create a community garden. Ceal Havemeyer began to work with the kids and helped create a garden, which was such an incredible thing. She just wanted to create a place where someone could help them with their schoolwork when they came home from school. What it turned into was a great effort at all levels. It wasn't just about reading, writing, and computation. She knew how important it would be for them to put their hands in the dirt and get that earth, and learn the lessons—some of the easiest lessons that you could possibly imagine by seeing something grow. She was very instrumental for me and my work and in our community with our children. God bless her.

And then there was Mr. Paul Fordham, who was a part of the community in a very important way. I'm not sure if Mr. Fordham was a manager or a trustee in one of the banks but all of his cultural and ethnic sensitivity was always trying to afford others the opportunity to "have the American Dream." Which is what? To own your own home. My grandparents always used to talk about Mr. Fordham because he was someone who could originate some money to help them be able to afford a mortgage. I think about all the redlining that goes on now in banking and real estate and, at the end of the day, that was there but you had to have someone who had that kind of courage. Of a Ceal Havemeyer to walk into a community and say, "Yeah, the school should be accountable for reading, writing, and computation, but I'm gonna show them how to make a garden." For Mr. Paul Fordham to say, "I have families of color all over this community working for me and the bottom line is: shouldn't they be able to afford a home?"

I found some of my grandparents' old stuff and I laughed because it almost looked like the contracts they had were put together on napkins. So much was done so informally back then and some stuff was even done with a handshake. I know that there was more to it than that, but it originated in these messages on these little pieces of paper. Now of course we do everything electronically, but I think about how big that was, in terms of what was happening back then and affording people the opportunity to not just make a living but make a life.

The Art of the Garden

Black gardens were truly works of art. Right on the highway, Route 39, there was a gentleman named Willie Banks. His house came right up to the edge of the highway but so did his garden. Truly, his garden was so beautiful it became a tourist attraction. Another man named Phil Seymour used the information that his father and his father's father told him about growing. His plants were so healthy and so big he actually went into his own business selling the product called Seymour's Super Green. Like most things, when he created it, guess what happened? Someone found out about it. The next thing you know, corporate America had taken it and created their own product. That's how it works, right? But they didn't call it Seymour's Super Green. They just bought his recipe—and the rest is history, and he's just a farmer.

It goes back again to the whole migration. People weren't coming from South to North just to make more money, they wanted to create a better opportunity. Everyone's idea is, "Can we create something better for our children?" And they did it. I became one of those children, I became a first-generation college student. With that we saw more children, young people like myself, taking advantage of the schooling and being able to go from there to college. Then the parents' dream was, "We'll build this little house, and we'll have something to leave you." It didn't materialize like that. It was a good thing that they created the opportunity. They worked hard, sacrificed like you wouldn't imagine, and all of a sudden we have all these first-generation college students.

Those students then decided, "We don't want to go back there." If I'm a music major, for example, I'm not getting the job in music. I'm not getting a job teaching anywhere. It was economically depressed here. The big employers were the hospital. So if you were a nurse, if you were in housekeeping, you could work in the hospital. After that it was about taking care of what? The big estates. First-generation college students weren't looking to come back and take care of the estates. They were looking to create their own lives, professional jobs. It just wasn't here. So what happened? The parents moved on. They would leave those homes to the children and the children would say, "Wow, this is Southampton." Those little houses were built in the village of Southampton. They were like shoe boxes with money because hardly any of them still had mortgages on them. So the children decided to sell the homes, cash out, and they moved elsewhere. Where did they go? Isn't that ironic? They went back South. They went to Georgia, Virginia, and North Carolina. Said the cost of living was cheaper, more opportunities. I can keep myself in sight because there's somebody who looks like me. They all went back.

In Sag Harbor we'll always have a community called Azurest, at the end of the beach. We always called it the bourgeoise Black. There were

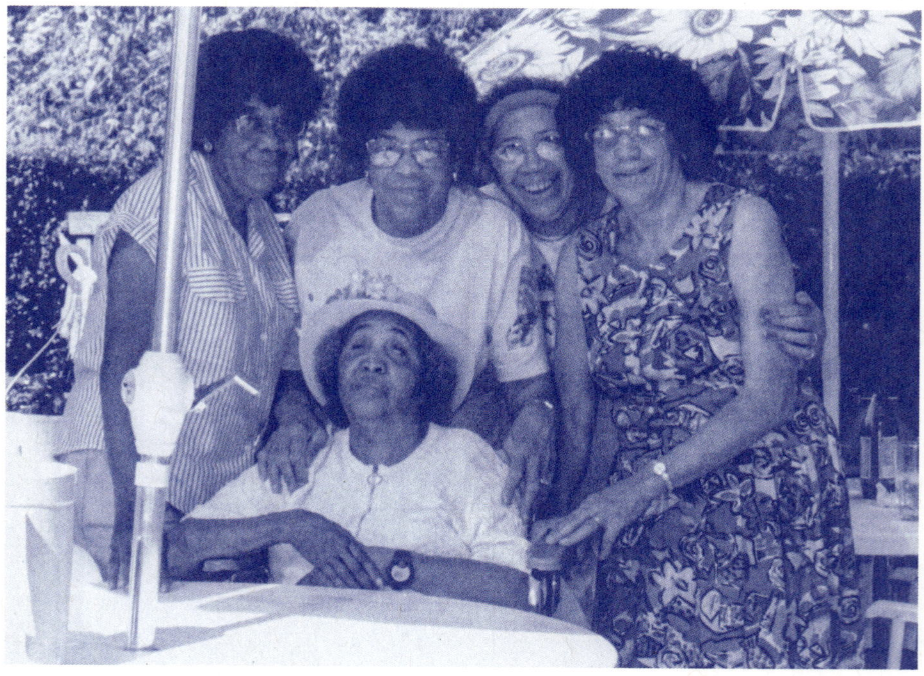

6.
The Wingfield sisters (standing, left to right) Alice Wingfield, Louise Barnard, Roxanne Dozier, Florence Brown, and Blanche Cherry (seated), 2001

Courtesy Richard "Juni" Wingfield

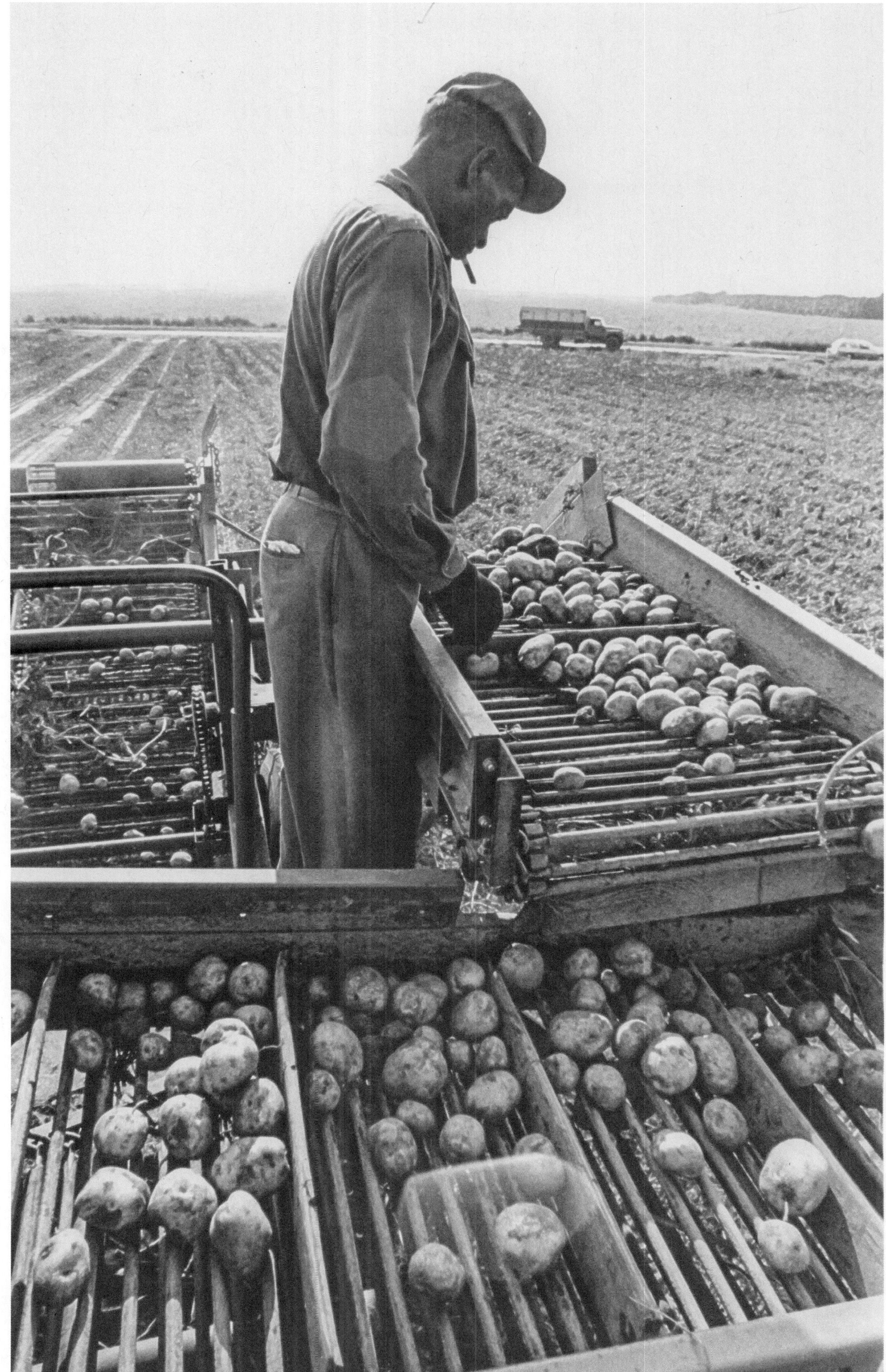

7.
A worker in a South
Fork potato field,
ca.1950

Courtesy Express
News Group

a lot of people who'd come out, who had already had that opportunity to afford an education from Washington, D.C., Baltimore, Delaware, New York City. This was a very middle-class, upper-middle-class group of Black people building houses out in Sag Harbor on Gardiners Bay, with the same idea: "We will allow our children to have something when we leave here." Guess what? The children had something. But those same children, afforded tremendous opportunities, went to some of the best schools in the country. Everything from Historically Black Colleges and Universities to Ivy League schools. When they had the opportunity to get those homes they said, "No. We're going to sell them." It was just young people who had come to a place where they now said, "No, no, no, no. Thanks, but no thanks, Mom and Dad. Thank you for giving it to us, because there's a lot of equity in it. We're just gonna cash it out and we're going to use it to establish our families and our lives somewhere else."

When I grew up there were migrant camps. All the migrant camps disappeared. Now you go into those communities and find out that the homeowners are people in town, and some people in the estate section, who have bought a few houses to put their workers in. I call it the sophisticated migrant camps. If you really want to see the workforce and how it looks, just follow the school bus through the community and three out of four kids that get off the bus are Latino. That's the manpower, that's the womanpower now. And they have to put their families somewhere. When I started in Southampton schools, the African American population in Southampton School District was approximately fifteen percent. Today it's less than two percent. The School District is now forty-two percent Latino, approximately nine to ten percent Native American, and the African American population has nearly disappeared, never to return. It breaks my heart.

Workforce housing, that's the new push, but we don't have any place to put it because the NIMBY (Not in My Back Yard) is there. There is an attitude that's so pervasive here in the East End that nowhere in government are you going to have someone with the courage to finally fight like they should for affordable housing. You got to go back to the way it happened when your grandparents came here. There's got to be one generous farmer who has land and can integrate enough social consciousness with economics and have the courage to say, "No way! I need to divide my land up so people here can have some building lots, knowing that I can sell an acre of my land for two million dollars." Who's going to step up and do that? Sooner or later, they're gonna have no choice.

Black Caucuses and Entrepreneurship

If you come into Southampton Town now, there's a Dunkin' Donuts on the right-hand side. That was a diner. The diner was important because it was a place where young people could go and hear the old guys tell stories. Some were legends in their own minds, some were tons and tons of hyperbole, but always an ounce of truth. The diner was this wonderful meeting place. That's when

I first learned about what a Black Caucus was. I realized they weren't just talking, they were caucusing. They'd talk about:
"Who needs what? Your family got groceries?"
"What do you mean, your truck broke down?"
"You need us to come over there and fix it?"
"Who's chopping that wood?"
"Somebody need to help you with that?"
"Oh, don't worry, we got an extra cup of sugar."

The diner had become a meeting place and they'd get a little bit of coffee. Interestingly enough, after the diner disappeared, some of the older men and the children of those men, who got older, like myself and some older than me, started using McDonald's to do the same thing. The diners in this little area always meant something for so many of the Black people. It was a place to be able to do a lot of soul work. It was a place to understand that most times, whatever you were going through, no matter how difficult it was, your experience probably wasn't just personal. It was also very similar and familiar to anybody sitting around. If you've got a common experience, you've got a common language. And that was happening. In this way it relieves some of the pain. There is a gathering of old, young, and middle-aged men and women to have that conversation.

"How do we fix it?"

It wasn't just about a diner and food, people needed to go there. They go there and find out: "Yes, we can maybe fix something here because we all have some similar concerns, similar feelings, and similar problems."

There was also Percy Kingsbury. We called him the King, he was still the Black farmer in our community. He also rented some land on the Shinnecock Reservation to do some of his farming. But in our community, on any given day or night, we could hear the tractor coming down the road going to one of his fields. Mr. Kingsbury planted a lot of cucumbers. He wasn't doing the potatoes, he had cucumber and corn, that was pretty much what he was doing. What was interesting was that King was a landowner, he wasn't just farming. The key for him is he owned that land. He also began building some of the homes in the community himself. Mr. Kingsbury looked like a giant up on that tractor—we call it the Iron Horse—just coming through the community going to plow his fields.

There's another gentleman, we call him Partner. Well, Partner's probably like ninety-five or ninety-six now. He gave me a book that he'd compiled called *The Black Book*, it just blew my mind. It was a book of all the Black businesses, from taxicab companies to little delis and grocery stores to restaurants and bars. We don't have any here now! There was Jefferson's Taxi, there was Seymour's Taxi. They understood, even to this day, that the one thing that the folks still needed was transportation. Not only did they create their own transportation system, that system allowed some of the men who were still farming their land to create their own businesses. Landscaping businesses. There were people who knew that, "Yes, there are white folks who created very nice and fancy landscaping companies." But there were Black men and women who would get lawn mowers and throw them on the back of the truck. The people who owned the mansions knew they could get their grass cut for half the price. They parlayed it into their own businesses: Noah Simmons Landscaping, Mr. Danny Quad Excavating, Robinson's Bar, Sherman's Bar, Patterson's Bar. It was amazing what came out of it.

The whole idea of transportation was always knowing that that would be a big need here. Sometimes the transportation would just turn out that you can get out of the field because somebody needed a chauffeur. The du Ponts, the Vanderbilts, the Fords. Ford owned the Ford Motor Company, but they still needed chauffeurs. It was always fascinating to see how they could parlay all these things and these needs into creating these businesses. We're still a service area to this day. I saw how it came about. They saw a need that was developed and created these entrepreneurs and this incredible Black business section.

Potato to Privet

For the farmer trying so hard to get that potato to the market, fighting that potato bug was a big deal. Then they made that shift, seeing how the wealthy now have a certain demand. The potato was something they could get another way. We live in communities that are private and for members only. They needed privet, better known as your hedges. They needed all kinds of privet. The next thing you know, you saw privet farms jumping up. But then guess what? They found out, "Wow, that's a pretty clean industry!" They decided to give big tax breaks for sod farms and privet farms for being able to grow big old trees so people don't have to start from scratch. When people built these McMansions they didn't want a little twig, they needed that tree to be half grown. Okay? So the shift was easy. Now you couldn't get the potato anywhere. Then what was the next big break? Let's make sure we give horse farms real tax breaks. Next thing you know, everybody and their brother have horses and horse farms. Next thing you know, you had big tax breaks on clean industry with what? Wineries. Big tax breaks.

We have a school district that is one of the neediest little school districts in probably the whole East End of Long Island, constantly not knowing if they're going to continue to function because they can't get the money for the budget because it's surrounded by eight golf courses. Who do they give big tax breaks to? Golf courses! Guys that are paying hundred-thousand-dollar initiation fees, green fees, and they got big tax breaks. A little Tuckahoe school suffers trying to meet their budget sitting in the most pristine area of eight golf courses. If you're building golf courses, you can't build no houses. If you're building wineries, sod farms, and privet, you can't use it for any

houses. So they really begin to shift, and it totally shut down development. If you didn't have two million dollars to buy an acre, game over.

Nobody wants to do affordable housing because the connotation that comes with affordable housing is always the same thing everywhere all over, right? It means you're going to allow poor people to come in. We know how that works: wealthy people are above the law, poor people are below the law. If you travel on the highway we already see the trade parade, don't we? The people who work here can't live here. Eighty-five percent of Southampton schoolteachers live outside the district. Think about what just happened with the pandemic: we had the Manhattanite diaspora, they fled. They fled, not to return. That's the thing that still blows my mind. They didn't just come hoping that this thing would pass over, they cashed out. Amazing, what's happened.

Tela Loretta Troge, Esq. is a member of the Shinnecock Indian Nation and the Hassanamisco Nipmuc Tribe. As an attorney she is involved in a number of economic development projects for the Shinnecock Nation. She has helped organize the Warriors of the Sunrise Sovereignty Camp 2020, to bring awareness to the plight of the Shinnecock people.

Her interview considers the traditional agricultural and whaling practices of the Shinnecock Nation relative to the community's emphasis on education, sustainability, and the recent historical connections between real estate development, land theft, and the desecration of Shinnecock sacred sites.

When you're on the highest point of Shinnecock Hills and you look around, you can see the Atlantic Ocean. You can see the Shinnecock Bay. You can see the Peconic Bay. It's beautiful and it was stolen from us. When you look at the newspapers and the commentary that people make: "You gave it away fair and square in 1640." While the Shinnecock Hills was actually in 1859. We're not talking about a first-contact early land theft, this is really a relatively recent land theft. What I have been trying to do is look at what else was going on during the 1800s. What you see starting in the 1850s is the expansion of the railroad system throughout the United States, and that's exactly what happened here. You start to see it on early maps before the railroad ever came through. You see them drawing it out over the Shinnecock Hills. There was this nationwide federal policy of removal during that period. That was their solution to the problem. You know, we have to run this railroad through these peoples' land. How are we going to do it?

We would look out from the highest point of the Hills for pods of whales. We were known to hunt whales that were swimming close to shore. We were especially skilled in hunting these whales, which were a primary food source. We would hunt deer. We would move around to different areas, going all the way up to the area now known as Brookhaven, all the way to the area now known as East Hampton. These are all of our hunting and fishing grounds. I think there's a bigger concept here: a lot of it is connected to the whales. There is a species called the North Atlantic right whale and they're currently the world's most endangered whales. There are only about 360 of these whales left, and only a small fraction of those are female whales able to have calves. New York State is looking at expanding its green energy and has made a huge commitment to producing electricity through wind farms, and the United States has leased a lot of the land surrounding Long Island to these wind farms. The only problem is that this area is directly in the migratory route of these whales and directly in their feeding grounds. We look at our existence as a tribal people being directly connected to these

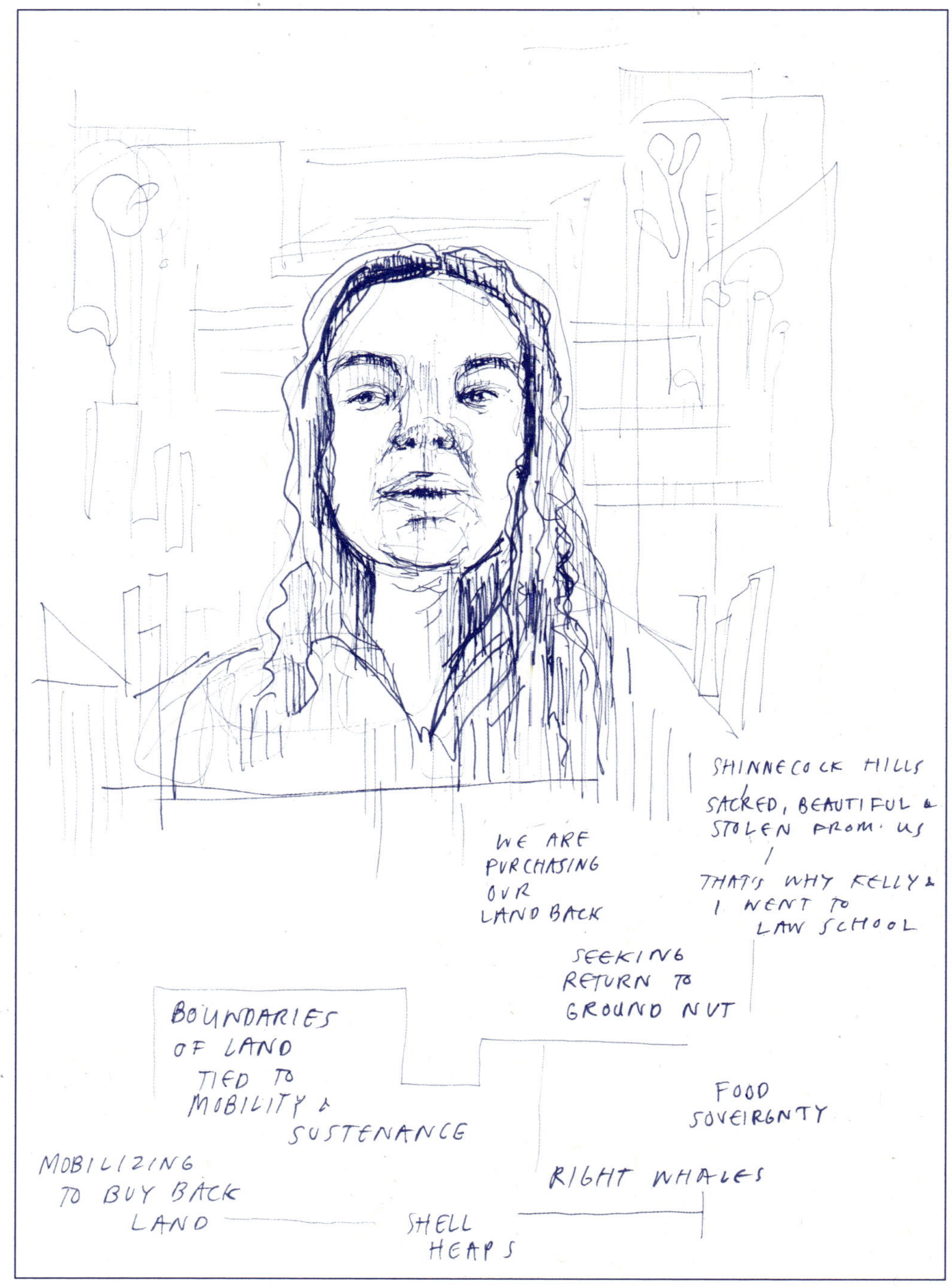

Martha Schnee
"Shinnecock Hills: sacred, beautiful, & stolen from us" — Tela Troge on purchasing back stolen land, 2021

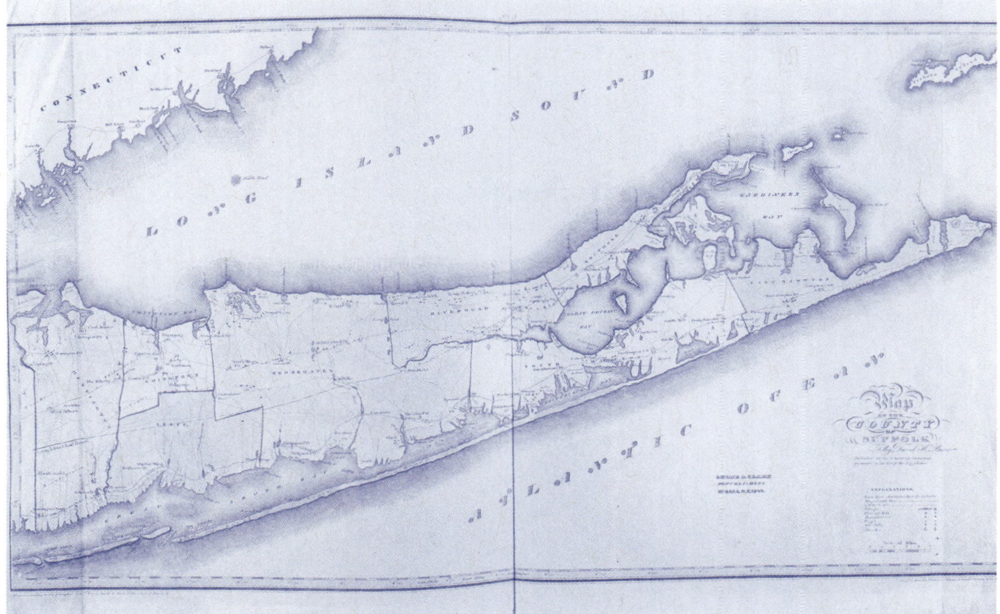

8.
David H. Burr Map
of Suffolk County,
1841

Courtesy Hope
Sandrow and the
Lionel Pincus and
Princess Firyal
Map Division, The
New York Public
Library

whales. They're called right whales because when the colonists first came here, we were really helping them learn the lay of the land and what species to hunt and fish for. We told them that these were the right whales to hunt and the colonists took it to an extreme level, which led to the whales' complete destruction as a species due to 280 years of industrial hunting.

In working to get this highest point restored to Shinnecock stewardship, the first response was that the only reason we would want our land back is to build a casino on it. For a while I was really offended. I've spent the past three weeks being horrifically offended and just angry. How could they try to say that is only why we want this land, which is proven to be a designated protected burial area, from decades of effort by Shinnecock activists? How could their first assumption be that we want this land back to build a casino on it? For a while, I thought that they were just being offensive and I was really angry. They don't value sacred sites. They have no connection to this place; they are not from here. These are not their ancestors and they don't care. That is what they would do because it is so beautiful. That is the first thing they would do—is build whatever they're going to build and that's what they've done. It's exactly what they've done. We're hoping that we can work cooperatively with the Town because they have $104 million in their holdings as a result of COVID-19. That's going to be the work that we have to do, to get people to see. There's some kind of huge disconnect here between these people who are not from here and us, and the way that we treat the environment, and the way that we value the land, and the way that we'll fiercely protect our ancestors and our children and our elders, in ways I don't think they can comprehend because it's about survival for us. And this is what we have. This is what we've been doing since they've gotten here. There's a huge amount of guilt too. I think that they're scared that, when we get our land back, when we get our economy going, and when we are powerful in the region—I think they're afraid of what we'll do.

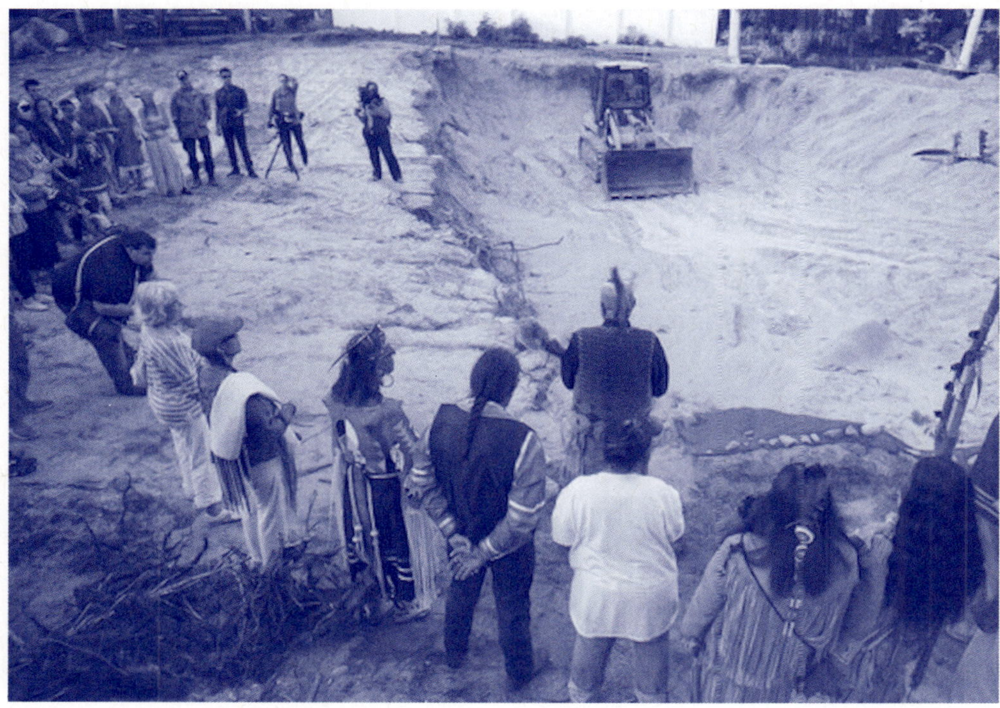

9.
Vigil held at
construction
site where
Shinnecock
remains were
found in
Southampton,
NY, 2018

Courtesy Bryan
Downey

Jeremy Dennis
To Belong to a Certain Place on Earth

Jeremy Dennis is a contemporary fine art photographer and a tribal member of the Shinnecock Indian Nation in Southampton, New York. His work interrogates Indigenous identity, culture, and assimilation through reconstructed visual narratives that challenge the hegemonic and selective histories of Long Island.

In his interview, Jeremy reflects on the concept of "home" in its connection to the landscape, emphasizing the cultural significance of communal living among the Shinnecock people, and the Shinnecock Reservation as a site of respite for many minority groups and the only affordable venue to host gatherings and cultural events on the East End of Long Island.

I think that home represents the Land. I think it brings a great feeling when you have a landscape that you can call home. The idea that you belong to a certain place on Earth is really special. The whole theme of the Land Claim is very much linked to that idea of home. As a Shinnecock person, whether you're into history or not, when you grow up you get very familiar with the landscape. We live on the border where Shinnecock becomes Southampton. The Land Claim is all about that idea of trying to regain that land, or that home, that was taken from us. The more you learn, the more you read about the Shinnecock-specific Land Claim, the more you can pinpoint it to the specific area of the Shinnecock Hills, which encompasses more than 3,200 acres.

Things like agriculture, art, and other community-focused events are what a lot of people have been demanding for a while. There have been issues of unemployment on the Reservation and I think that having a community farm would resolve a lack of job opportunities and save a lot of money. One could walk down the road and dedicate a couple of hours to taking care of a community plot and be able to eat at the end of the day. Our land is so small, it's 800 square acres. In reality, when walking on the southern tip of the Reservation, I would say one third of that 800 acres is marshland. It's not sustainable for residential or agricultural development, so the amount of land that we're able to use as a community is even smaller.

My mom always says that back in the day we used to have potato farmers. Going back to the 1900s there were probably a couple dozen families and houses here on the Reservation. It was all fields. We would lease land to potato farmers. There was a pesticide called Temik, which was a really toxic chemical they sprayed all over the Reservation's fields. There is one spot near all of our public buildings where they dumped a lot of the raw pesticide. That's the spot where nothing ever grows because it's been a toxic cesspool. There are all of these issues of space and land pollution. We are trying to come together and get the resources to do agriculture and farming. I think

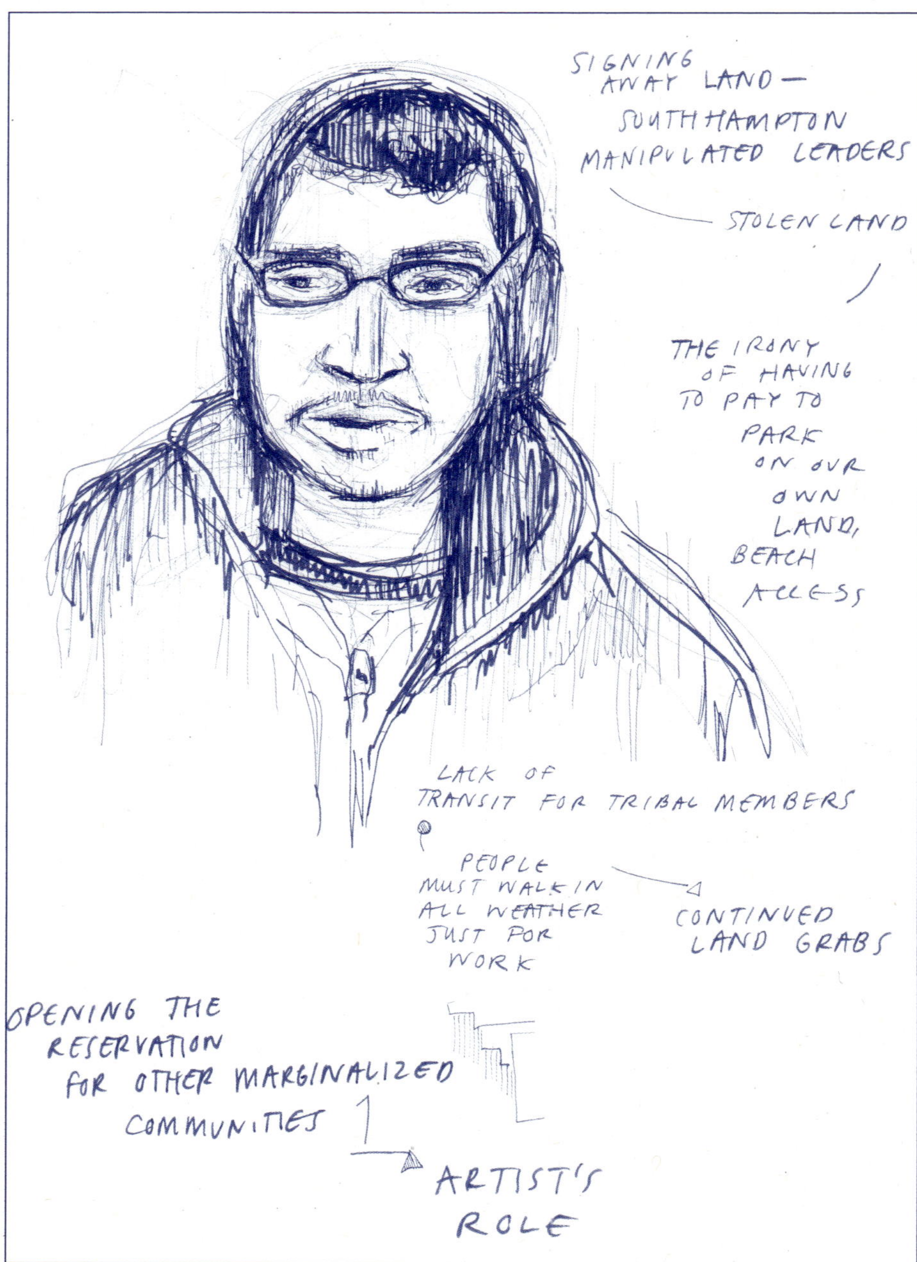

Martha Schnee
*"The irony of having to pay to park on our own land"
— Jeremy Dennis* on stolen land, transportation, and opening the Reservation, 2021

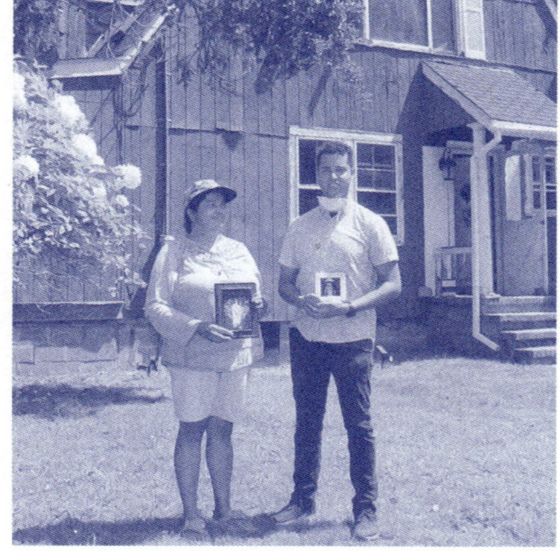

10.
Denise Silva-Dennis and her son, Jeremy Dennis, in front of her mother's house, otherwise known as Ma's House, on the Shinnecock Reservation, Southampton, NY, 2020

Courtesy Durell Godfrey

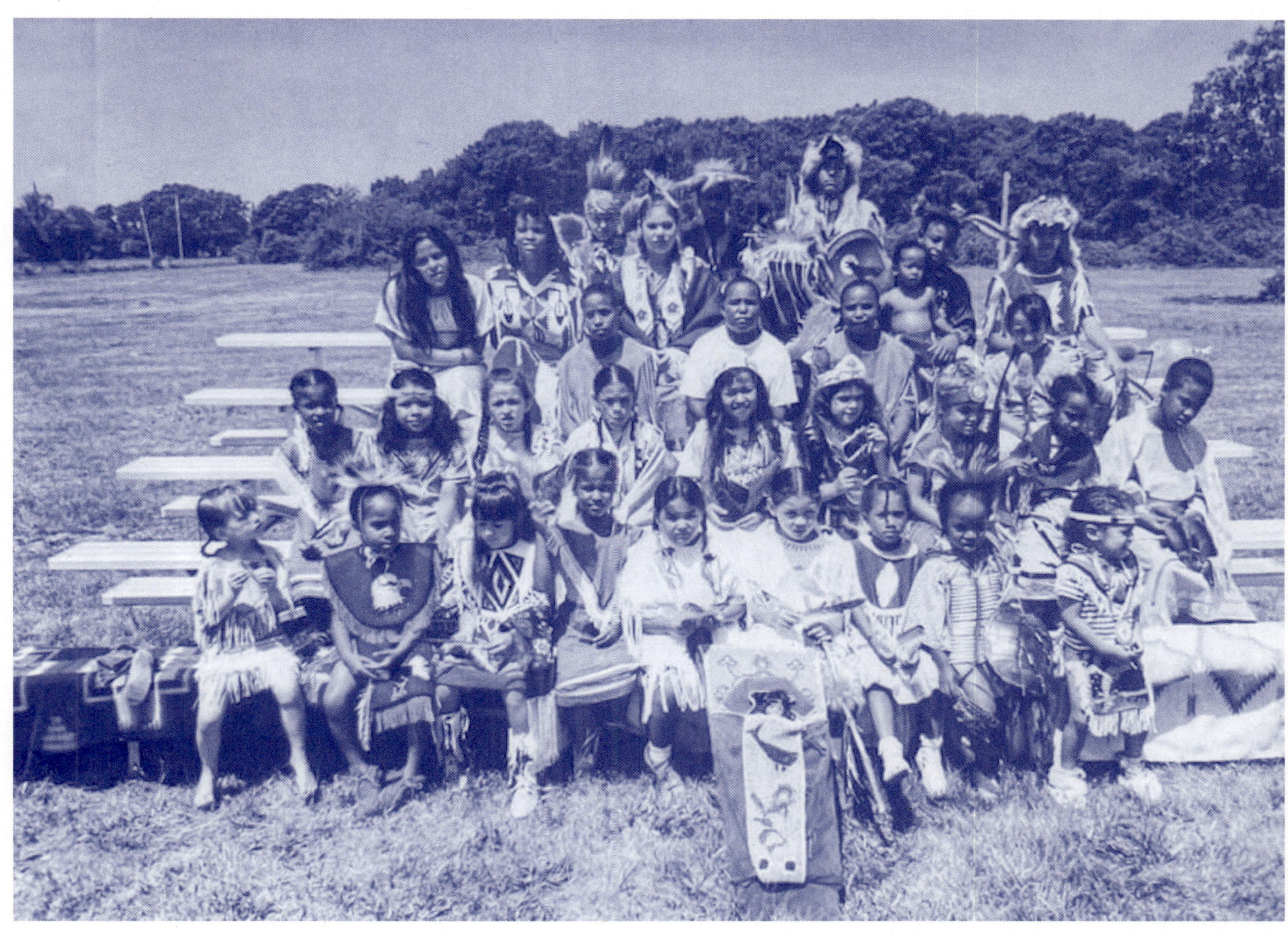

it's something that we all want, but we just have to try to figure it out.

On the issue of transportation: we have no postal service, no police patrols of our own, no ambulance, emergency medical technicians, or fire service. That also includes bus services and taxis. There's no Lyft service that comes and idles on the Reservation. I think about that every day. You see tribal members, no matter if it's snowing or raining, who are walking along the margins of the road going to their places of employment. I think about how resilient and how determined they are to attend their jobs when other people are able to hop on the bus for a couple dollars to get to their destination. That whole support system is there for them. But for us it's more than an hour each day spent walking while wearing business or work attire and probably getting sweaty. That's a detriment to those who are just trying to do some honest work.

Bonnie Cannon
That Village Type of Mentality

Bonnie Cannon is Executive Director of the Bridgehampton Child Care & Recreational Center (BHCCRC), where she seeks to provide crucial resources to children and young adults in communities of color on the East End of Long Island. She is Chair of the Town of Southampton Housing Authority and a cofounder of the Southampton African American Museum.

In our conversation, Bonnie describes the advantages and obstacles associated with growing up on "The Hill" in Southampton, New York. Further, she explains how she and her team at BHCCRC are navigating the educational struggles that minority communities have confronted during the COVID-19 pandemic.

I was born here in Southampton, and my mom and dad are from the South, both from North Carolina. My father migrated up here and lived in Brooklyn for many years, and my mom migrated up from the South and lived in Southampton. Mom and Dad met and Dad moved out to Southampton, and then you have me. A lot of my ancestors migrated from the South because there was work up here— cooking, cleaning, and farm work.

A lot of wealthy white families would come from Europe. They had big houses here and they would hire help to tend their lawns or to take care of their children, to clean their houses, and to cook. That would be the labor force that would take care of them. If there were parties, you had a lot of cooking engagements, catering engagements, the lawn, and landscaping. Then, of course, you had the agriculture. Out here are potatoes and corn, so you have a lot of individuals who worked on the farms digging for the potatoes and the corn harvest. My family worked in the houses and did landscaping. There were construction jobs working on the roads. A lot of my family worked in construction. Joining the union was a big thing because you would get union work on the highways. My father was a construction worker and a jazz musician, known out here as King Charles. His passion was music. He did a lot of playing in Brooklyn, but what brought in the money was the union job. My uncle worked in the union as well and some of my uncles did landscaping work and upkeep of houses.

A lot of my aunts and uncles migrated from the South, and we all lived in the same neighborhood called The Hill. I lived on Miller Road, my grandmother lived up a few houses on Miller Road, and I had two uncles that lived farther up on Miller Road. I have an uncle that lived on Hillcrest but it was known as Hill. It's a Black neighborhood, and everybody knew everybody, so it was great growing up on The Hill. It was like a family culture neighborhood. The playground was a gathering place. That's definitely where all of the kids in the neighborhood played and we all got together then. Teenagers met there and it was a lot of fun. It was a neighborhood and you couldn't get away with stuff on The Hill because Miss Madeline,

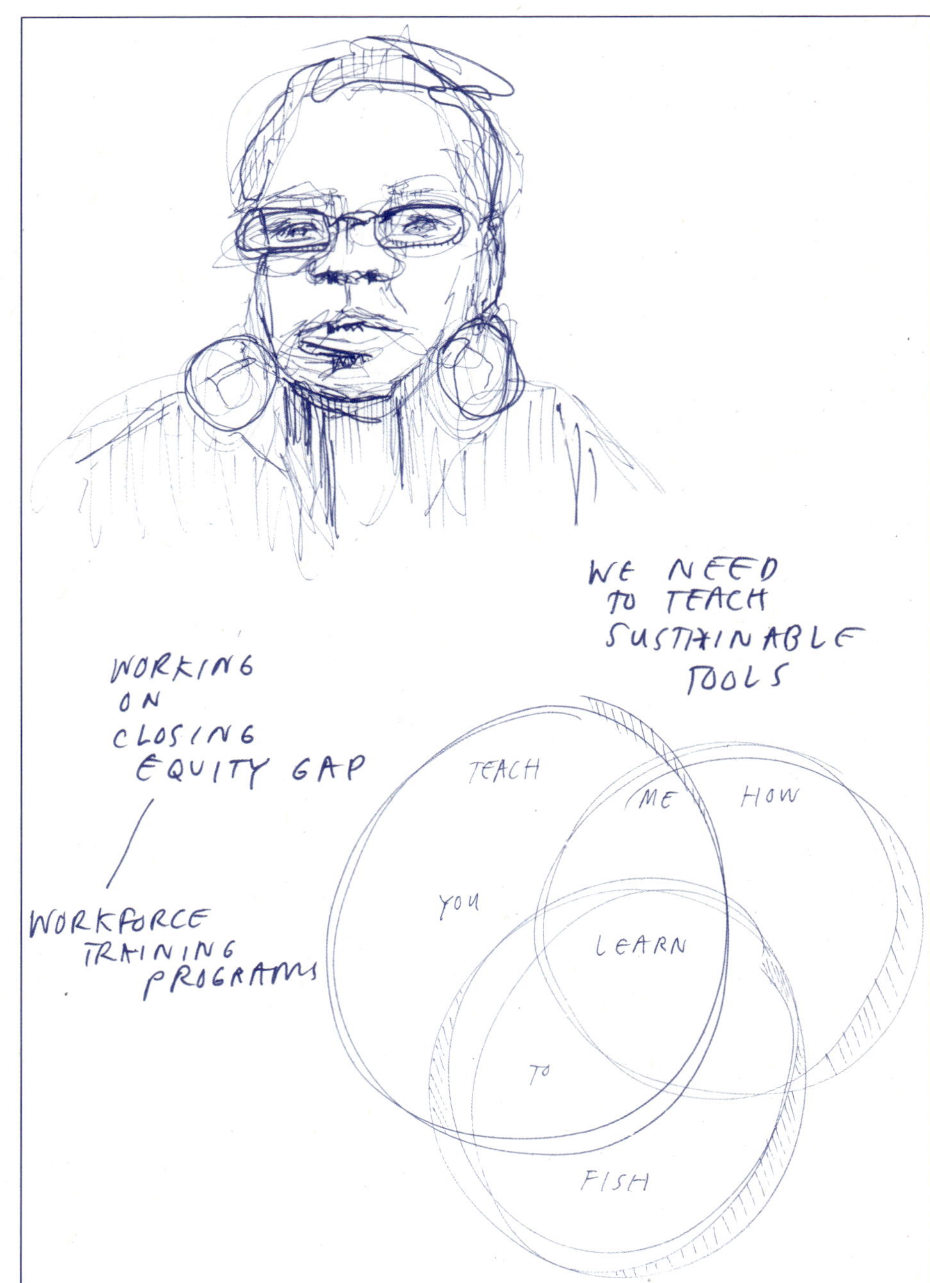

Martha Schnee
"We need to teach sustainable tools"
— Bonnie Cannon on closing the equity gap, 2021

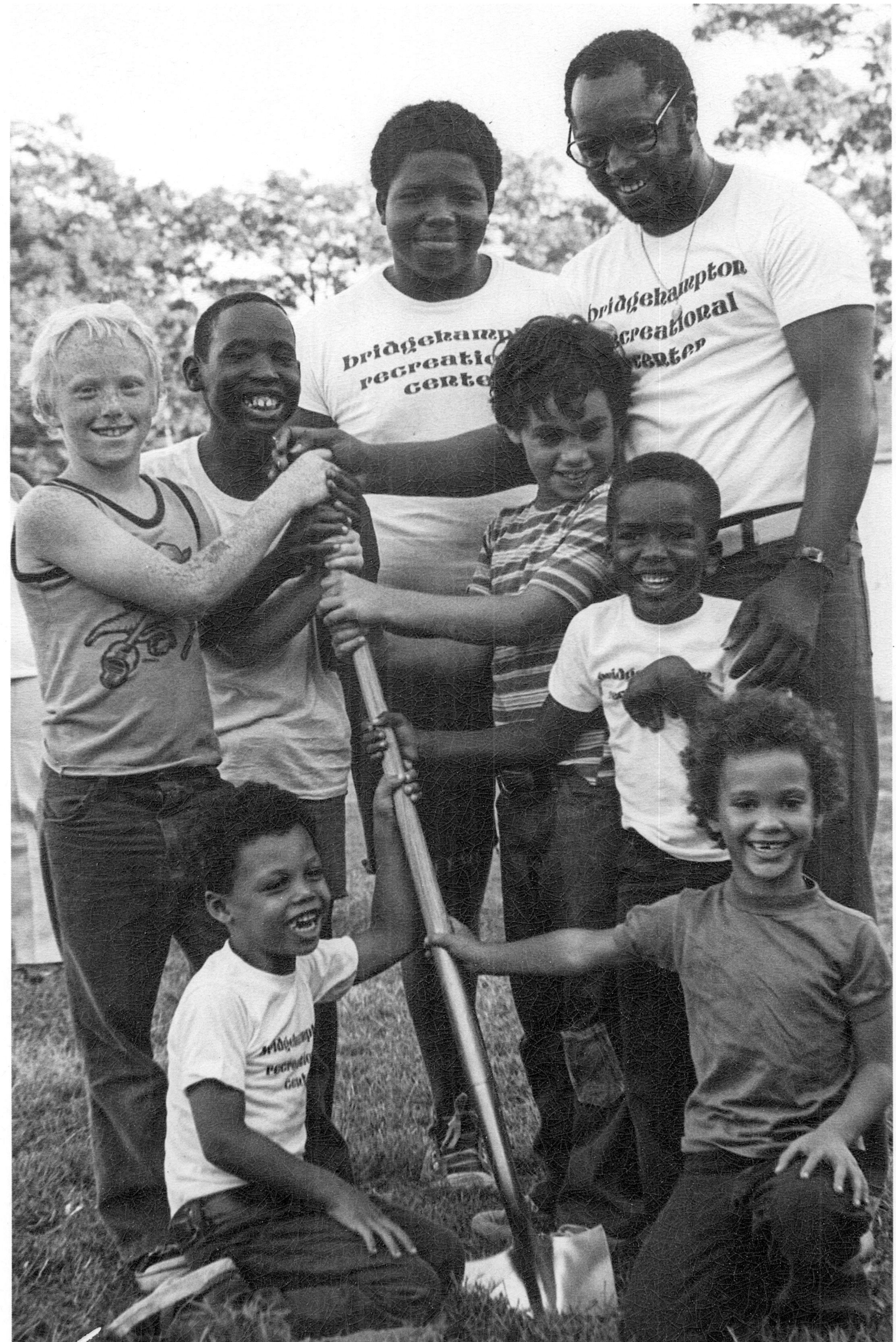

12.
Marvin Dozier
and students
from the
Bridgehampton
Childcare &
Recreational
Center, ca. 1970

Courtesy the
Southampton
Youth Association

up the road, if she saw you do something: "I'm gonna tell your grandmother that you did this or you did that!" Everybody just knew everyone. A lot of people went to the same churches. There were only two or three churches that were around. In some sort of way, when you talk about the village raising the child, it was definitely that village type of mentality on The Hill. That does not exist anymore because The Hill has changed a lot.

King's Chapel Church of God in Christ on Hillcrest Avenue, First Baptist Church of Southampton, Community Baptist Church in Southampton, First Baptist Church in Bridgehampton as well. You'd be surprised there are quite a few churches, Padgetts Temple that is over in Tuckahoe, and the First Church of God in Christ in Bridgehampton. A lot of churches have closed down, but that does not mean that we are not connected. The church inside me is what makes me a part of my home and there's a connection there. So the home or the spirit of that family still exists because it's not based upon what is physically around me, it's a spiritual type of connection.

The Hamptons thrive off the farms and what the farms produce: potatoes, corn, you name it. It was a main thing here but we didn't own the farms. White people owned the farms, but they had a lot of Black people that worked on the farms, migrant workers that came up here from the Carolinas and they say, "You working at a tater grater." They didn't get paid much money and a lot of them didn't have decent living conditions. But the labor, that agriculture, is a big part of what's out here, and it's interesting because a lot of the farms have sold their land and now you see, in place of the farms, big houses. A lot of second home owners that come from the city, a lot of the Wall Street money. The farmers sold the land to them, so there aren't many farms as big as they were before, but now there is more housing for the rich out here.

People are working to pay for a roof over their head, and there are other necessities. If you ever looked at the Housing Choice Voucher program, and what the qualifications are for the Section 8 program, you will be like, "Well, dang, that's not Section 8." But there are nurses and teachers that qualify for the program out here because that's how high the medium income is. So somebody making $60,000 to $70,000 a year could possibly qualify to get a Section 8 voucher. It's really crazy.

We gotta come up with something to keep everything at a balance, because you can't just have all wealthy people and no other people that are here; it has to be a community. When we were coming up, you had a lot of rentals that were available because everybody, especially young people or new couples, can't start out just buying a home. We rented. There's a lack of rental housing that's out here. That's why I'm the chair of the Southampton Housing Authority, and we're working to make more affordable housing out here. So it's changed, everything has changed. Everything.

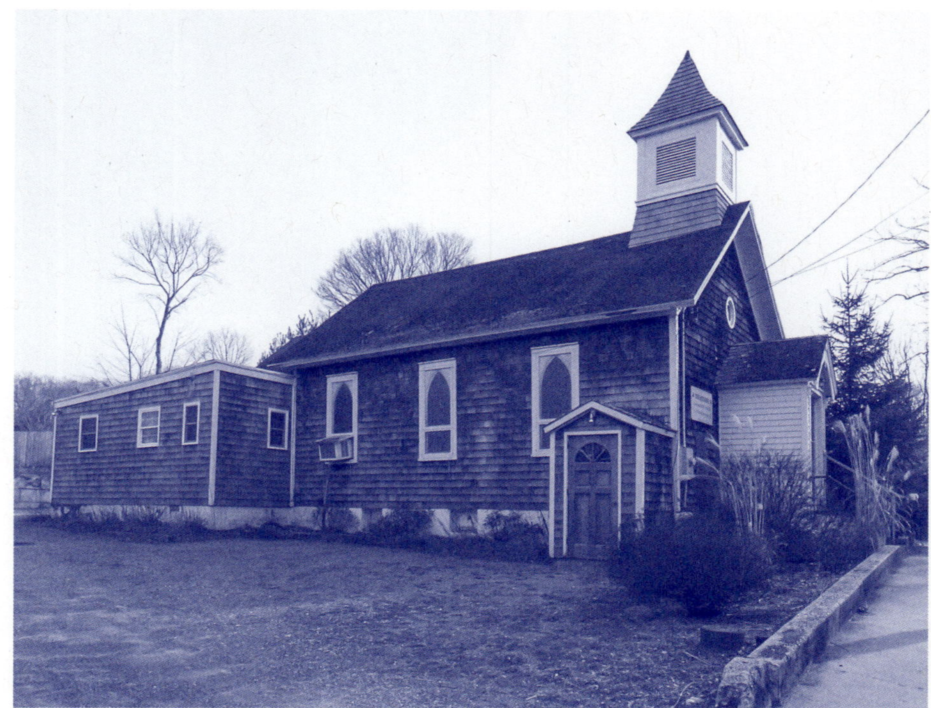

13.
St. David AME Zion Church in Sag Harbor, NY. Founded in 1840, current view

Courtesy the Eastville Community Historical Society Collection

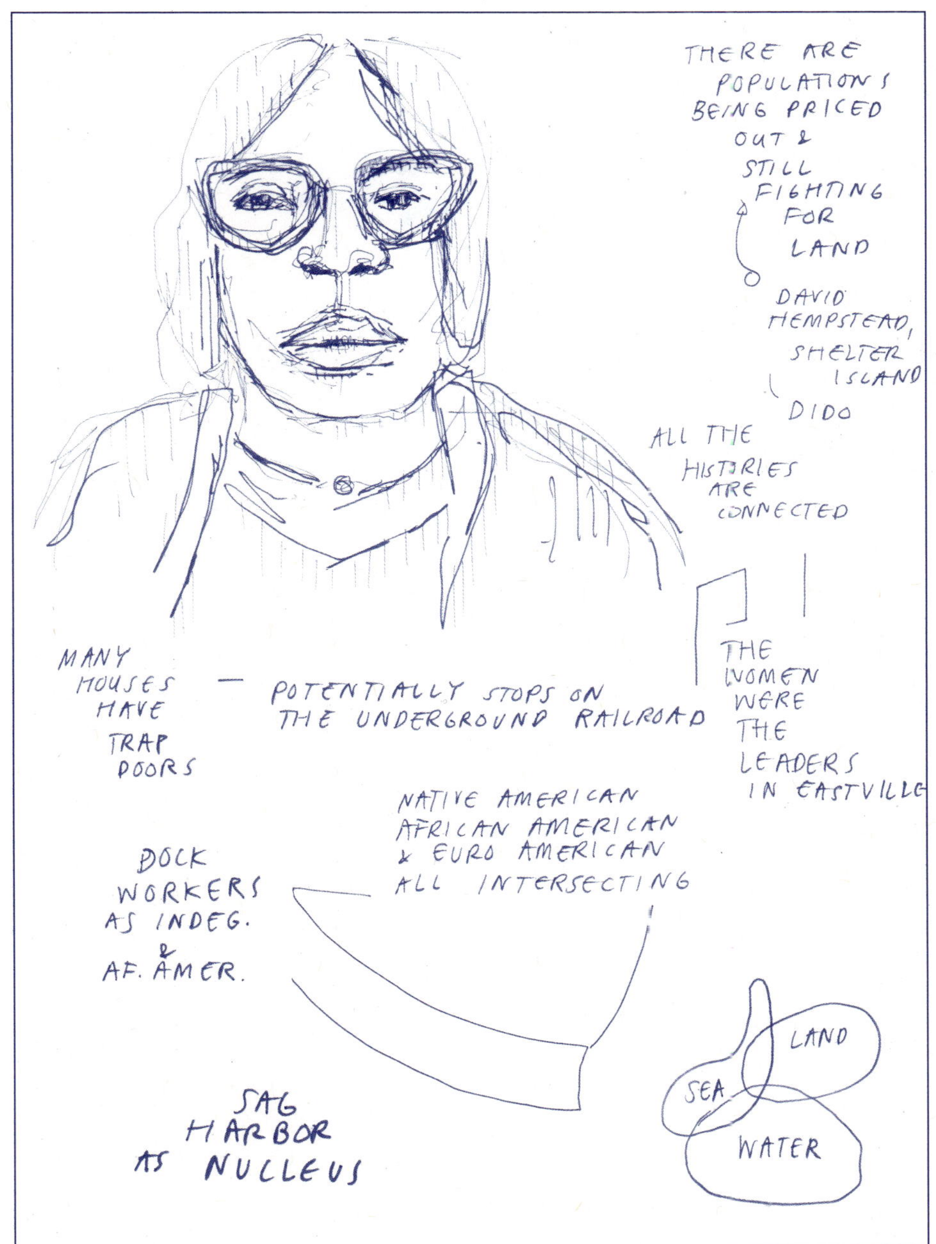

Martha Schnee
"All the histories are connected"
— Georgette Grier-Key on intersecting cultures and the ongoing fight for land, 2021

Georgette Grier-Key
We Are Still Here

Dr. Georgette Grier-Key, Ed.D., M.Ed. is the inaugural Executive Director and Chief Curator of the Eastville Community Historical Society of Sag Harbor, New York. She is also a cultural partner of Sylvester Manor Educational Farm on Shelter Island, New York, and President of the Association of Suffolk County Historical Societies.

In her interview, Georgette reveals the rich narrative of the historically Black Eastville and SANS communities on the East End of Long Island and details her ongoing efforts to protect and preserve local landmarks associated with them.

Sylvester Manor, the first provisional plantation in the Northeast, is one of the most important sites for marking a period in time in relation to the sugar trade between Barbados and here. From there you see generations of enslaved Africans and their children that are also born and enslaved. You see patterns of different generations that are now going free and migrating from Sylvester Manor over to Sag Harbor. Those connections between land, water, and sea are really important. On the land you can see the African burial ground and a Quaker cemetery there.

Most of the people we see who live in these historic places were the Indigenous peoples who were part of British colonial America before we were the United States. You see African American populations that are born here. Some of their descendants no longer live in these places because they can't afford to, and when opportunity opened up for people to move about some people moved and disappeared, so a population got lost both ways. Between 1843 and 1865 you see African Americans fighting for land that they had that was either given to them because they were taking care of the property or land that they had bought in little pieces. David Hempstead comes over to Sag Harbor after actively fighting for land in Shelter Island and not winning. He was a part of taking care of the land, with an agreement that it would be his land. When he wanted to formalize relationships, everything went awry.

He moved on to Sag Harbor and then he was able to help them successfully establish the Eastville community, anchoring the David AME Zion Church that is there in his namesake. There's a couple disbursements from the Sylvester Manor going east. Then we see a presence go west with Jupiter Hammond, who ends up in Lloyd Harbor. Going manor to manor, that was really important in the early founding of the East End. There were thirteen land-grant patents that were given to folks for the establishment of these manors. These manors were huge, like the Manor of St. George, Lloyd Manor, and Sylvester Manor. All of Shelter Island belonged to Sylvester Manor. You would see those relationships, sometimes people were working with others, people were lent out to work for other slave owners of these sites.

Dido, an enslaved person, actually inherited her land. Then, slowly but surely, the Sylvester family descendants bought it back piece by piece because she didn't have money. There was no way into work. What are your resources? How were they able to keep it? Just keeping the house wasn't providing enough money for Dido. Selling off the land was a natural thing, she thought, not realizing that she was actually being taken advantage of. She died destitute in Sag Harbor. She died with nothing.

In Sag Harbor most of the property that is there belongs to the Black people. The beach property is the only real beach in the SANS [Sag Harbor Hills, Azurest, and Ninevah] neighborhood. When you talk about travel you think about the real Green Book, because that was one of the known areas that is associated with places like Idlewild. If it wasn't for this early history of Eastville, the SANS community couldn't happen. It all started with the provisioning plantation and the outskirts of the people on the provisioning plantation. Then you see a change over, that some of the people were still here, and then you see modern-day people still trying to keep their land. The modern-day SANS communities were built in the 1940s. Again a very great story: two women approached the young man who wanted to go off to college and didn't want to be bothered with his family business, Daniel Gale real estate, which is currently Sotheby's. These two sisters, Amaza Lee Meredith and Maude Terry, created a syndicate, a company, to distribute this land to distinguished second home owners of the professional Black class where they bought the property. The women were leaders of the community.

We see matriarchal community patterns coming out of Eastville because the men were whalers, they were away. Women owned land before they were legally allowed to own land. The women were normally encouraged to marry. Nope! The sisters didn't marry, they accumulated wealth together, they bought things together. You see these patterns, the strength, and the growth out of Eastville. Making those connections between these large plots of land, the people that worked and lived there, then seeing where they went once slavery was over or there was freedom. How did they go there? Two places were East Hampton, Freetown, and Sag Harbor, Eastville. You see that relationship happening, but then you see Sag Harbor really being a nucleus to it all. Why did they decide to place the church there?

We have a few people where we know all of their names. If you go on Sylvester Manor's website, you'll see that on the stairs Donnamarie Barnes did an exhibition where all we had was the names. We asked, "How do we honor this?" The names are going up the staircase to the attic, where the enslaved persons and servants would have moved about the house (see Fig. 16). You see, the treads on the stairs were different from enslaved folks and the ladies of the house. So Donnamarie had the first names written in calligraphy on the stair risers]. You don't have a face and you don't have a last name, you just have that name. Honoring those women in that space was really important.

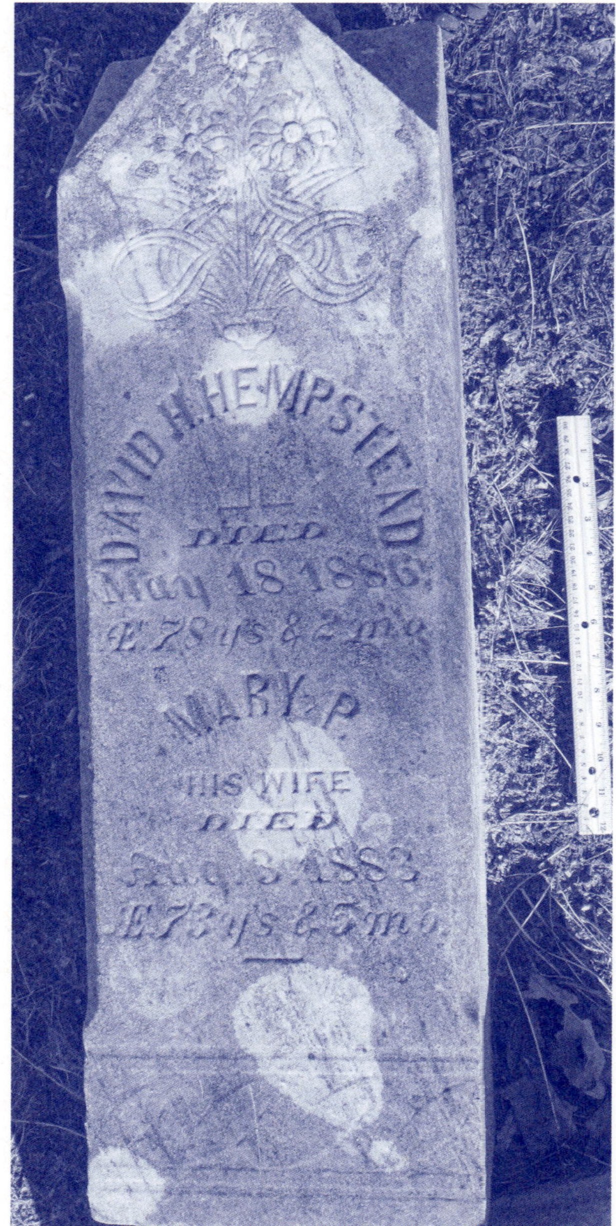

14.
Gravestone of David H. Hempstead, Mary P. Hempstead, Henry Green, and Mary J. Hempstead, current view

Courtesy the Eastville Community Historical Society Collection

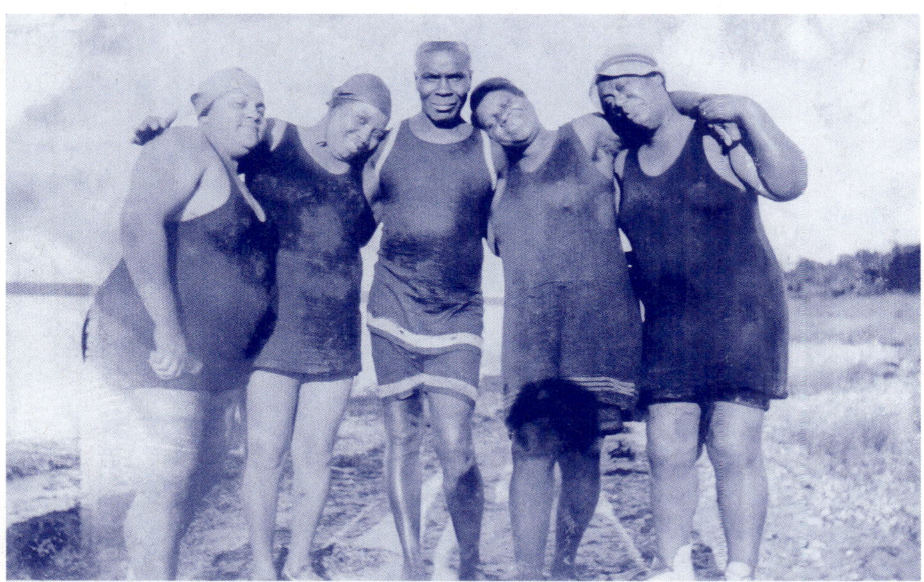

15.
Group on Azurest
Beach, Sag Harbor,
NY, date unknown

Courtesy
the Eastville
Community
Historical Society
Collection

Back then, the border lines between these communities weren't as strict as they are now. Sag Harbor and Eastville are directly in the middle of Southampton Township and East Hampton Township. Why is it important? We would have been like the South Street Seaport. We have the first custom house in the nation, so people would bring down their cargo and register it in Sag Harbor. Who would be working those docks? Of course, it would be the People: Native American, African American, Indigenous people would be working those docks. They were the expert whalers, who were whaling well before contact with Europeans in that area. The importance of Sag Harbor is that it brought everybody together.

There is a Historic Trails group in the village that's associated with the government and the township. A lot of times, you'll see these little gravestones or gravesites, some of them off the beaten path. I consider these cemeteries, these stones, to be documents that are very important to our understanding because a lot of the time they aren't there. How do we find a lot of the stuff in those records? A lot of the stuff is hidden. The Plain Sight Project is focused on saying, "It is here but it's very hidden. Who was literate? Who were the keepers of the information?" A lot of the time it wasn't the government, it was the private holders who held vital records. Shipping records and logs, account books of things recorded in the churches, you'll see it. Sometimes you can find a mention of an enslaved person or a name, but it just stops cold there. Our connection to them is really the land where we are actually walking where they lived or where they were interred. That is the connection to a lot of the land.

In the book *The Land Was Ours*, Andrew W. Kahrl talks about all of the land that Black people had after Reconstruction and how we have it now. It makes you remember Dido and how she had land, but there's an effective procedure to try to get this back, to turn back the clock and take the land. This did happen in SANS too, where we had a developer by the name of Black Rock, a big-time company, come in and try to gentrify all of the Black communities that have access to the water. In Sag Harbor Hills they have the beach on their actual deeds. It's a lot, but you can trace it through different time periods of enslavement to Reconstruction, Jim Crow, and now gentrification.

Donnamarie Barnes
A Place Held Together by the Work of Women

Curator and Archivist Donnamarie Barnes uncovers the histories and identities of enslaved and Indigenous people through the artifacts left behind on the grounds of Sylvester Manor Educational Farm, located on Shelter Island, New York. She is Co-Director and Chair of the Plain Sight Project, an ongoing endeavor dedicated to acknowledging and researching individuals who were once enslaved on the East End of Long Island.

In our conversation, Donnamarie unpacks Sylvester Manor's significance as one of the first provisioning plantations on eastern Long Island for the West Indian sugar trade, and recounts her experiences growing up in the SANS community of Ninevah Beach, in Sag Harbor, New York.

I live across the water from Shelter Island in Sag Harbor. I've lived here all of my life and so I'm very deeply tied to this land. It is home and my soul. It's what informs my art. It's my family's home and so I have these very personal connections to it that get reflected in this work that I have suddenly fallen into. In 1651, Nathaniel Sylvester and his partners bought the entire island. They bought the 8,000 acres of Shelter Island for 1,600 pounds of sugar and established this provisioning plantation. Nathaniel Sylvester is the partner who's tasked with building a house and making this a commercial enterprise of felling trees for timber, farming the land, and raising livestock. It's a complicated story, but they do eventually lose it to debt and Shelter Island then gets established as a town, with the family retaining a thousand acres and the present manor house that's there now. The thousand acres is the basis of the land that we still have today, which is now down to 235 acres. It was sold off in different ways and at different times of need.

Around 1820, a Black man named Comus Fanning, who was manumitted from his enslavement, bought twenty-three acres of prime land from the family on Shelter Island. He was a Black man who owned property on Shelter Island that he then passed on to his stepdaughter Julia Dyd Havens, who worked at Sylvester Manor in various ways throughout her life over three generations. They systematically bought back her land at far below market value and swindled her. She's the last known person buried in our Afro-Indigenous burial ground. It's this amazing history that is so broad, so wonderful, as well as horrible. Four hundred years in one place is a long time, and there are many, many different stories. It is a place of enslavement. It's a place with a connection to the Caribbean. My ancestry is Caribbean, West Indian, and from Barbados, so I'm very connected.

When Europeans started coming to the East End, or all of Long Island, it was immediate and purposeful. They were here to stay, and as David Rattray and I point out in the Plain Sight Project, everybody enslaved people; it was ubiquitous. If you were a landowner you were a slave holder.

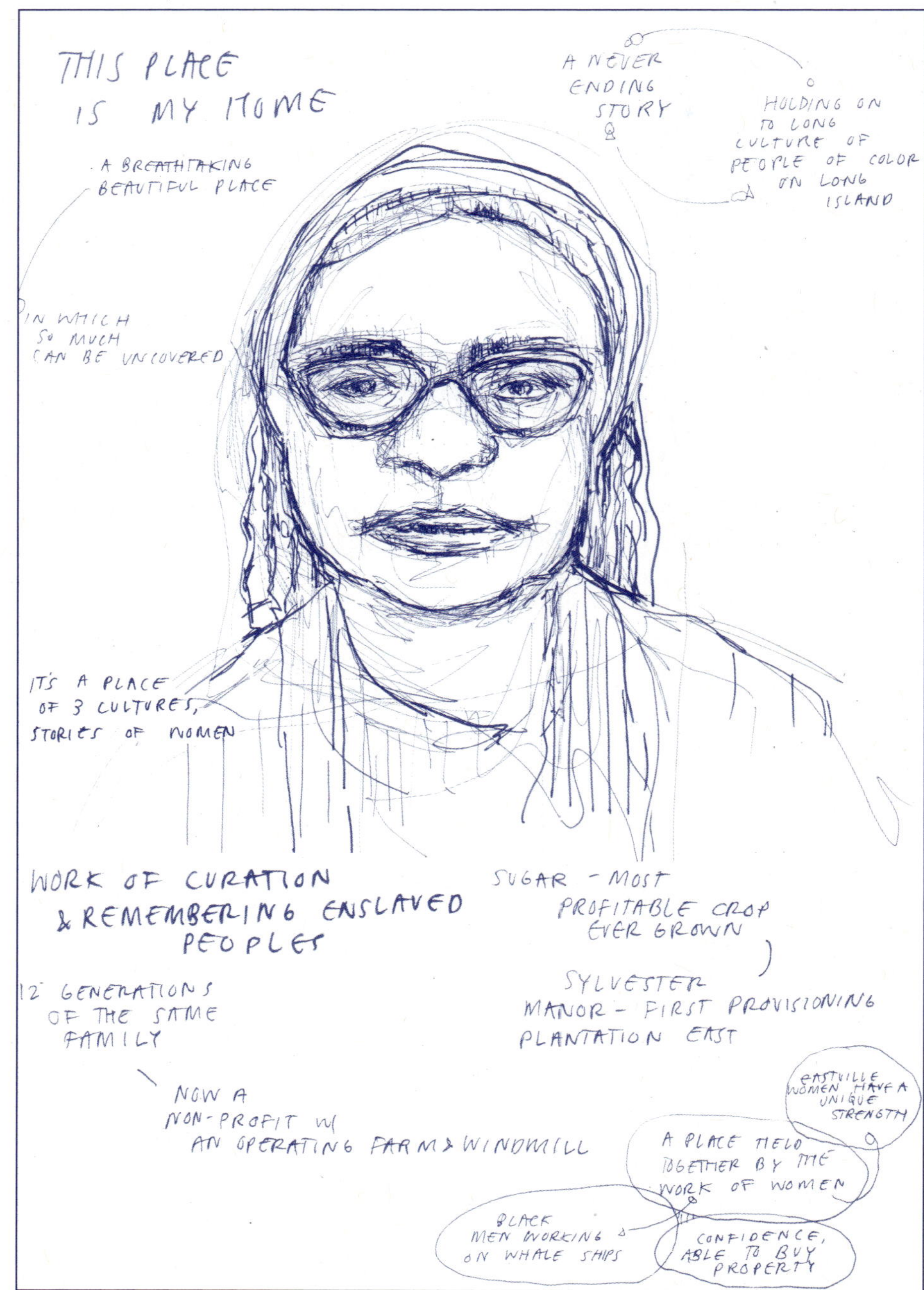

Martha Schnee
"A never ending story"
*— Donnamarie Barnes
on remembering and
uncovering histories
of people of color
on Long Island,* 2021

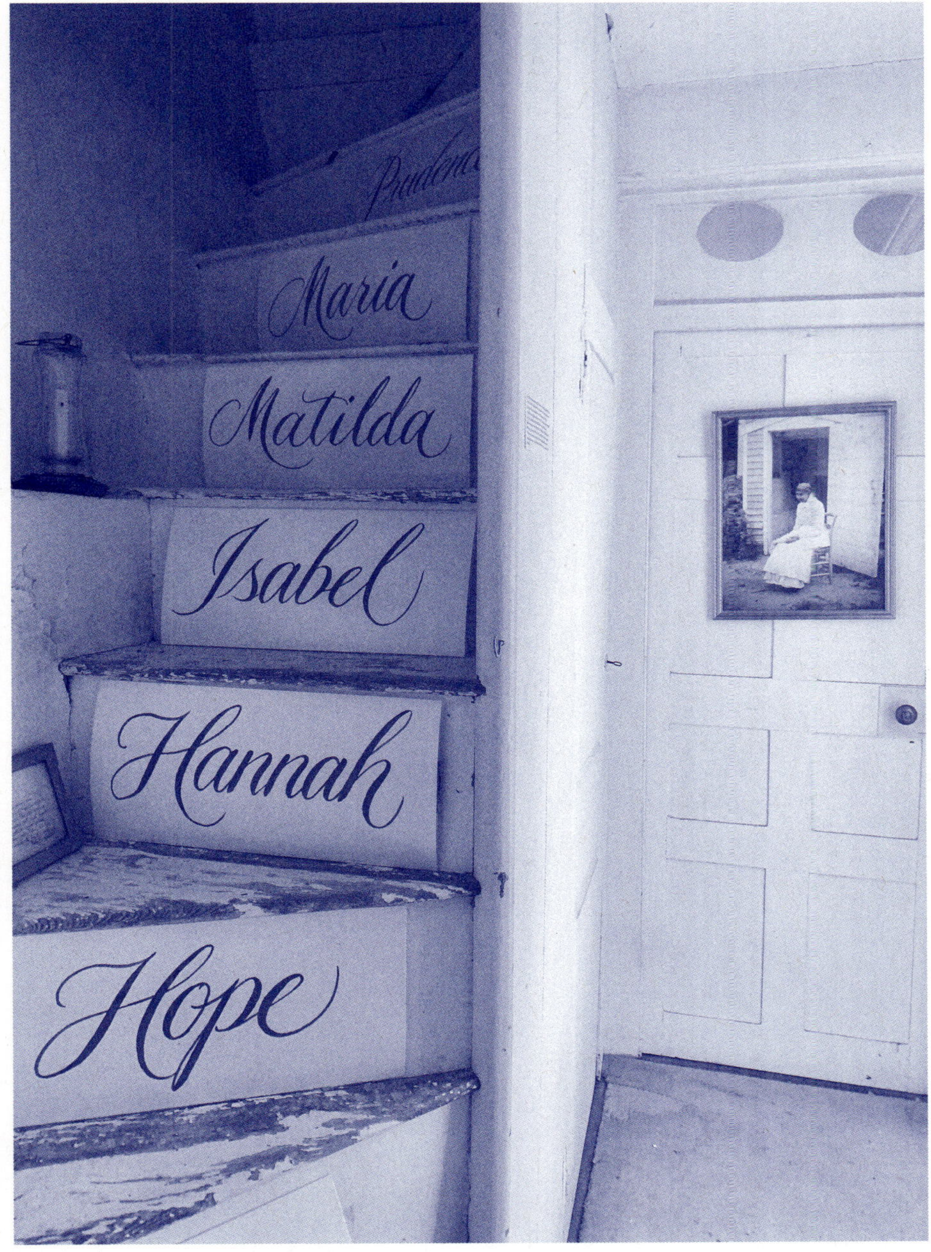

16.
Slave staircase
at Sylvester Manor
Educational Farm,
Shelter Island, NY,
current view

Courtesy
Donnamarie
Barnes/Sylvester
Manor Educational
Farm.

Today streets are still named for people who have held people in bondage. That part of the history was just starting to be told. The purpose of the work that we do is to bring these stories to the forefront because the subject of Northern slavery is not taught. When people come on tours to the manor and learn that slavery was abolished in New York in 1827, nobody knows that, because they weren't taught that—old people, young people, white people. I've had Black people say, "I didn't know there was slavery on Long Island. I didn't know there were slaves in New York. I didn't know there were slaves in the Northeast or what they did, or how many there were, I thought that was just in the South." This is a history that's been hidden, forgotten, or that's slipped through the cracks, not to be told because of many factors.

The Sylvesters (Nathaniel, his brother, and two partners) owned sugarcane plantations on the island of Barbados. Sugar became the greatest cash crop in the world in the mid–seventeenth century. All the land was used for the production of sugarcane, which was worked by transported enslaved Africans. Food was not grown on the island, and so they had to import all of their supplies. Foodstuffs, livestock, raw materials were provided to them by the site's landowners, specifically the Northeast, in New York, upstate in the Hudson Valley, in Connecticut, and on Long Island. Sylvester Manor was among the first provisioning plantations of the Northeast and probably the first on the East End of Long Island. It's what fueled the economy of the Northeast; it was the Northeast's position in the triangle trade.

Sugar was brought from the Caribbean, molasses was then distilled into rum in Rhode Island. Sugar was then transported back to England, raw materials were sent from the Northeast, from Shelter Island, to the Caribbean to provision the plantations there with barrel staves from the trees cut down to make the barrels to house the sugar, for food stuffs to feed the enslaved workers, livestock, et cetera. Sugarcane was grown and processed in Barbados and then shipped to the Northeast of America and then to England. When sugar was introduced to Europe for the first time, people literally lost their minds and became instantly addicted to it the way that we are now—and it literally became the most profitable crop ever grown. Whole industries evolved from sugar, everything in the British Empire was driven by the profit of sugar, including the slave trade. Sylvester Manor originated from two plantations on Barbados and those were the African people who were brought there after being transported from Africa to the Caribbean, they were then brought to Shelter Island to live a totally alien life in this place. It's those people that my research is really based on, finding out as much as I can about them even with the lack of documentation. Because although the Sylvester descendants kept every piece of paper they ever wrote on, the documentation specificity about the lives of the enslaved people is scarce, beyond just their names on last wills and testaments or inventories and account books or mentions.

Jupiter Hammond was an enslaved man who lived at a place called Lloyd's Manor in Queens Village in Huntington. He became the first published African American poet as an enslaved man. His father, Obi, was born in Sylvester Manor, and Obi's parents, Tammero and Oyou, were among the first enslaved African people brought to Sylvester Manor from Barbados; they were African-born. We have a ceramic pot that was made by an African woman and a Native American woman that was unearthed in the archaeological dig. Was that Oyou? There is a tradition of women being potters among the Yoruba people of Nigeria, which is where we think they were from. Did she bring that skill with her? Did she make this pot? Was that artistic tradition passed down to Jupiter Hammond? Just how did he become a poet? Was storytelling a part of his family and a tradition passed on to him? All of those are really specific and important facts and imaginings. Just to say that Jupiter Hammond was the first published African American poet is a statement. How do you become a poet? What influences do you have? And so it's a family, Jupiter Hammond's family, it's unique not just because he became a poet but because we can trace his family back three generations to Africa, which in itself is incredible. So it's a connection between Sylvester Manor and Lloyd Manor.

I have these names and I have to imagine them in this landscape that has not changed in four hundred years because the same family lived in this place. I am a photographer. I've been trying to interpret their lives through the photographs and images that I make of the place because their memories are fused in the very landscape. Despite the fact that I don't have documentation, we have artifacts uncovered through archaeological digs which don't specifically point to enslaved people but their articles of work. So if I have artifacts that are sewing needles and thimbles and buttons or clay pipes and nails, those are symbols of work that was performed by enslaved women and by enslaved men that represent the origins of the place—which is then inherently tied to the people that lived and worked there and were, in fact, imprisoned there. This is the most breathtakingly beautiful place, but it's also a place of imprisonment, of enslavement, of being held on this land. That memory for me, and for all of us who work or visit there, is infused in the very soil. It's something we tangibly feel and celebrate.

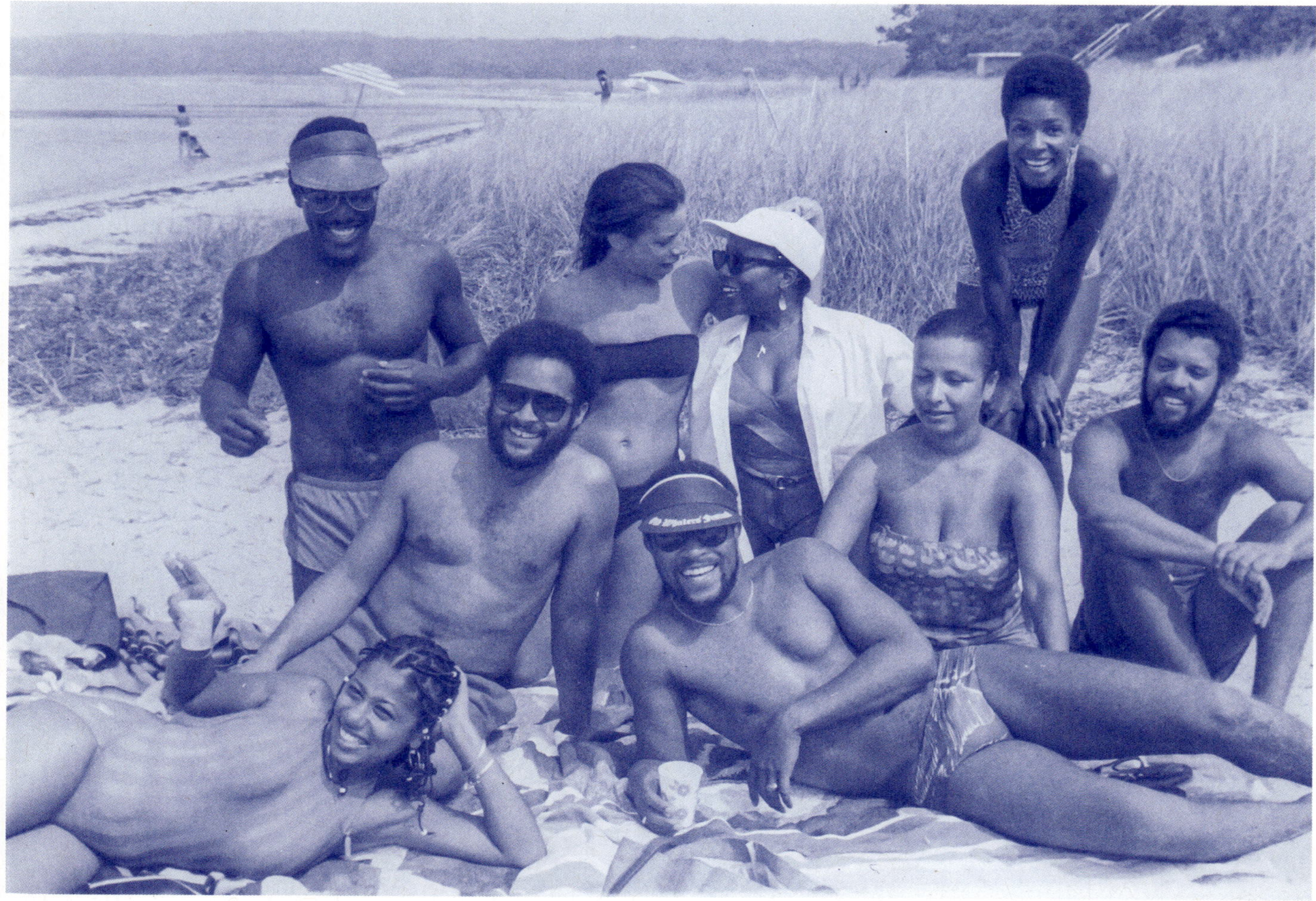

17.
Group on Ninevah Beach in Sag Harbor, NY, 1987

Courtesy Donnamarie Barnes

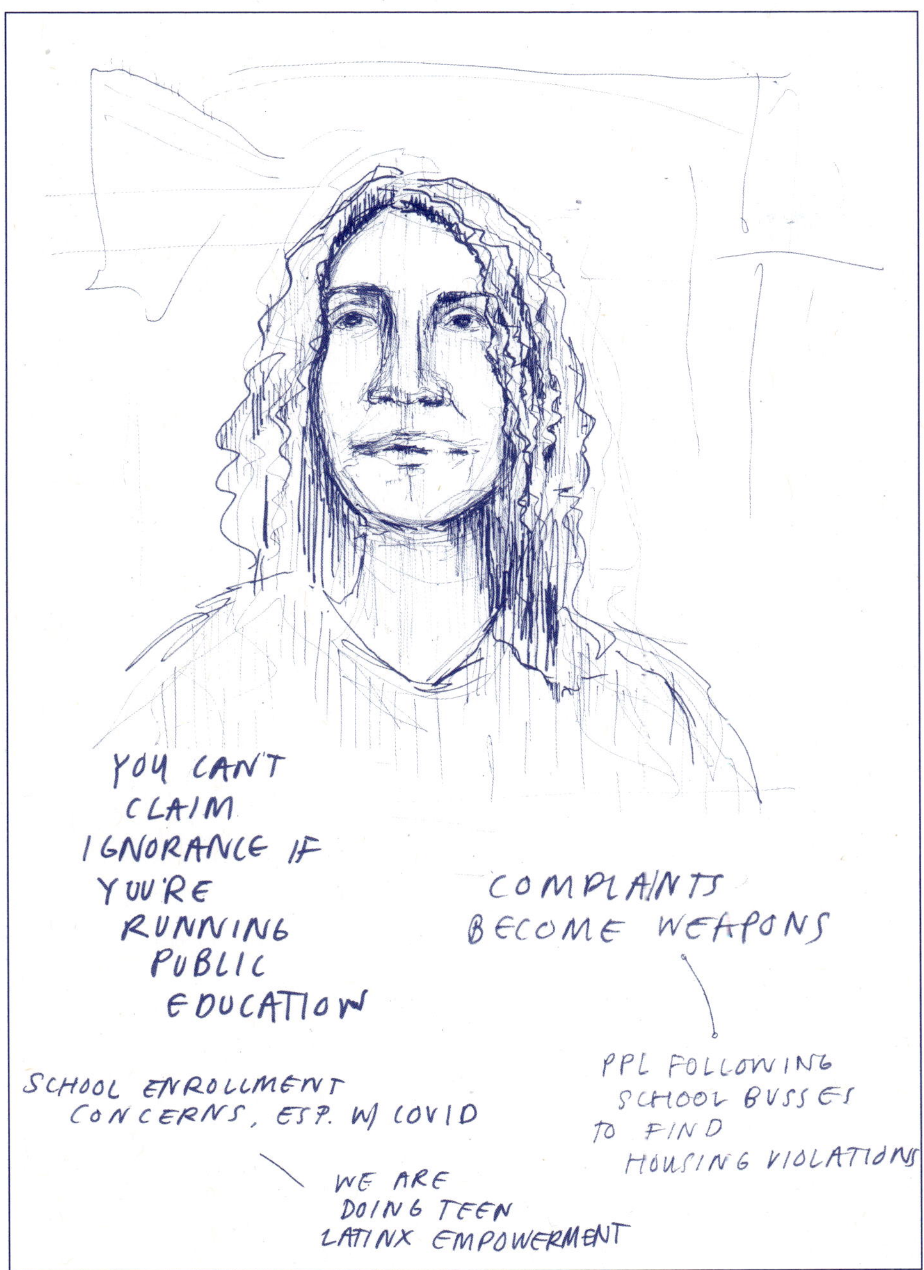

Martha Schnee
"Complaints become weapons"
— Minerva Perez
on public education and school enrollment concerns, 2021

Minerva Perez
For the Good of the Entire East End

Minerva Perez is Executive Director of OLA (Organización Latino-Americana) of Eastern Long Island, where she focuses on the protection, empowerment, and celebration of the regional Latinx community. As an active member of this community, she advocates against the growing exploitation of Latinxs in the workforce and the lack of affordable housing for immigrant families.

Minerva's interview details the ongoing difficulties that immigrant families face in the East Hampton Union Free School District, as well as the constant racial profiling of Latinxs by local police in the Hamptons.

We had concerns around racial profiling and we filed a Freedom of Information Act (FOIA) request to study the types of traffic stops that were happening where the pretext for the stop was rather small. Perhaps you didn't signal before you turned or something like that, yet the actual charge of the traffic stop was something else and mainly related to driving without a license. We were really studying what initiated the driving-without-a-license charge and seeing what level of profiling was potentially going on. We definitely feel there's racial profiling going on but what we didn't expect to learn was that, in certain police departments, certain officers had a much higher proclivity to pull people over who happen to be Latino.

Those charges that were brought were ultimately more significant because that could land you in Suffolk County jail. At that time, when we were studying that data, that jail time wouldn't be a simple "Spend ten days in jail and go home." That would be "Go to that jail, ICE [Immigration and Customs Enforcement] is waiting, you never come out." It was very important that simple policies and procedures with local law enforcement don't have to result in someone being taken from their home. We are not talking about life and death, we are talking about a traffic stop. Those were the concerns but not so much anymore. ICE doesn't have the same access that it did before, because of some things that happened through some lawsuits. Driver's licenses are now possible for undocumented people, so that has changed that quite a bit, which is great.

There's a federal guideline that basically says you have the right to some type of transportation. When we're living in an area that's as remote as it is here and you don't have a way to get to the doctor's office, you don't have a way to go to the grocery store, you don't have a way to go to your child's school, or to do something for your child, or a way to get to work and home again safely. All of these impediments exist because of a lack of public transportation. We learned that, at the height of all the fears around being stopped by police for driving without a license, Suffolk County was cutting bus lines. Cutting bus lines at the very same time that police were ratcheting up pulling people over. At the same time that ICE is running raids out here. All that was happening at the same time.

That's when we decided to advocate very strongly for replacing or reinstating those bus lines. Also looking at a forward-thinking mode of transportation that actually fits our region, which is a combination of those folks who might be out here at a resort or to relax for the weekend, those folks who are working and supporting the needs of the folks that are second home owners, and those folks who are just year-rounders and have a life here. We wanted to look at what it might take to create a transportation system that is both environmentally conscious and accessible to everyone. Something more like a rideshare, an on-demand type of scenario that doesn't have this bus spewing all kinds of things, riding around half empty, and then too full at other times.

That's not where leadership is at the moment, we're way behind the ball, but the big problem for us was that there just wasn't access. We started a free medical transportation service to meet at least some of these needs, and we're still running it. With COVID it's very tricky because we work with a lot of volunteers who are still willing to put a stranger in their car to get to a doctor's appointment and then get them back home again. We're transporting cancer patients, children's visits to their doctors that are related to cerebral cancer, children with kidney-related issues, cerebral palsy, and OB-GYN visits. Visits

for which there may be no eligibility for transportation. We help those who are eligible to call the Medicaid taxi, but many are not.

We just took about a month to wrangle transportation for a sixty-seven-year-old woman to get to her eye doctor appointment. We finally were able to get her signed up for SCAT, which is a Suffolk County transportation system only available if you've got certain kinds of ailments or long-standing chronic conditions or you're a certain age. Those kinds of things make life unlivable. When does someone say, "You are not providing any type of regular or accessible transportation?" We're not there yet. OLA, with the strength that we have, we're getting there. Transportation has been that much of an issue out here, and COVID-19 is compounding everything.

As growth happens on Long Island, so does labor and so does immigrant labor, and that is a historical piece of what Long Island has been. The last twenty to forty years have shown that our region has built to the point that extended families from areas of Mexico, Chile, and Ecuador understand that the plan is to come out here and participate in the building of this area. That is formal and informal; becoming businesses and corporations that are developed. That has been going on now for a long period of time in agricultural areas, be they vineyards or farms on the North Fork, and all of the other industries that are the engine of success in this area. Specifically the Hamptons, but let's say the full East End: restaurants, landscap-

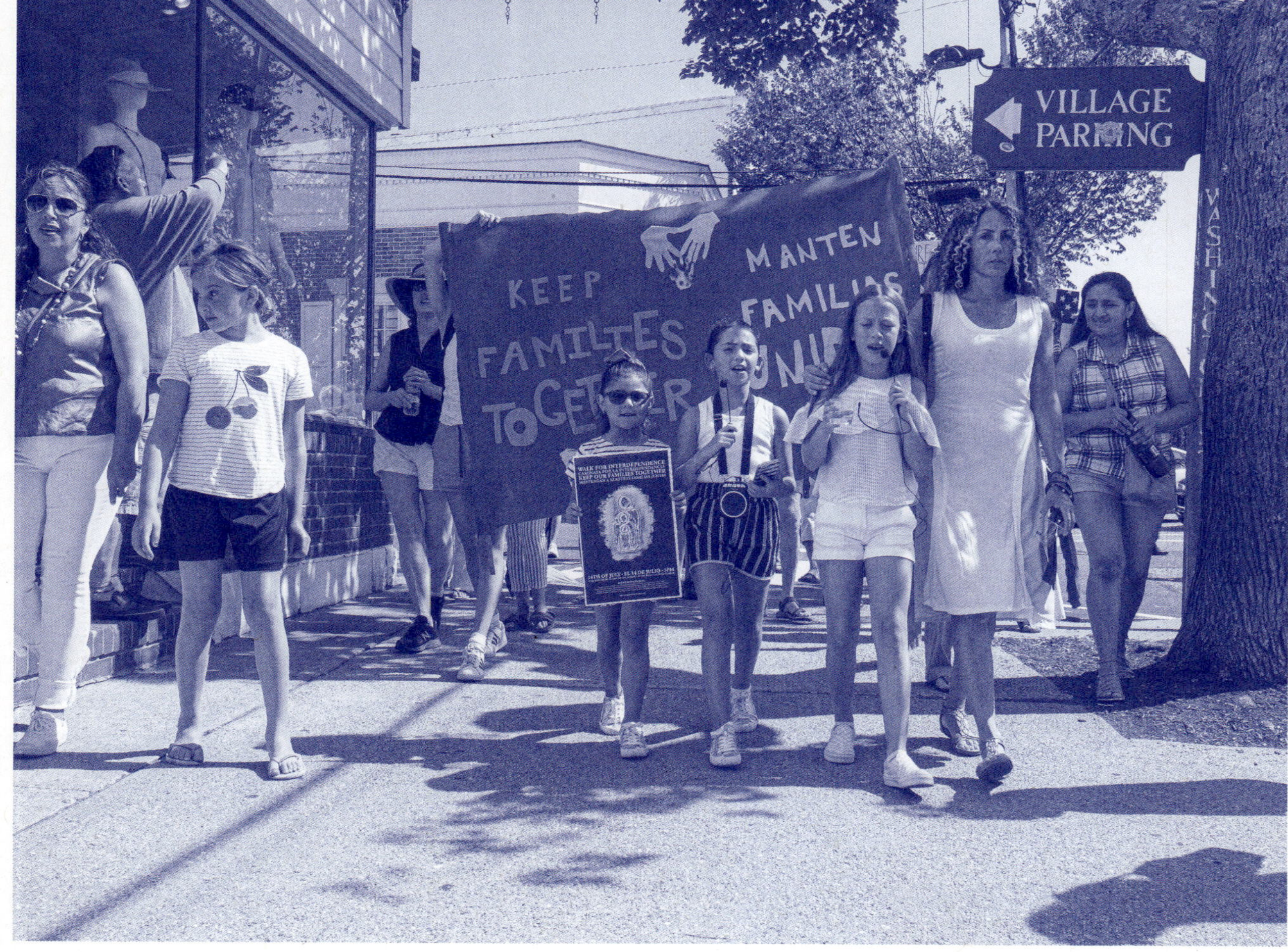

18.
The Interdependence
March in Sag Harbor,
NY, 2018
Courtesy
Christopher Patrick

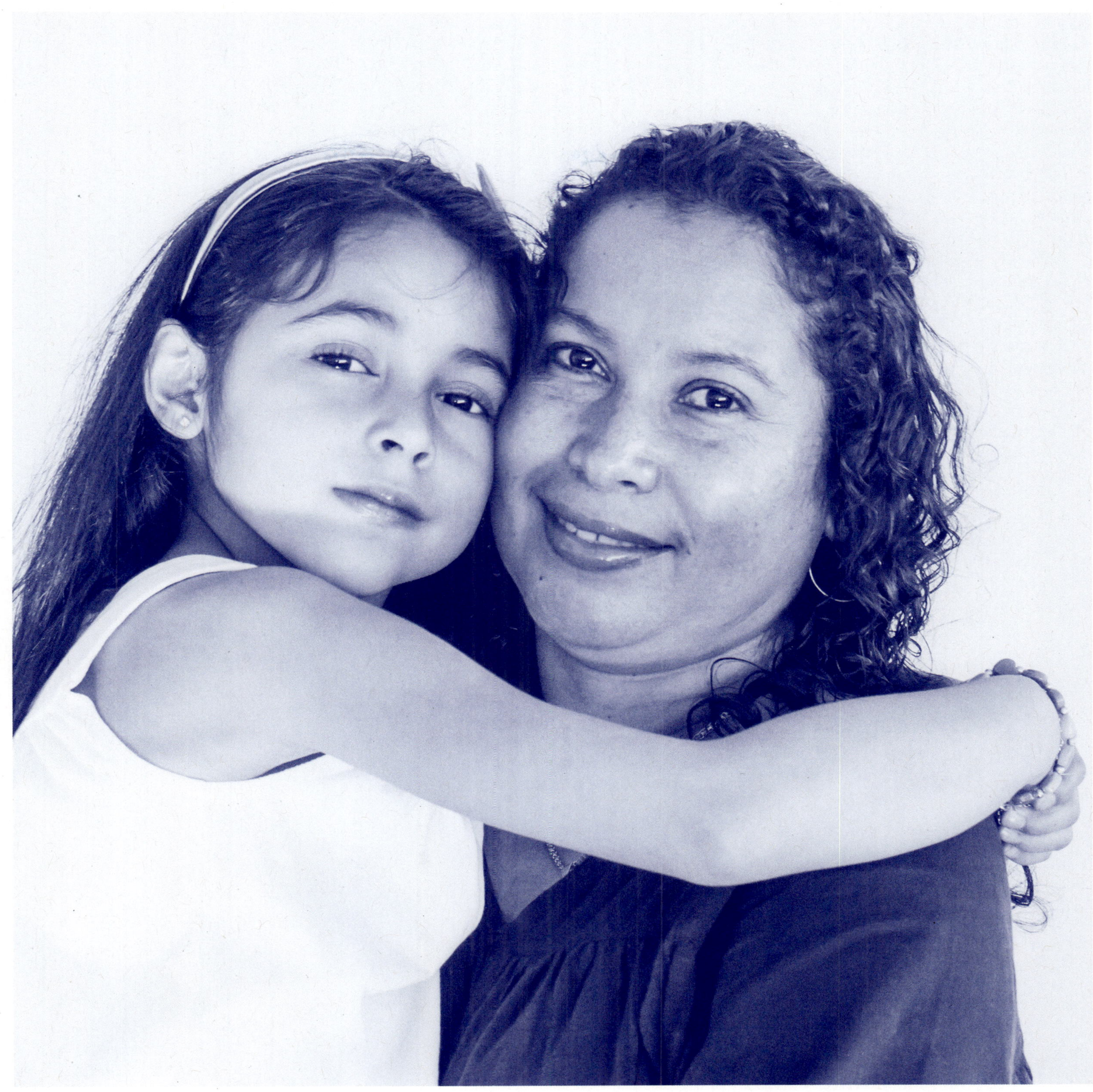

19.
Philippe Cheng,
Untitled, 2018

Courtesy
©Philippe Cheng

ing, construction, child care, domestic work, and cleaning. All these are positions predominantly held by immigrant labor. Whether they're more recent immigrants or maybe long-standing in the community, those are positions that are held by majority immigrant labor.

What is OLA? COVID-19 has shifted the axis a little bit here, and I think it's shaken out from our organization kind of what we really are. We are here for the good of the entire East End and we're still Latino focused. We are focusing on communities that don't have equity in the areas that are the most important: health care, education, safety, and protection from law enforcement. Our role on the East End is to look at all those systems that can be made stronger for the health and the betterment of all the lives on the East End. The leaders in our organization are about ninety percent Latino. It's important that we show in our actions that we are here for the entire East End and to shift the paradigm on Latino leadership doing those things. Latinos are leaders, they are bringers of solutions. The Latino involvement in this community and the growth of this population in this community is a good thing. They've been doing that, but you're not paying attention. So we're going to help you pay attention. By doing that we hope to grow other leaders so that they can feel good and young people can stand up.

During COVID-19 we were meeting the needs of over a hundred families, working with volunteers to get food shopped for and delivered to people that couldn't get out of their homes every single week, and connecting with the county to create hotlines that didn't exist before, for anyone in Suffolk County no matter who they were or what language they spoke. I helped put together a town and county collaborative so that food would be dropped off between twenty-four and thirty-four hours if a person couldn't get out of their home and had no way to get food. Nonperishable foods that let you survive another few days. That kind of work didn't come naturally, we never did things with food, but when COVID-19 happened, we realized that this is where we needed to be. It wasn't just to make a sandwich, it was to find out why this person doesn't have access to that food pantry. Does that food pantry understand that only being open from twelve to two on a Wednesday is going to make it impossible for a person to get food, when the person is trying to eke out the last little bits of work? Does the county know that? The county that's funding the people who get the food to the food pantry—do they all know that some pantries are only open at these hours? Advocacy around food was never something that we thought we were going to suddenly jump into, but it really showed us who we were.

On Long Island, there is a dearth of affordable housing for everybody. Immigrant families and people within the Latinx community that find that they have any place to live out here to serve the need and to meet the great demand for their labor means that immigrant families make it work wherever they can. There are some areas thought of as slightly more affordable but they're really not. Immigrant families are often intergenerational. It's the traditional and historic model of how people make it happen. It happened with Italians and Irish. Having Grandma, an aunt, and an uncle provides extra hands for helping with the kids. You've got the family together. In America we have a short cultural memory and attention span regarding how we were formed, including the decimation of Indigenous peoples. We have this stigma around families living together in that way. It doesn't stop at a social stigma, it goes beyond that. You've got to be careful and safe, you don't want people living in a dangerous situation. However, sharing their housing is the only way that people can live out here. Otherwise the rents are astronomical.

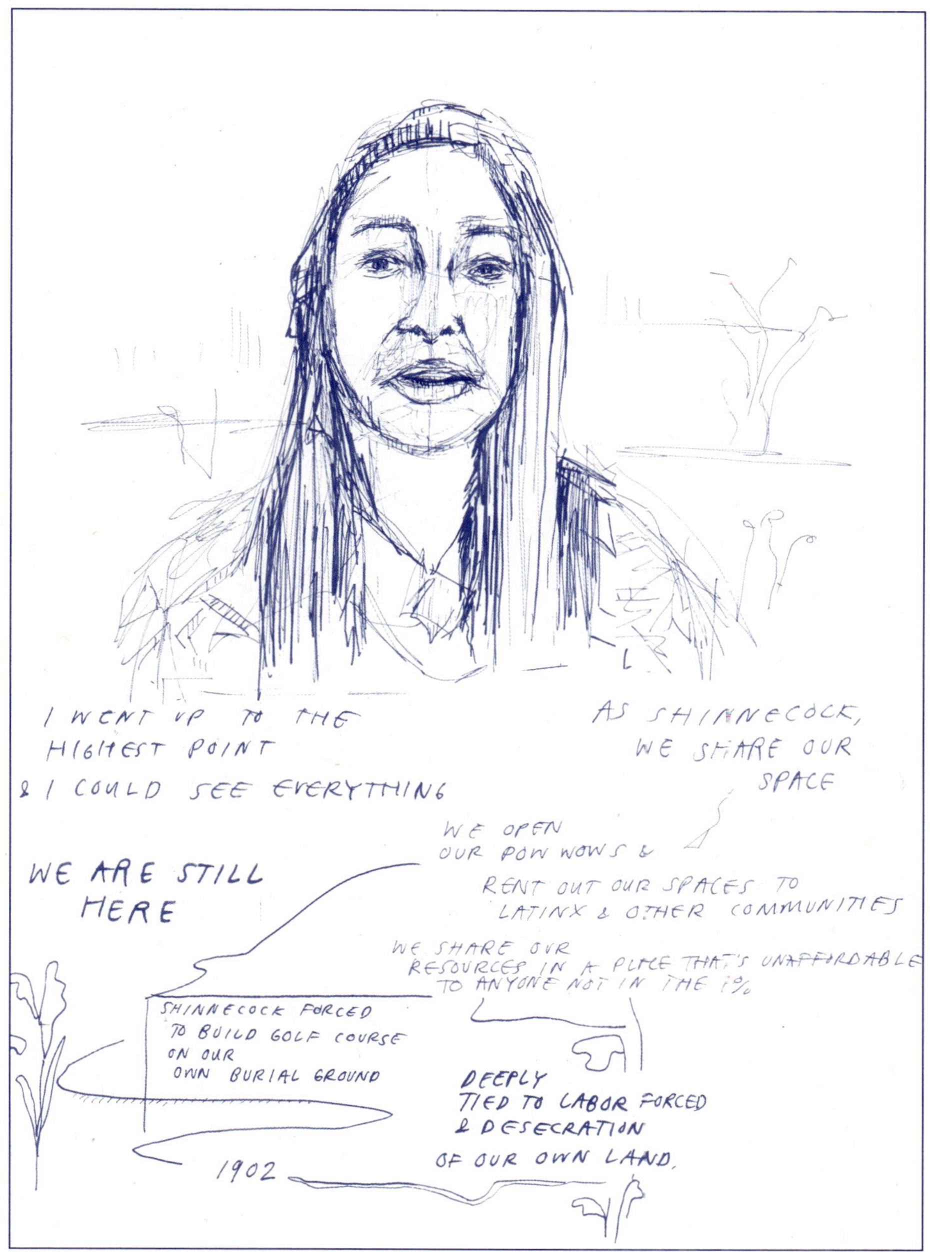

Martha Schnee
"As Shinnecock we share our space: we are still here,"
— Kelly Dennis on Shinnecock resource sharing, 2021

Kelly Dennis, Esq.
Our Leader Women, the Backbone of Our People

Kelly Dennis, Esq. is an attorney specializing in Federal Indian law who has represented the Shinnecock Indian Nation and other sovereign tribal nations on matters related to land rights, civil rights, and cultural and natural resource protection. She is also the Public Programs & Residency Coordinator at The Watermill Center. On April 6, 2021, Kelly was elected Secretary of the Council of Trustees for the Shinnecock Indian Nation.

In our discussion, Kelly chronicles the history of the Shinnecock Indian Nation's movement to reclaim stolen land and the thirty-two-year fight for federal recognition. She also speaks about the lack of affordable housing on the East End.

We come from a matriarchal tribe where our leader women, Sunksqua, have been the backbone of our People. Quashawam was one of the first women leaders. Nowedonah's daughter as well. There have been strong women forever in the Tribe. Princess Nowedonah, who was my grandmother's generation, was one of the people to inspire me to keep on working toward the Land Claim. Even though women weren't able to speak or vote in Tribe meetings, she would always be the one to break the mold and say, "When are we getting our Shinnecock Hills back?" She'd also stand up against other encroachments on the lands that were happening.

The women were looked to as part of this hunter-gatherer society, and corn, beans, and squash were what we were often planting. Before colonization, men were hunters and the whale was what they would go after. That was often a very difficult process of trying to whale, but that was what we were known for. That was what we taught the colonists to do when they arrived and what made the whaling industry such a huge thing before they found gold out West.

Women are still the backbone of our Tribe. I think we would have had federal recognition a lot sooner had women actually been in charge. My mom loves to do a talking stick workshop with Quashawam on respect and always goes back to her for those teachings. Quashawam first made the opposition of an illegal settlement in Southampton in 1652. She filed a complaint against the Dutch and English to demand compensation for lands that were illegally occupied. Unfortunately, there was a determination made that the land was validly taken, but that all happened when Southampton was still part of Connecticut and not New York. So, it's a whole other kind of crazy situation happening here, but that took over thirty years for that land settlement to recur after Quashawam had filed the complaint.

The Land Claim boils down to what happened in the year 1859, when New York State passed legislation to authorize Southampton to illegally get rid of the thousand-year lease promising us the Shinnecock Hills, which was over

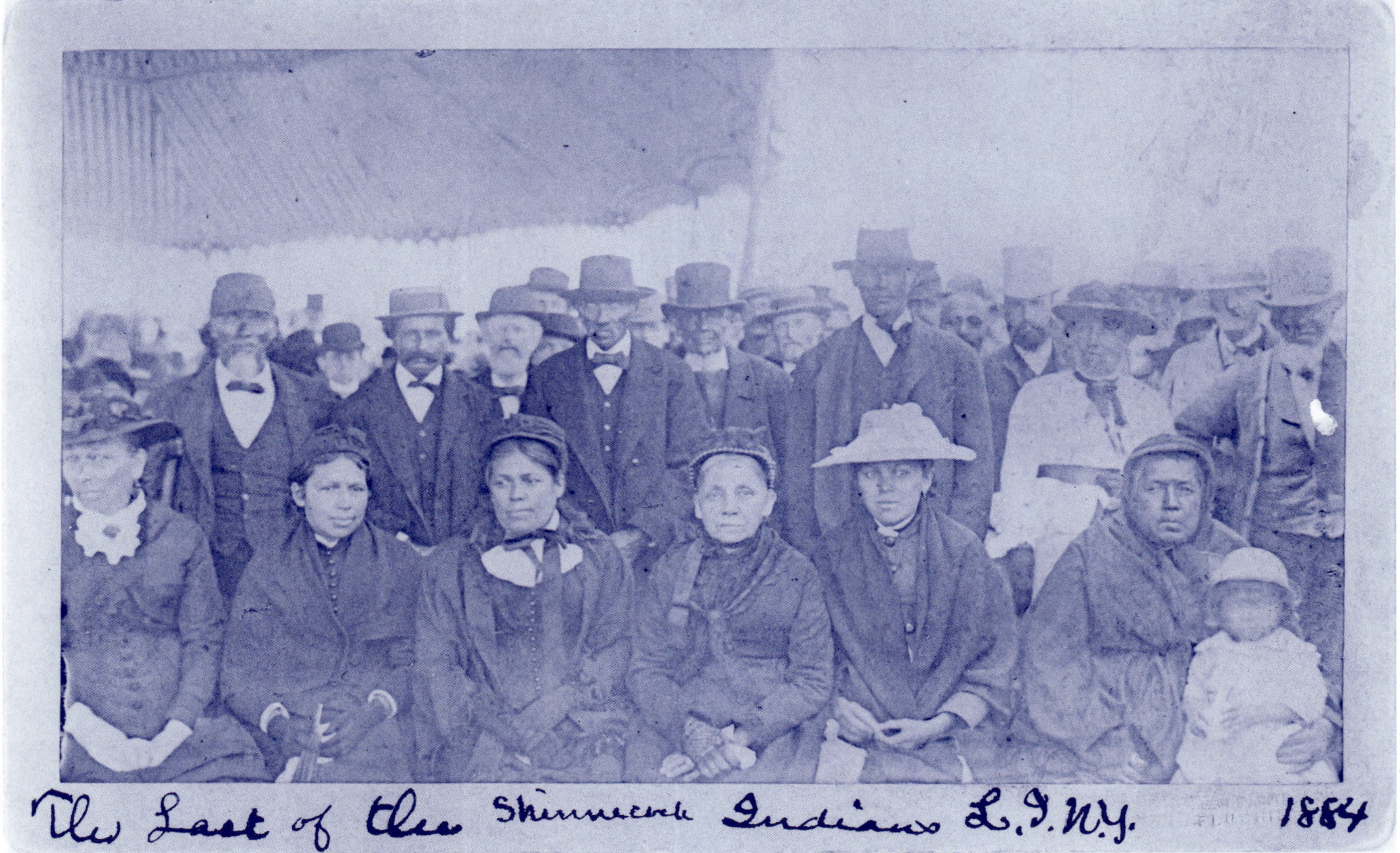

4,000 acres of land. They promised that to us for a thousand years in 1703 and they broke that promise in 1859. When the transaction occurred, our ancestors immediately denied that the transaction was lawful. Only a minority of the Tribe whose names were on the petition were accurate, others were forged, and the ones who did sign were made by undue influence: alcohol involved oppressive conduct. They hired an attorney to put in a complaint on July 25, 1859, about three months after the illegal transaction took place. That complaint was ignored and the case never went to trial. The lawsuit was pending and has been ever since, even after we submitted a petition to the U.S. Supreme Court in 2016. That never got heard on the merits, and as long as nothing gets heard on the merits, it's still alive.

We never had our day in court about what was promised to us and was illegally taken from us. That is the land where there's so much happening. I, for the first time yesterday, went at sunset to an area called Sugarloaf in the Shinnecock Hills. I always think about going up there but I don't want to trespass or get arrested. It is the highest point of the Shinnecock Hills, at Sugarloaf, and it's been recorded by archaeologists as very sensitive to the Shinnecock Nation. We buried our ancestors in that area. There was a massive archaeological dig that uncovered many of our ancestors' bones and ceremonial objects. I was able to just go up there yesterday. I could see everything.

I could see from one side of the South Fork to the other, I could see to the Peconic Bay to the north side, all around to the Shinnecock Bay on the south side. I could see the canal that opens up into the Atlantic Ocean. I was like, "Oh my God. This is where Creator knows that my ancestors would gather and hold ceremonies. This is where our ancestors were. The sun sets there and they were buried there and their graves were facing west so that they would be on their journey to the spirit world with Creator." Thankfully there is more protection there. Still, it's the entire Shinnecock Hills and all the high points on the western side where we have many of our ancestors buried. That's what we believe and continue to do on the land that we still own and occupy here on the Shinnecock Neck adjoining the Shinnecock Hills.

They put us on a peninsula after 1859. It is beautiful and we love it, it's our home. It's only 800 acres in comparison to the over 4,000 acres up to the Shinnecock Canal, where we would drag our canoes because we are people of the ocean, the bays, and waters. We make do with what we can here on the Shinnecock Neck Reservation. It's marshlands so you can't really build up on it or farm it too much, it's susceptible to flooding. We've had realtors come up here and try to take it from us still even despite all that. It's just the reality of how we've been able to survive in this space where we are surrounded by the one percent. This is where segregation began in the Hamptons and it still exists today. This is the only place where I'm ever going to be if I continue to try to live out here and work out here. This is the only place I can afford to live.

The Shinnecock Hills golf course was developed after the Land Claim but it's still a horrible

20.
The Last of the Shinnecock Indians L.I. NY. / B.M. Franklin, Flushing, NY, 1884

Courtesy the Library of Congress Prints and Photographs Division

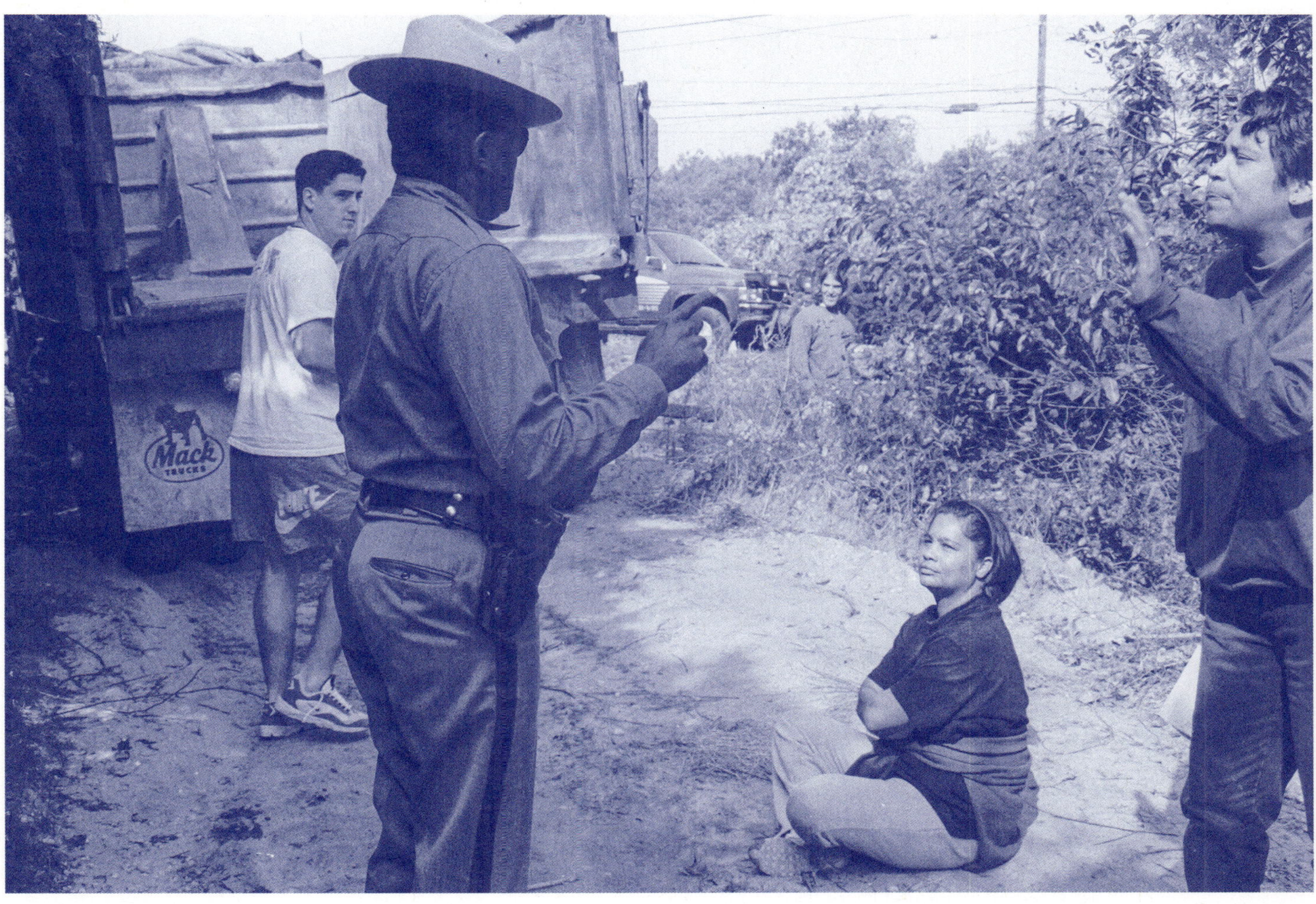

21.
Doreen Dennis-
Arrindell of the
Shinnecock Nation
sitting in the path
of a truck to protect
Shinnecock land,
Southampton, NY,
1996

Courtesy Express
News Group

thing. Shinnecock people were made to work to build that course, and in 1891, it was said that 150 Shinnecock tribal members assisted in weighing out the first totals of what was to become the golf club. They were the only available labor, and William Dunn, the Scottish course developer, said several years into development, "The place was dotted with Indian burial mounds and we left some of these intact at bunkers in front of the greens. We scraped out some of the mounds and made sand traps. One never knew when an explosion shot out a sand trap that would bring out a couple of firewater flasks or perhaps a bone or two." It was said that at least sixteen graves were removed from where the Shinnecock Hills Golf Club announced that happened in 1902. I have records of the different pits. The Town of Southampton has long acknowledged the presence of our Shinnecock remains in the Shinnecock Hills. The Town records show that we had a large cemetery near the front, about halfway between Southampton Village and the Shinnecock Hills. That was a considerable settlement about Canoe Place where those graves are still. That is in the 1918 records of the Town of Southampton. They know.

Our people have been fueled by alcohol and substance abuse. It continues on and is a huge issue still for us. It's tied to the labor issue and how we were the only available labor to help in the desecration of our own lands, building this golf course, and the railroad through it. We did so with flasks full of whatever liquor they were providing us—the firewater flask. In June 1884, Shinnecock Tribe members attended the celebration of the fif-

teenth anniversary of the Long Island Rail Road at the Shinnecock Hills train station. A photograph of Shinnecock people taken that day states: "The Last of the Shinnecock Indians." They were saying in 1884 that we were already an extinct People, and we're not. It's a long history of pursuing this Land Claim because we're still here and we're asserting our rights. We exist. It's a continuation of this paper genocide that is happening. We assert who we are and continue on. The Land Claim is a part of that.

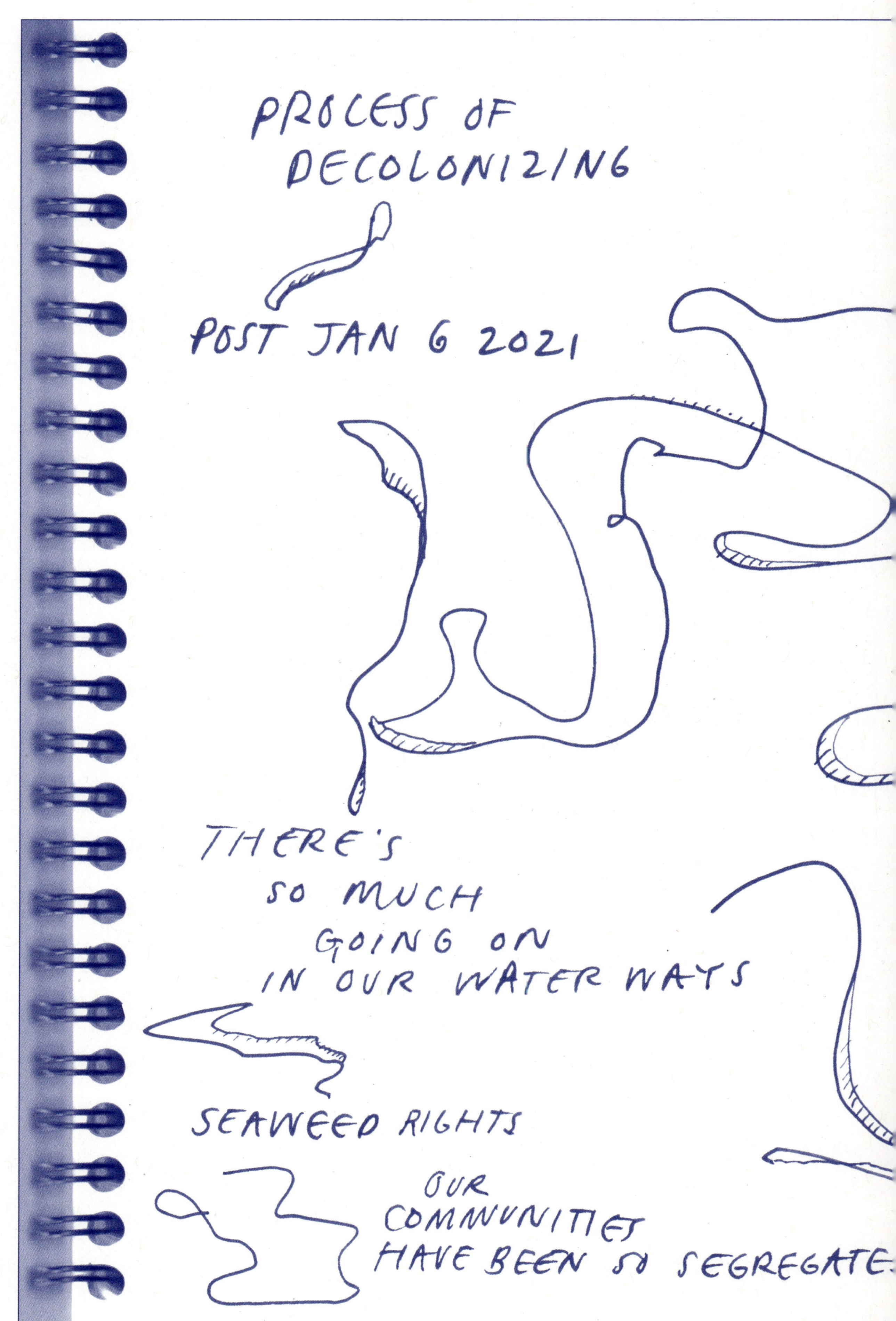

22.
Martha Schnee
*"There is so much going on in our water ways"
— Kelly Dennis on the ongoing process of decolonization*, 2021.

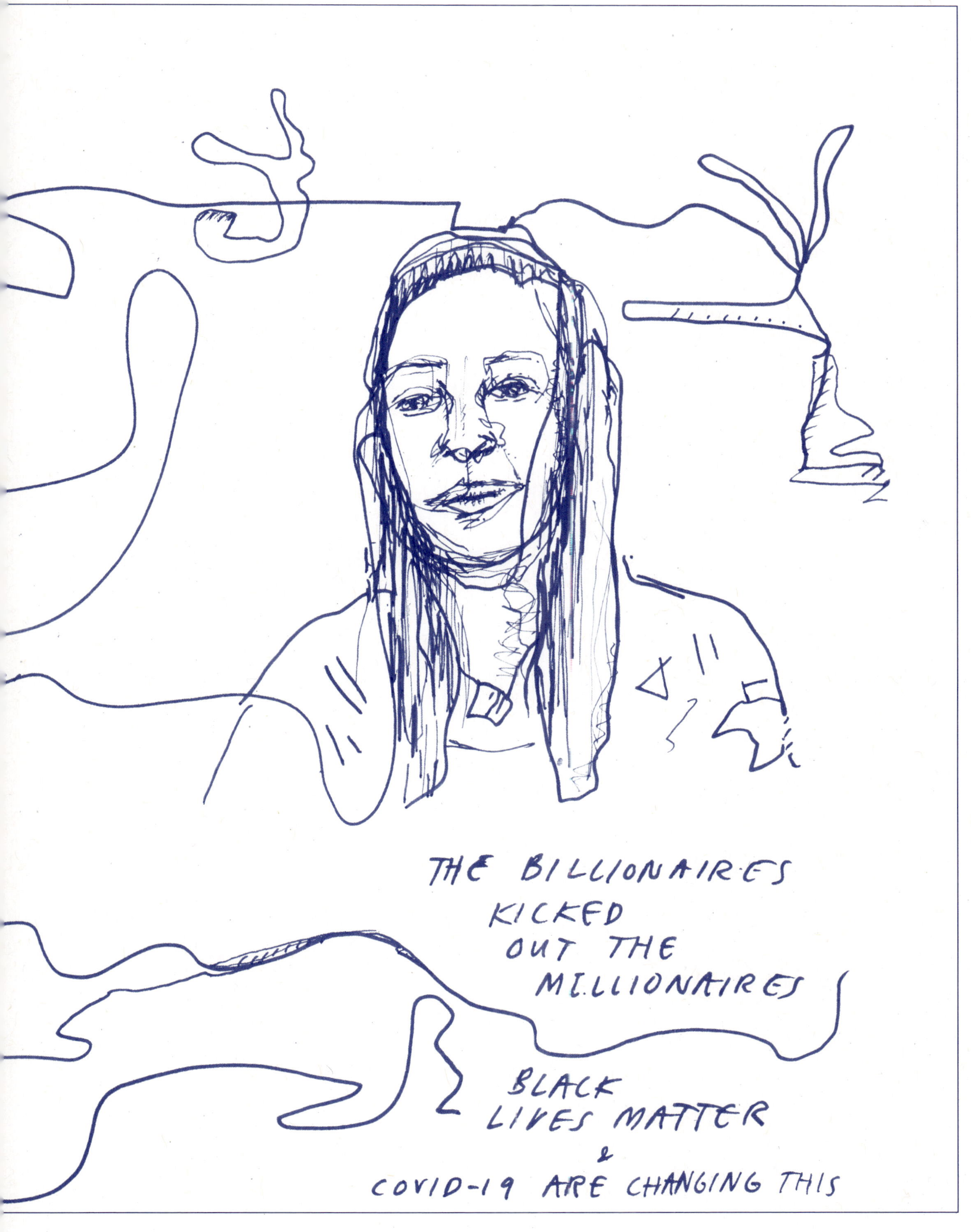

THE BILLIONAIRES
KICKED
OUT THE
MILLIONAIRES

BLACK
LIVES MATTER
&
COVID-19 ARE CHANGING THIS

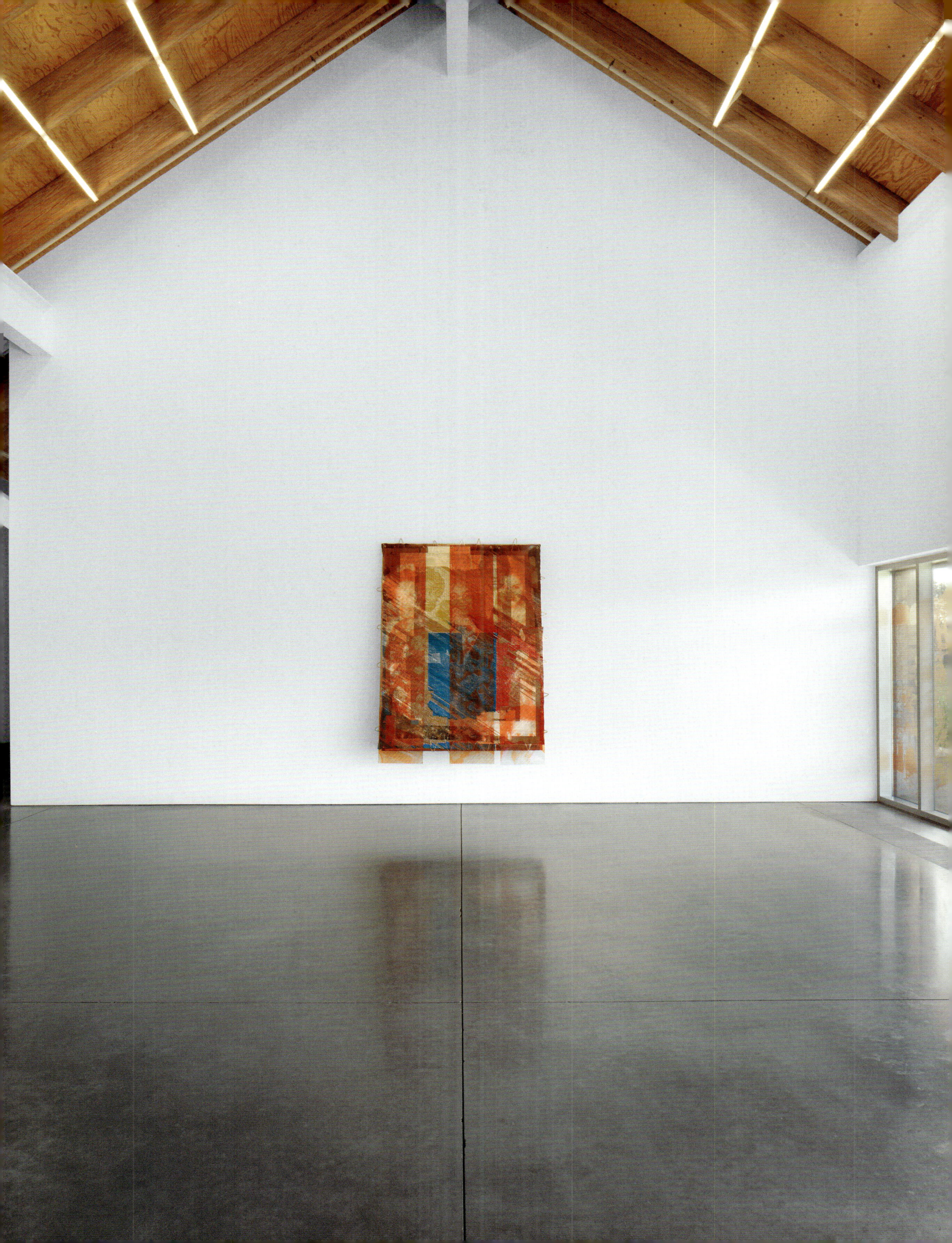

The Three Sisters, 2021

Acrylic, wampum dust, and soil from the
Parrish Art Museum grounds, a former potato
field, on canvas, cotton textiles, paper potato
bags, and paper bags with archival prints on
PVC marine vinyl mounted on a handcrafted
walnut, Douglas fir, and redwood awning
structure with brass hooks and grommets

95 × 66½ × 12½ inches

Courtesy the artist and Tilton Gallery,
New York

Transformed halftone line image painted on substrate:
Eastville residents, between 1880–1915, tintypes.
Courtesy Eastville Community Historical Society

Cropped halftone line image printed on PVC marine vinyl:
Loretta Hunter-Silva, Dorothy Dennis, Denise Silva-
Dennis, Pauline Kirby, and Jeremy Dennis gathered at
the Hunter-Silva home (Ma's House), 1992.
Photo: Avery Dennis, Jr.
Courtesy Silva-Dennis Family Archive

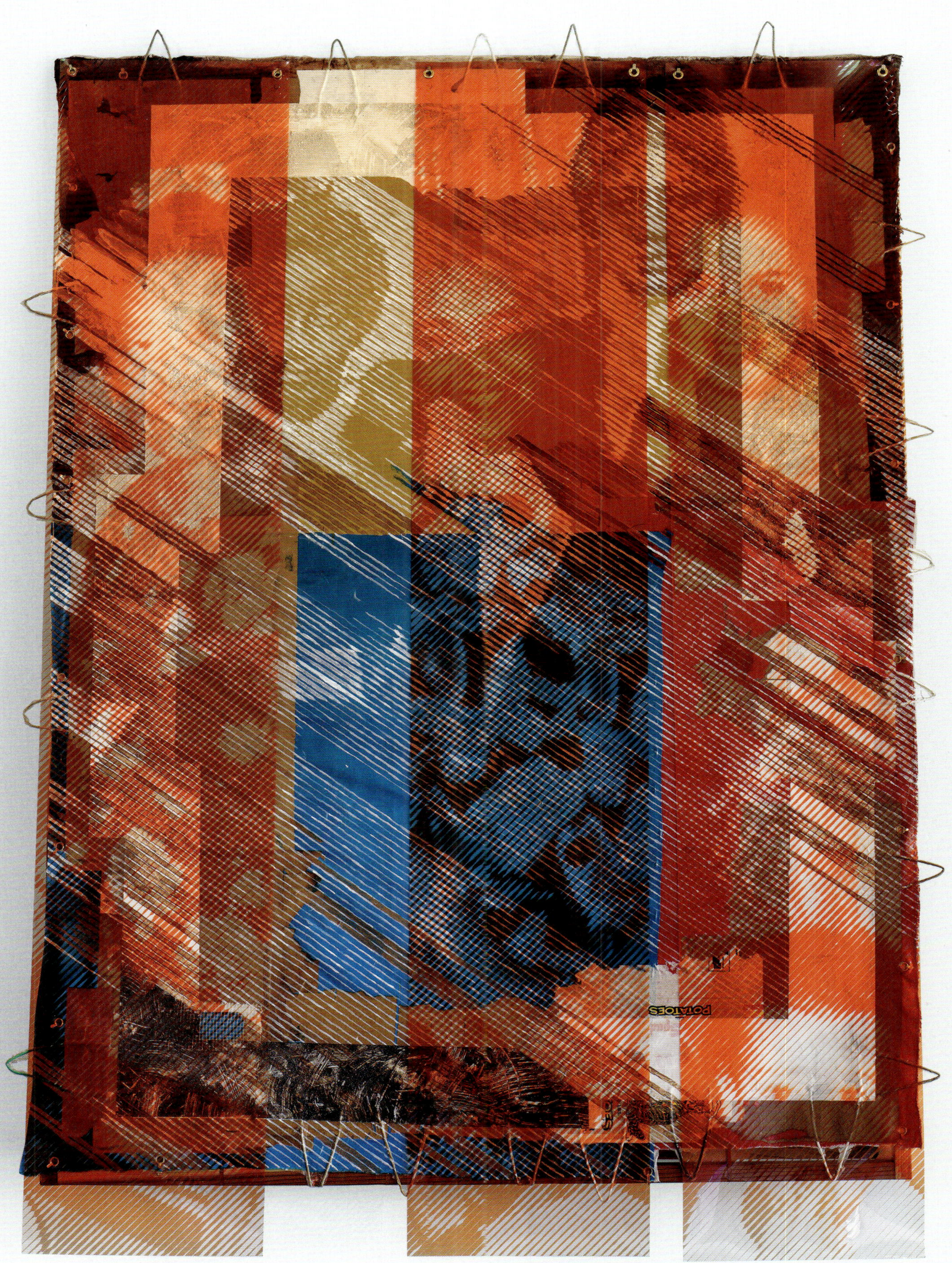
POTATOES

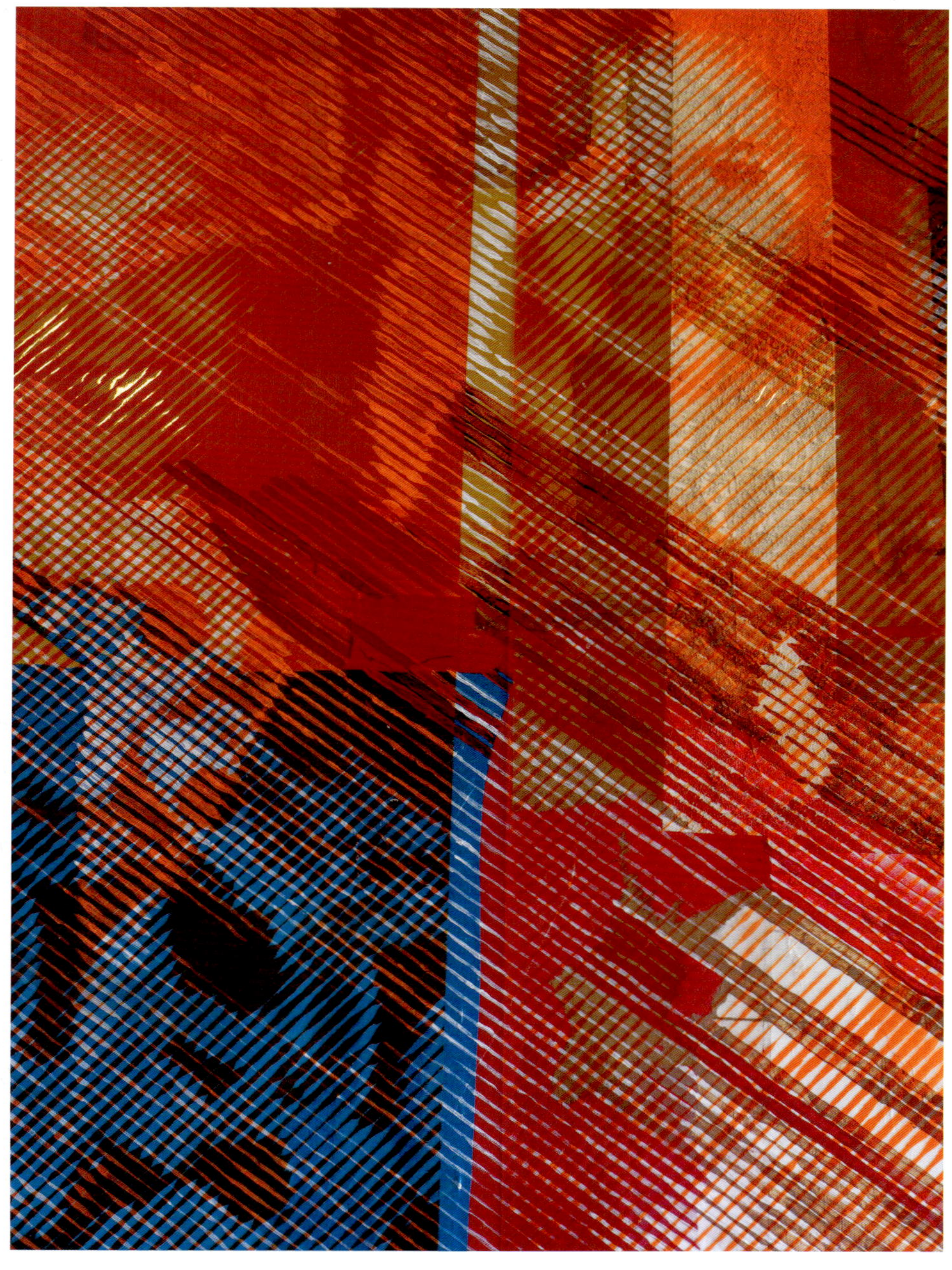

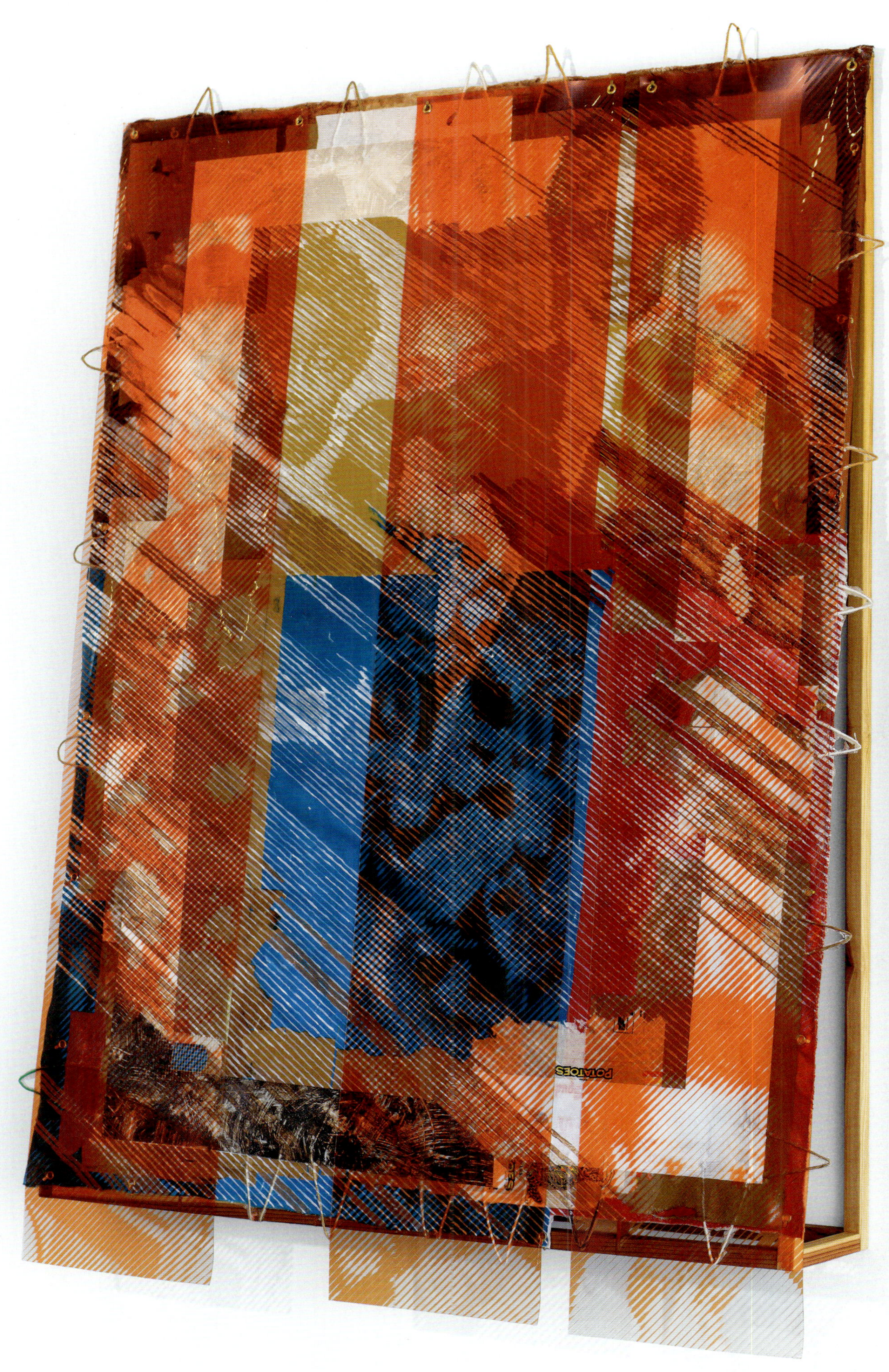
POTATOES

*Among Fruits (Big Shane and
the Farmer)*, 2021

Acrylic, wampum dust, and soil from the
Parrish Art Museum grounds, a former
potato field, on canvas, paper potato bags,
and paper bags with archival prints on PVC
marine vinyl mounted on a handcrafted
walnut awning structure with brass hooks
and grommets

93½ × 65½ × 12¼ inches

Courtesy the artist and Tilton Gallery,
New York

Transformed halftone line image painted on substrate:
Shane Weeks with hen of the woods mushroom.

Cropped halftone line image printed on PVC marine vinyl:
A worker in a South Fork potato field, ca. 1950.
Courtesy Express News Group

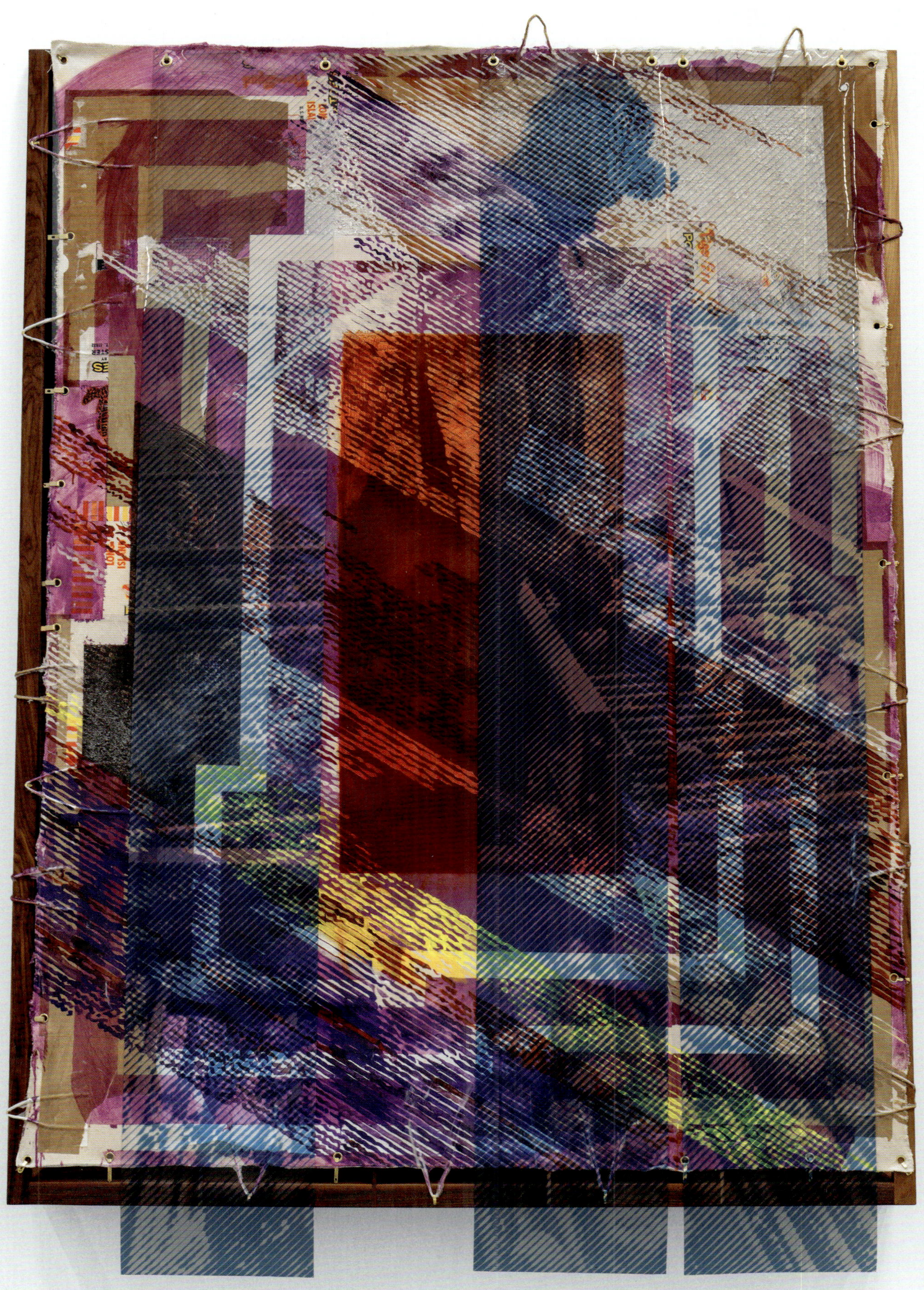

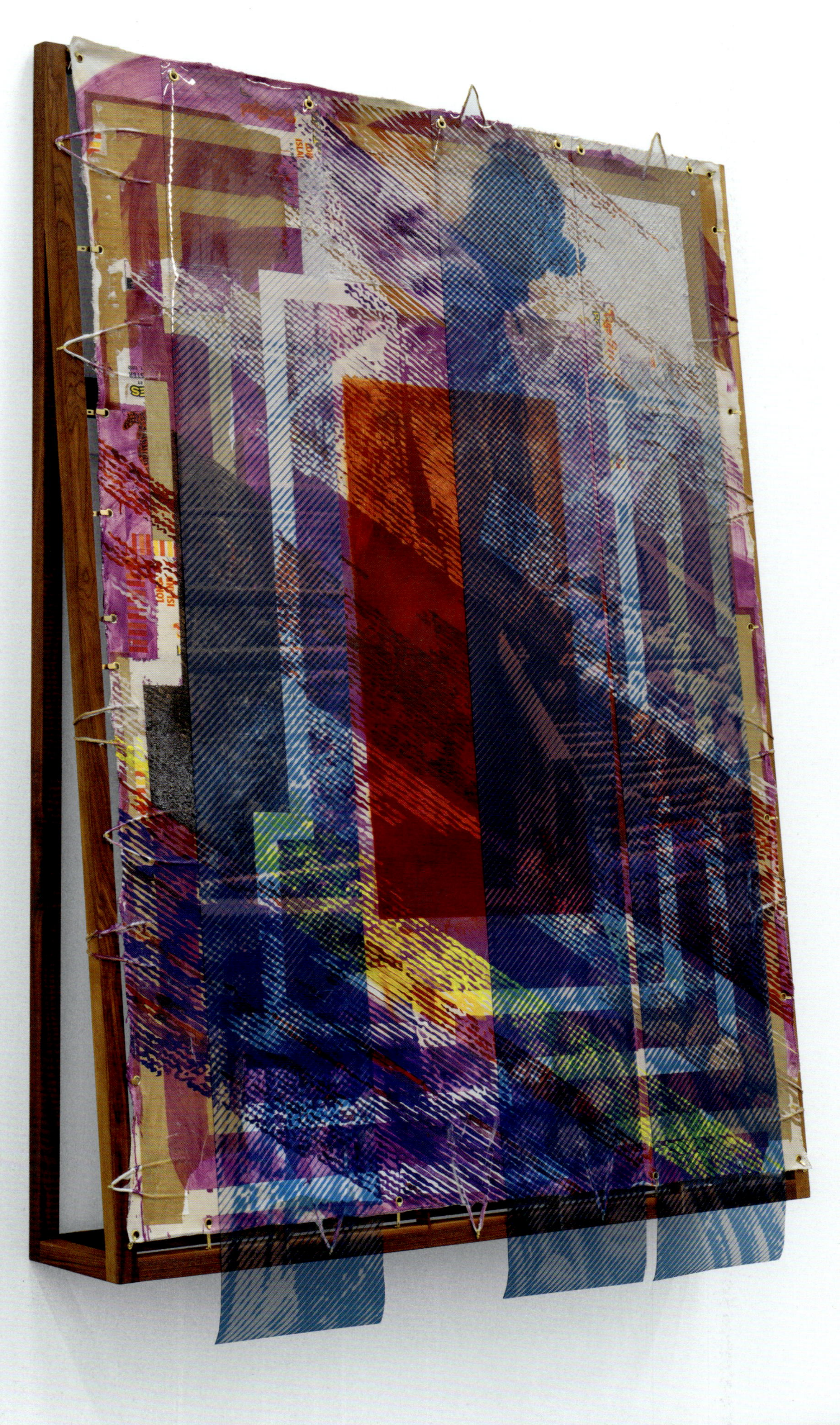

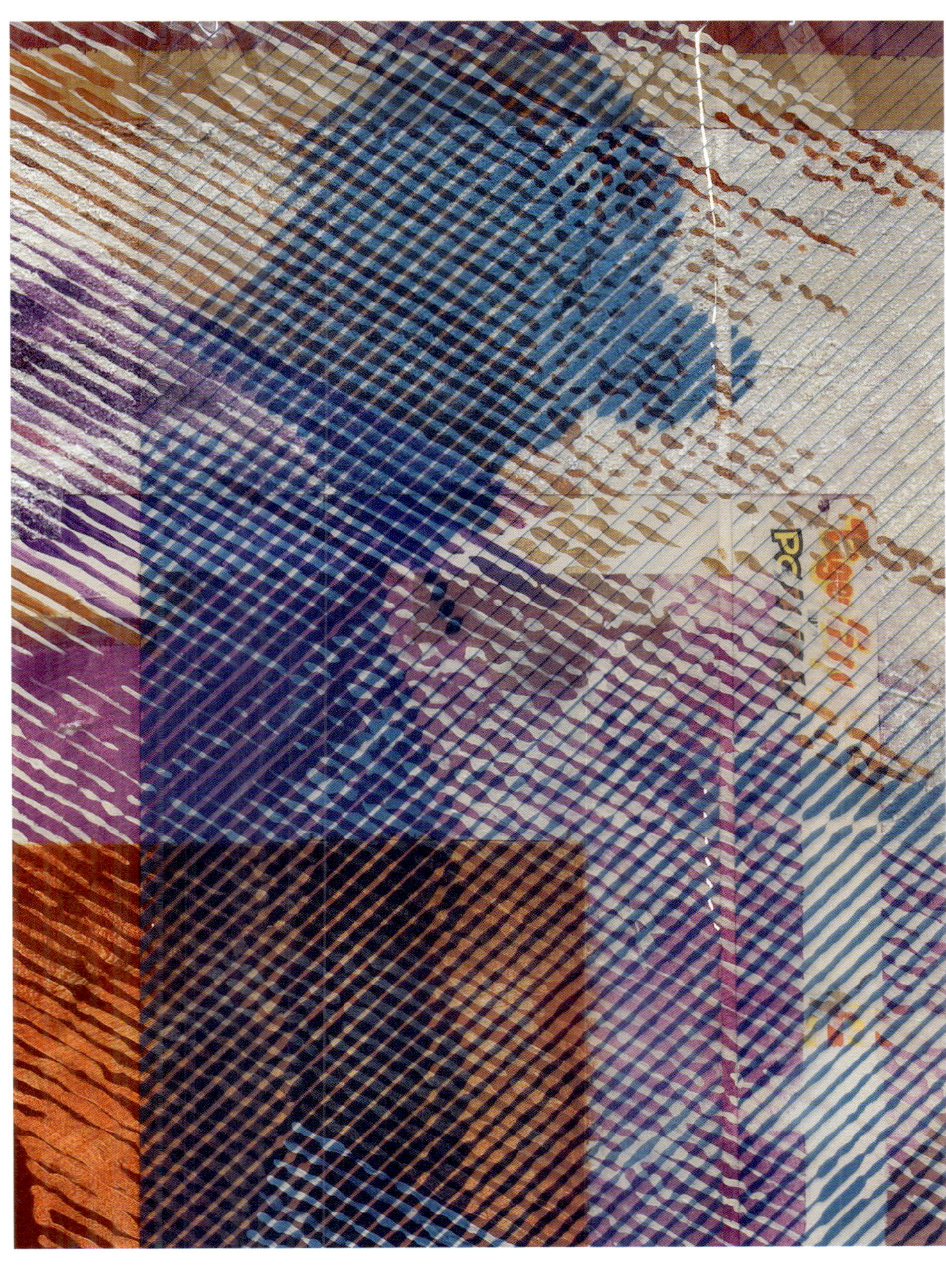

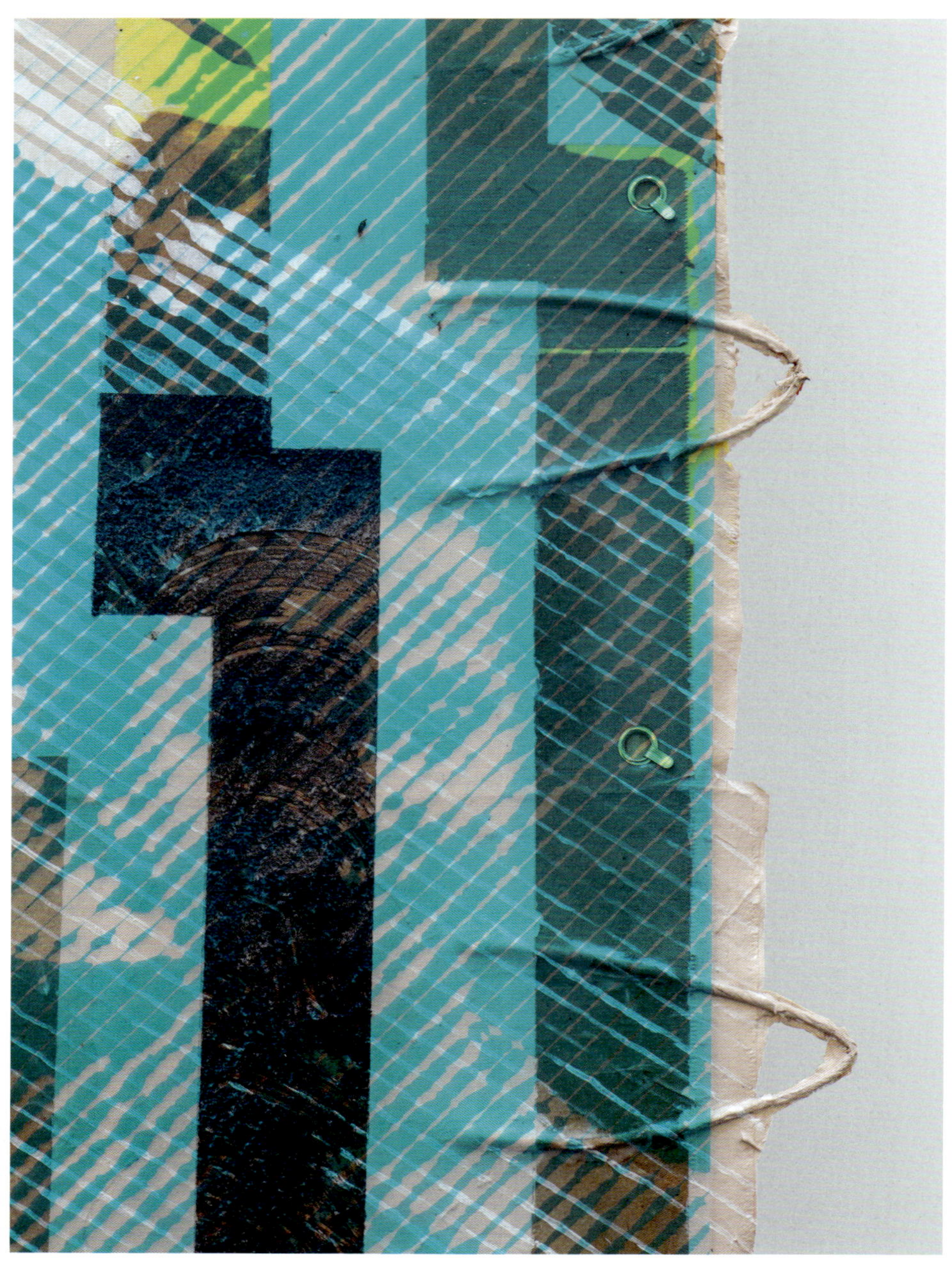

Among Gardens, 2021

Acrylic and soil from the Parrish Art Museum
grounds, a former potato field, on canvas,
cotton textiles, and paper bags with archival
prints on PVC marine vinyl mounted on a
handcrafted Douglas fir and redwood awning
structure with brass hooks and grommets

92 ½ × 67 ½ × 12 ¼ inches

Courtesy the artist and Tilton Gallery,
New York

Transformed halftone line image painted on substrate:
Steven Molina Contreras, *Mi Familia Inmigrante, in my
Mother's Salon, New York, USA*, 2020.

Cropped halftone line image printed on PVC marine
vinyl:
Marvin Dozier and students of the Bridgehampton
Childcare & Recreational Center, ca. 1970.
Courtesy the Southampton Youth Association

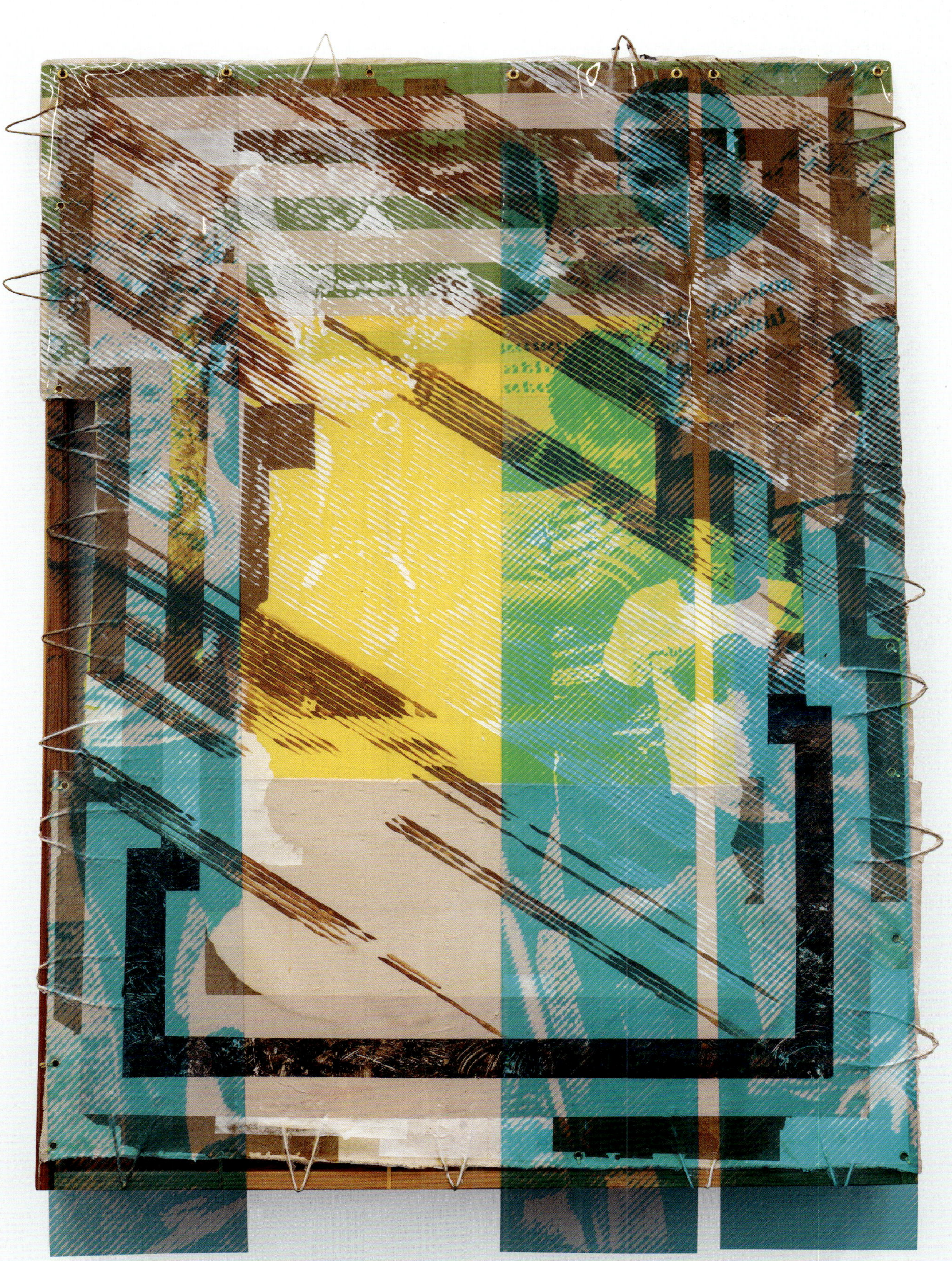

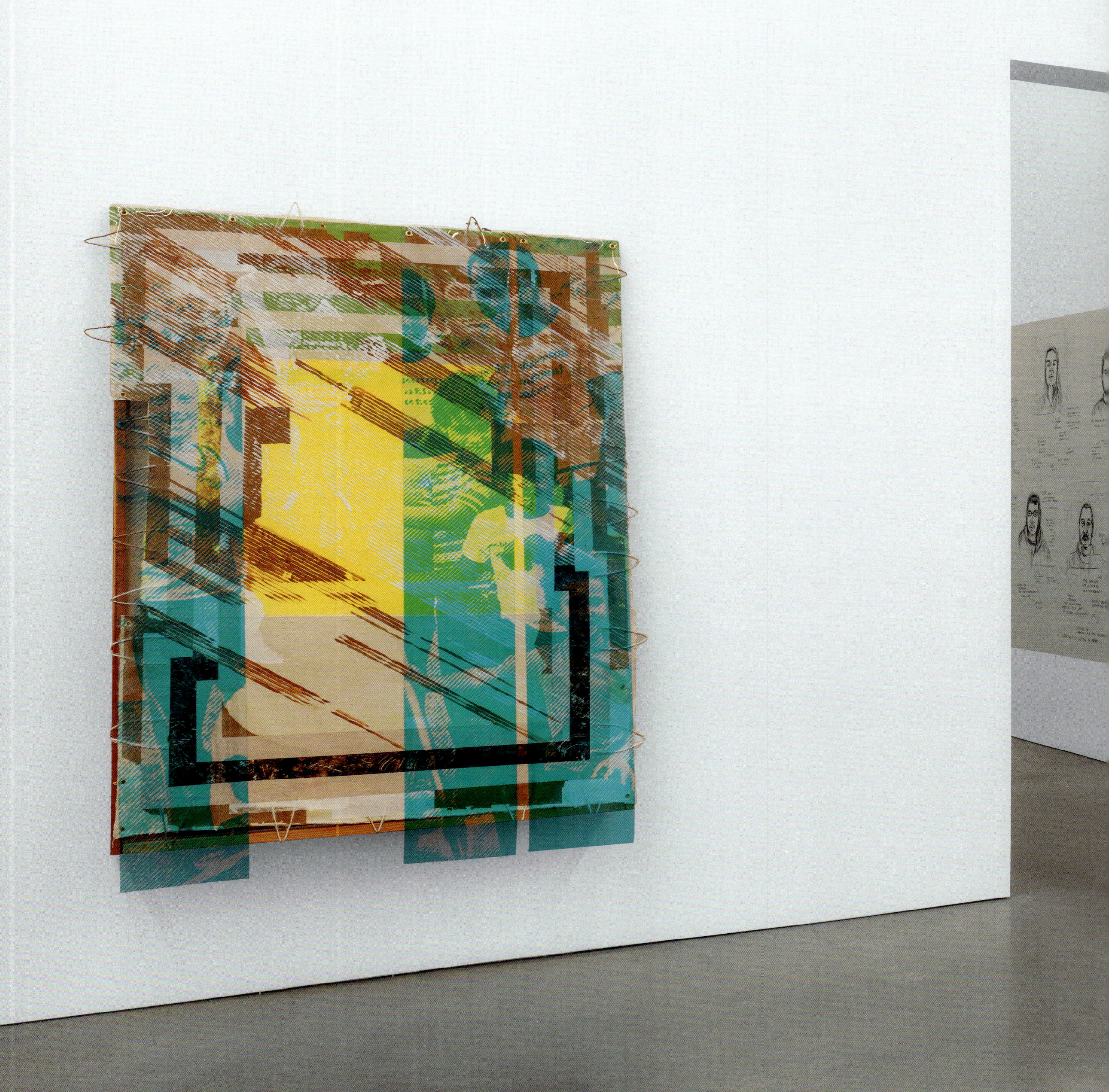

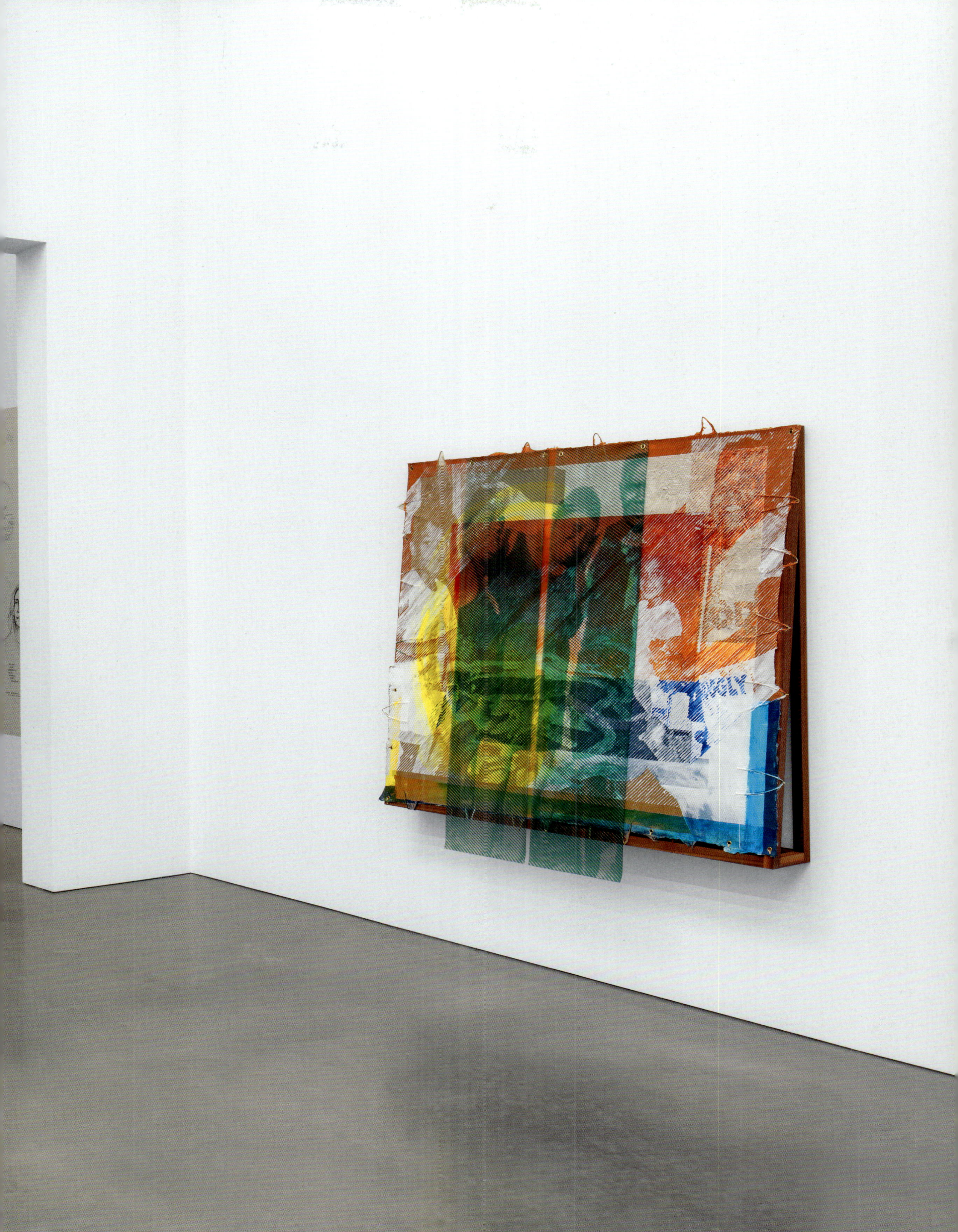

Among Heirs (Niamuck and Azurest), 2021

Acrylic and wampum dust on canvas, cotton textiles, and paper bags with archival prints on PVC marine vinyl mounted on a handcrafted walnut awning structure with brass hooks and grommets

75 × 77¾ × 9¼ inches

Courtesy the artist and Tilton Gallery, New York

Transformed halftone line image painted on substrate:
Ethan Smith, Kelly Dennis, Peter Smith Jr., gathered at the Hunter-Silva home (Ma's House), 1991.
Photo: Denise Silva-Dennis.
Courtesy Silva-Dennis Family Archive

Cropped halftone line image printed on PVC marine vinyl:
Group on Azurest Beach, Sag Harbor, NY, date unknown.
Courtesy Eastville Community Historical Society Collection

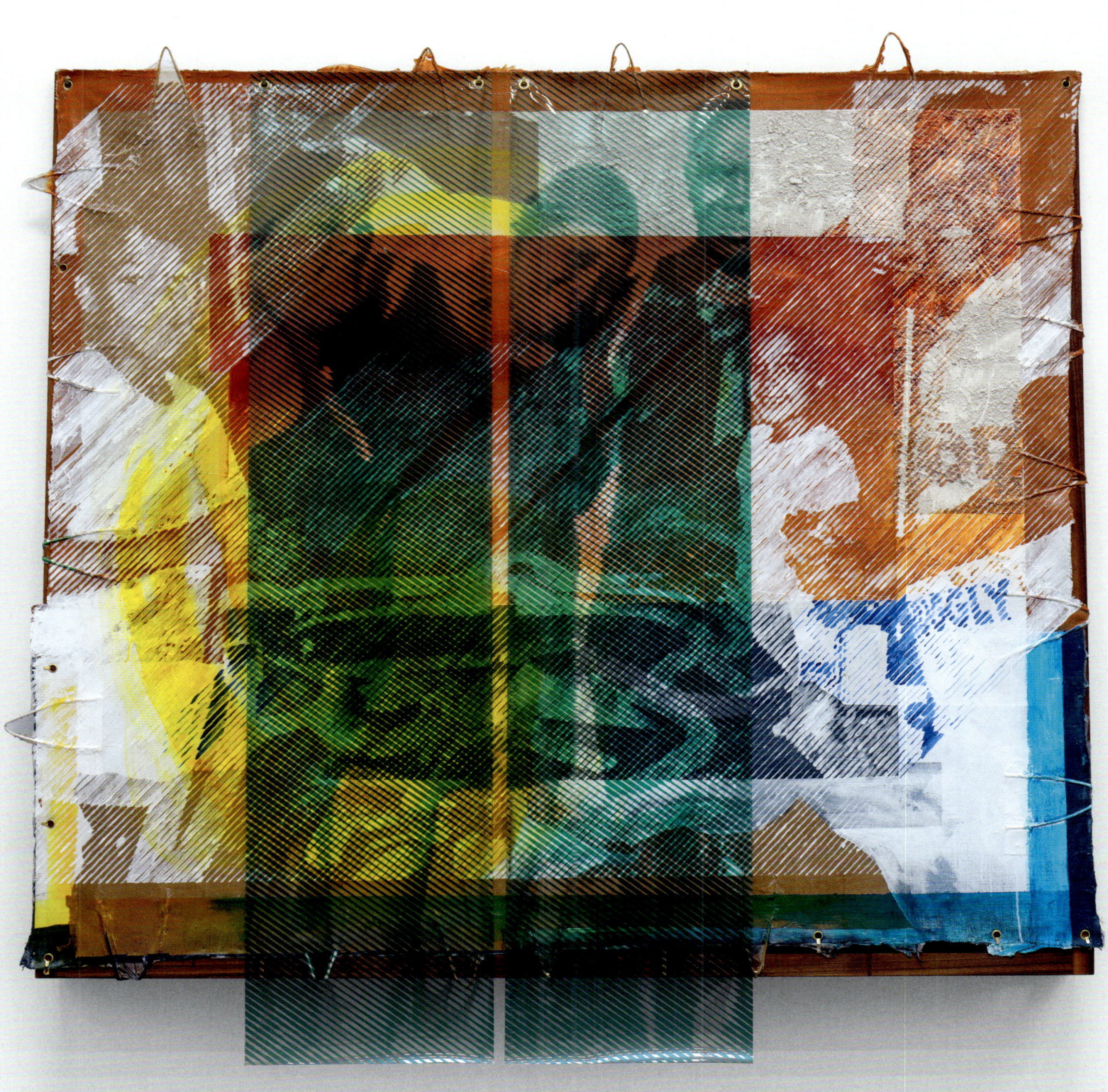

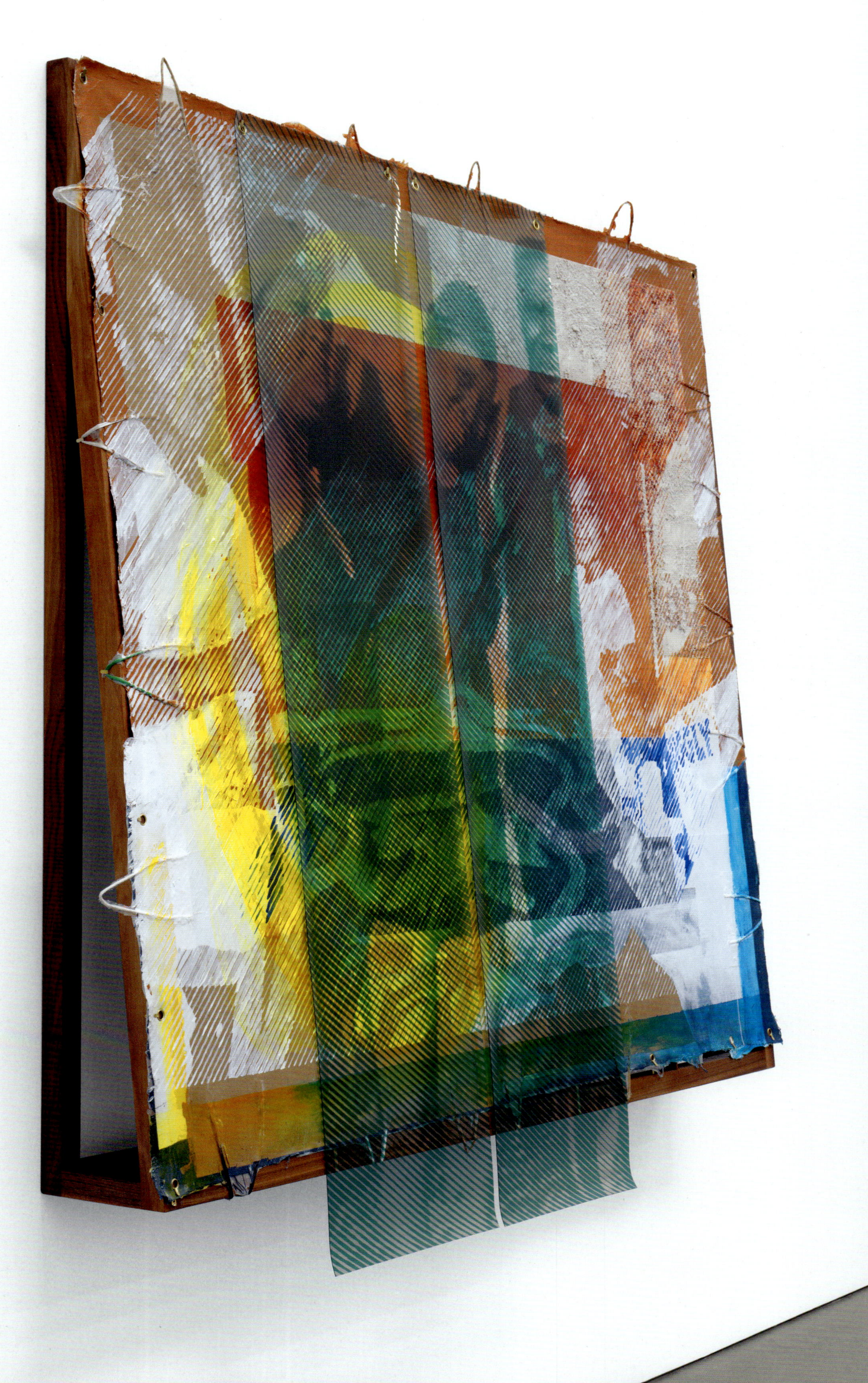

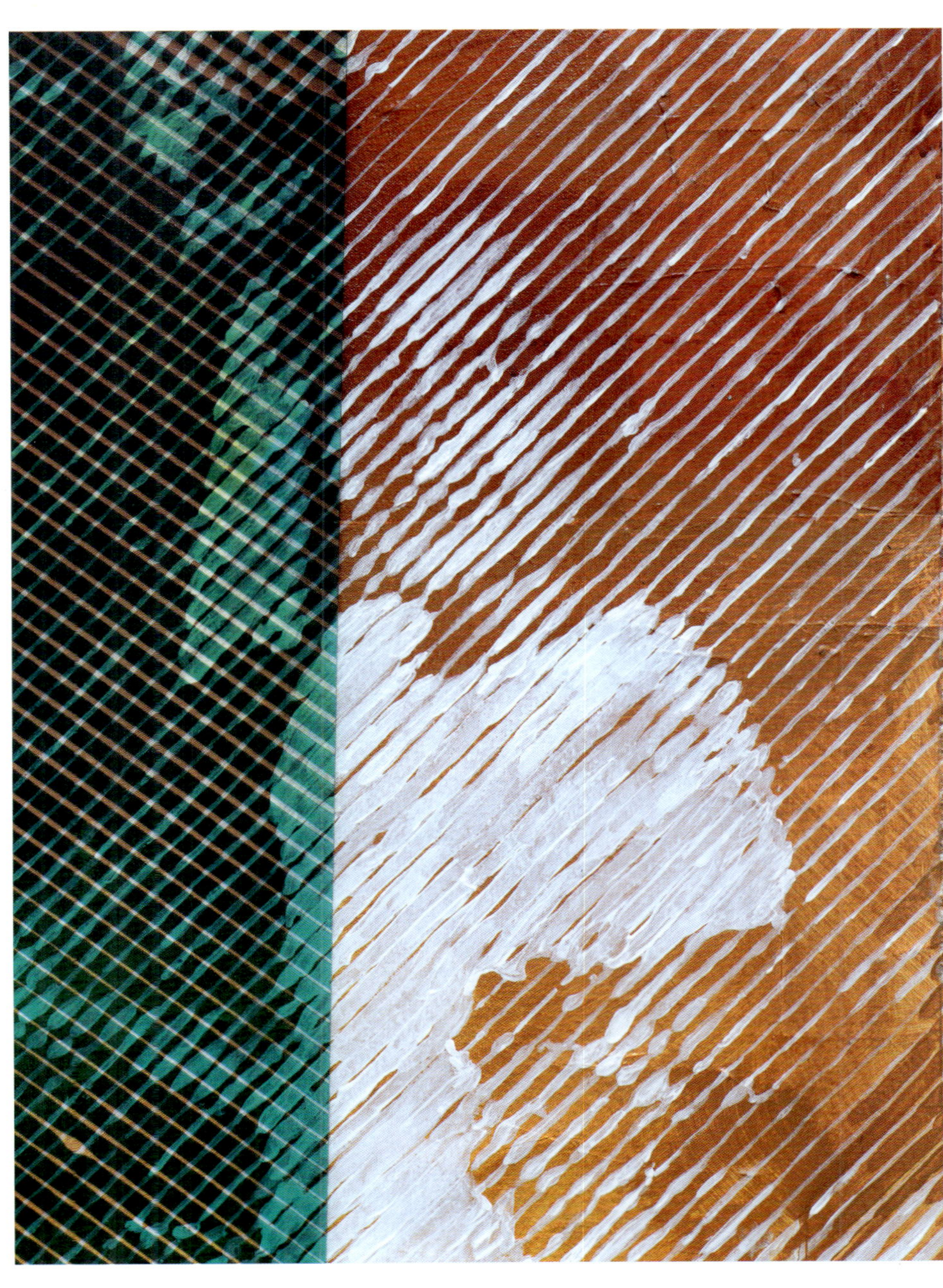

*Among Sisters and Brothers
(Three Families)*, 2021

Acrylic and soil from the Parrish Art Museum
grounds, a former potato field, on canvas,
cotton textiles, paper potato bags, and paper
bags with archival prints on PVC marine vinyl
mounted on a handcrafted redwood awning
structure with brass hooks and grommets

74½ × 75½ × 9¼ inches

Courtesy the artist and Tilton Gallery,
New York

Transformed halftone line image painted on substrate:
The Wingfield sisters (standing, left to right) Alice
Wingfield, Louise Barnard, Roxanne Dozier, Florence
Brown, and Blanche Cherry (seated), 2001.
Courtesy Richard "Juni" Wingfield

Cropped halftone line image printed on PVC marine vinyl:
Group on Azurest Beach, Sag Harbor, NY, date unknown.
Courtesy Eastville Community Historical Society
Collection

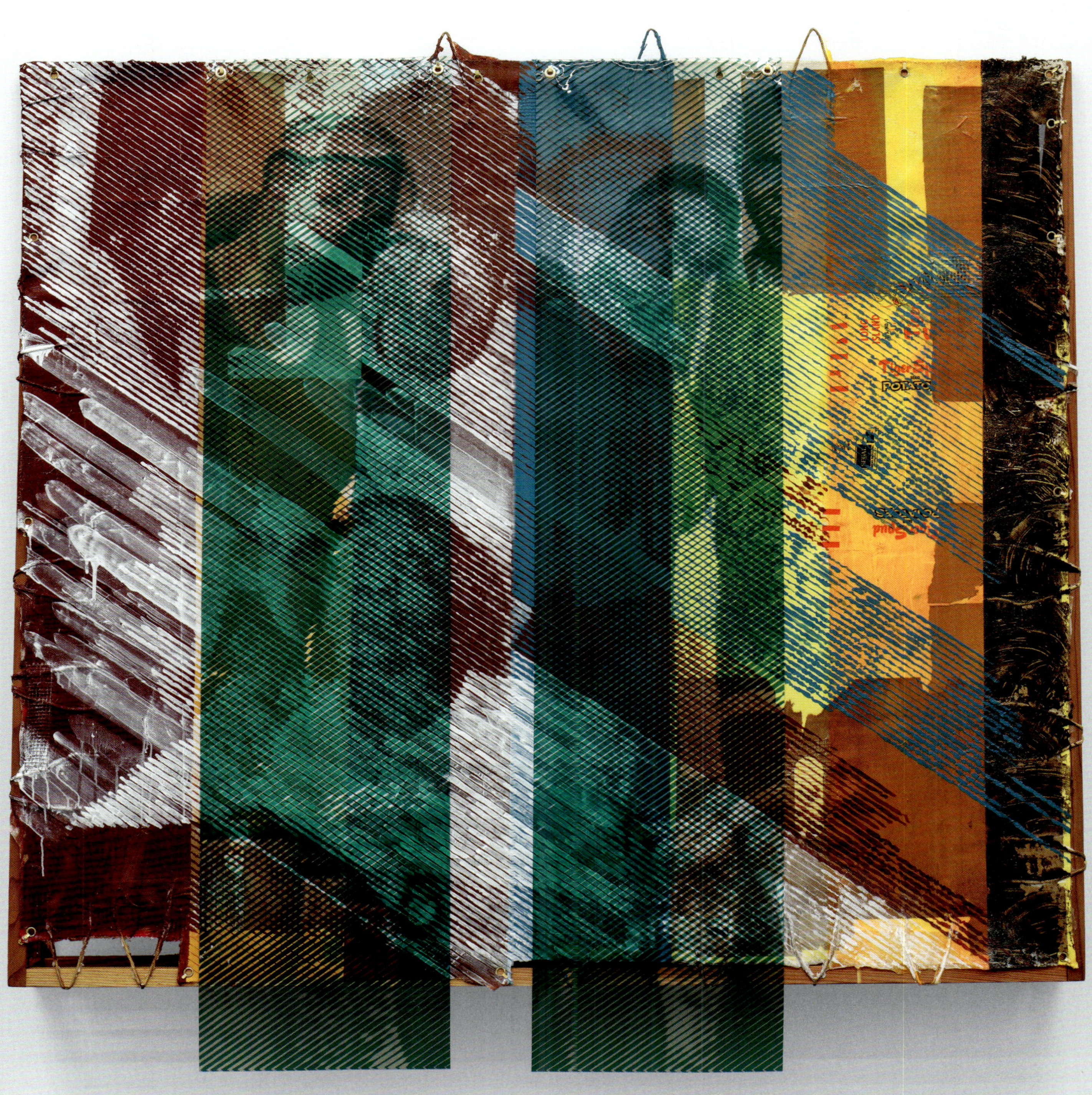

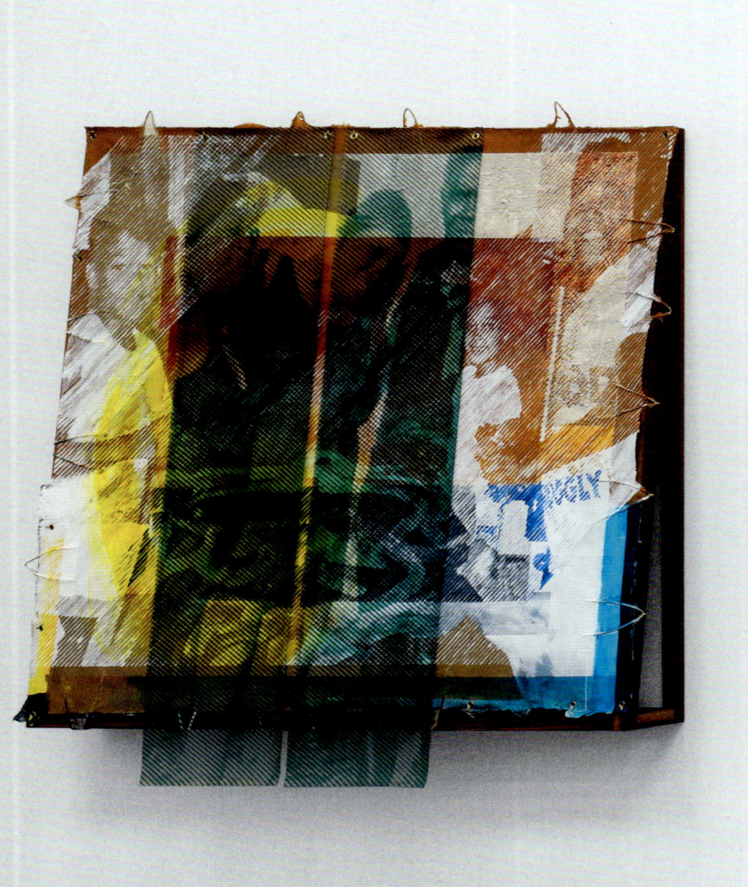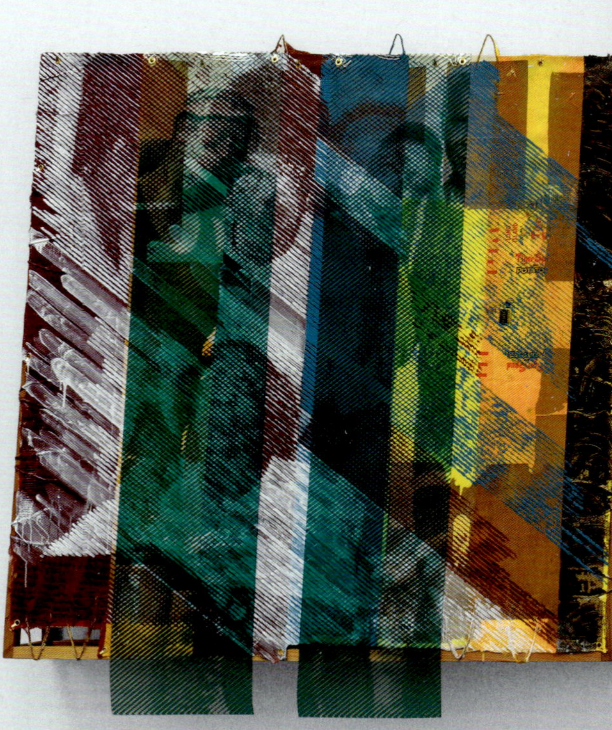

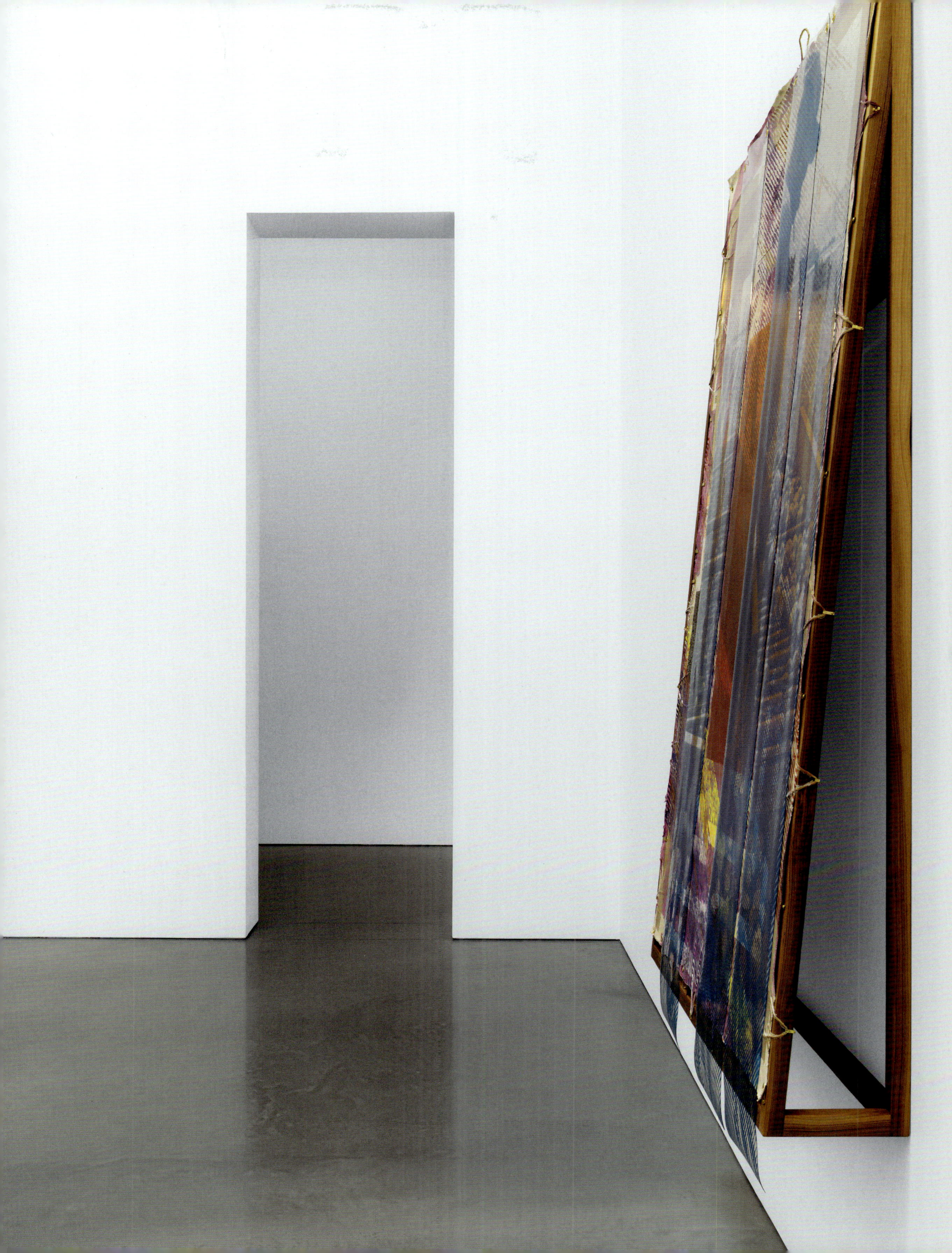

*Among Harvests (Aserrin
de colores),* 2021

Acrylic and soil from the Parrish Art Museum
grounds, a former potato field, on canvas,
cotton textiles, paper potato bags, and paper
bags with archival prints on PVC marine vinyl
mounted on a handcrafted walnut awning
structure with brass hooks and grommets

73½ × 78 × 9¼ inches

Courtesy the artist and Tilton Gallery,
New York

Transformed halftone line image painted on substrate:
Puerto Rican immigrants working on a potato farm,
ca. 1950.
Courtesy the Migration Division Collection at the
Archives of the Puerto Rican Diaspora. Center for
Puerto Rican Studies, Hunter College, City University
of New York

Cropped halftone line image printed on PVC marine vinyl:
"Most migrant workers now coming to Long Island are
from Guatemala, México, El Salvador and Colombia,"
according to a state Department of Labor spokesman,
2013.
Courtesy *The Suffolk Times* / Barbara Ellen Koch (file
photo)

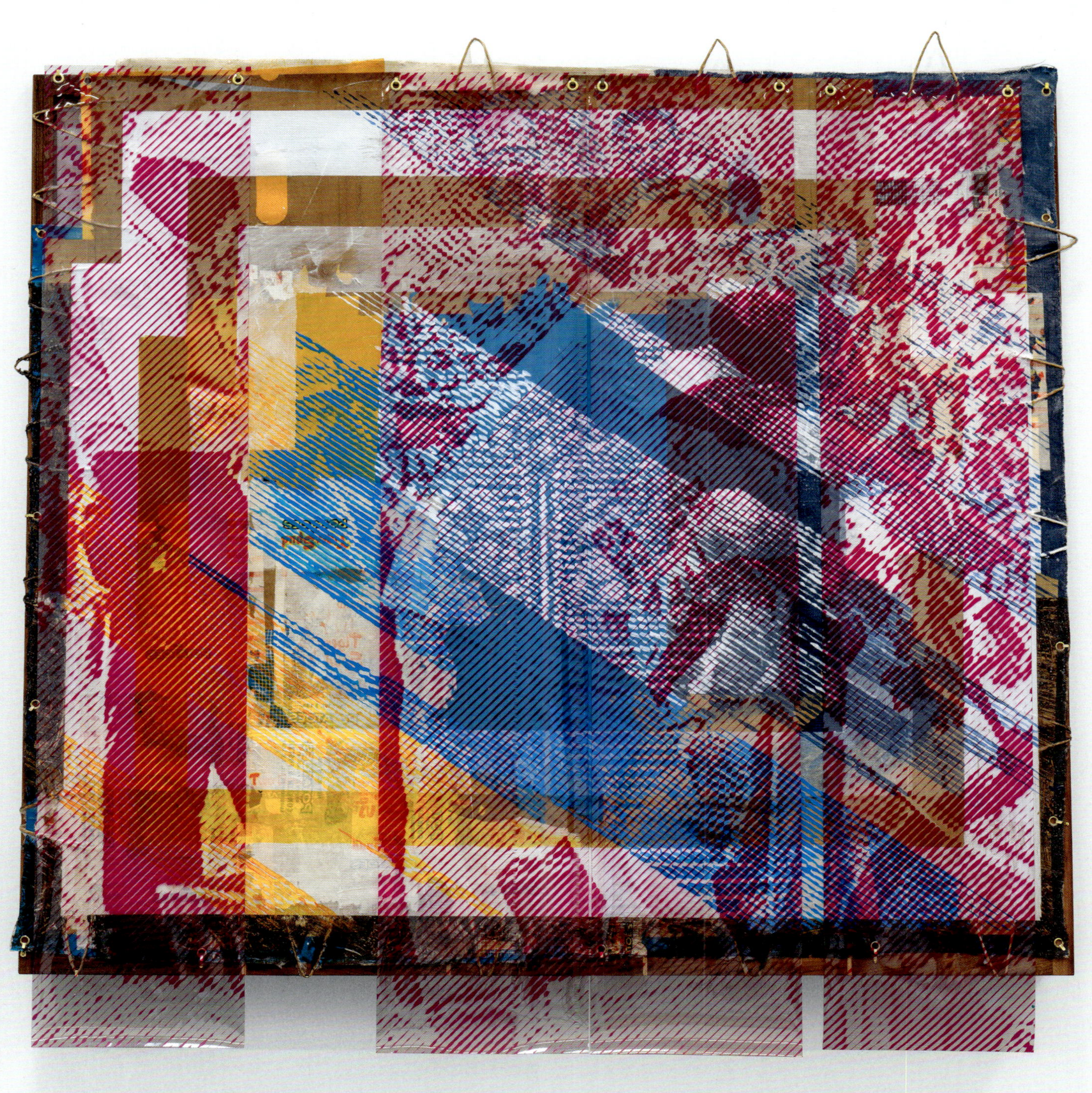

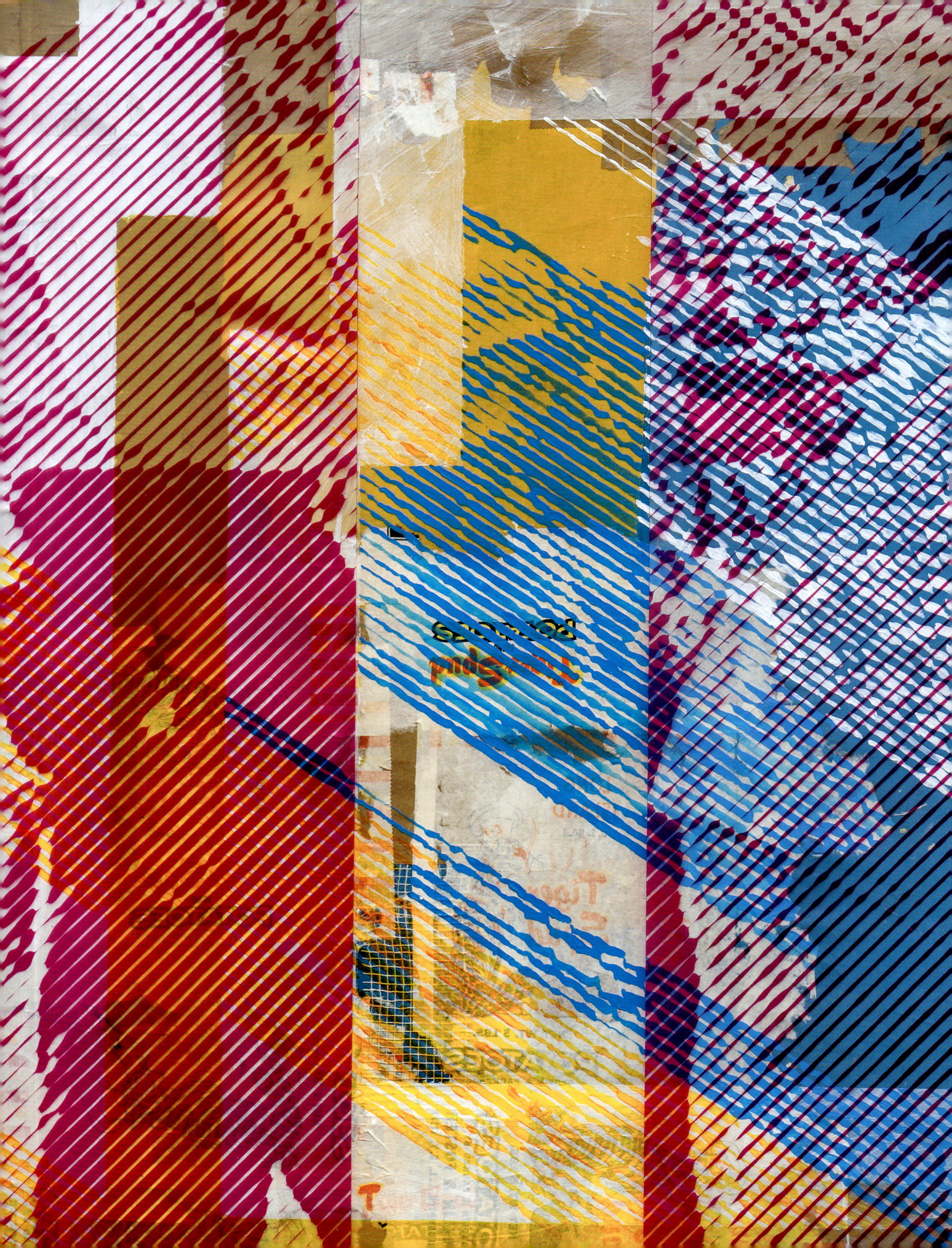

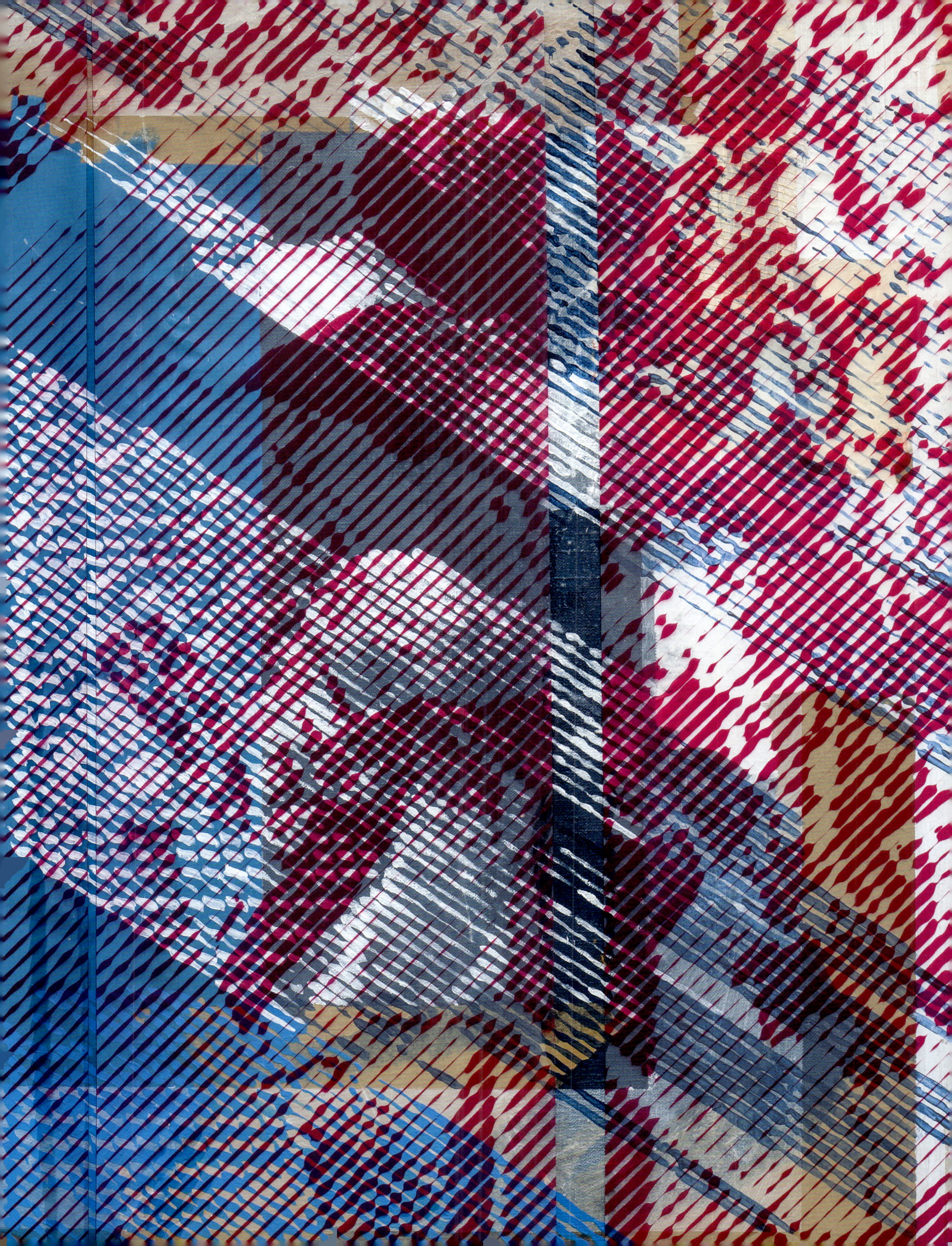

*Among Protectors (Hawthorne
Road and the Pell Case)*, 2021

Acrylic and wampum dust on canvas, paper
potato bags, and paper bags with archival
prints on PVC marine vinyl mounted on a
handcrafted Douglas fir awning structure
with brass hooks and grommets

74 × 76¾ × 9¼ inches

Courtesy the artist and Tilton Gallery,
New York

Transformed halftone line image painted on substrate:
Doreen Dennis sits in front of a bulldozer to protect
against illegal development on the Shinnecock Neck
territory, 1996.
Courtesy Express News Group

Cropped halftone line image printed on PVC marine vinyl:
Chenae Bullock sings a song to ask for protection of
the ancestors and for help from the universe to protect
sacred Shinnecock burial sites in the Shinnecock Hills,
2018.
Courtesy *Newsday* / Thomas A. Ferrara

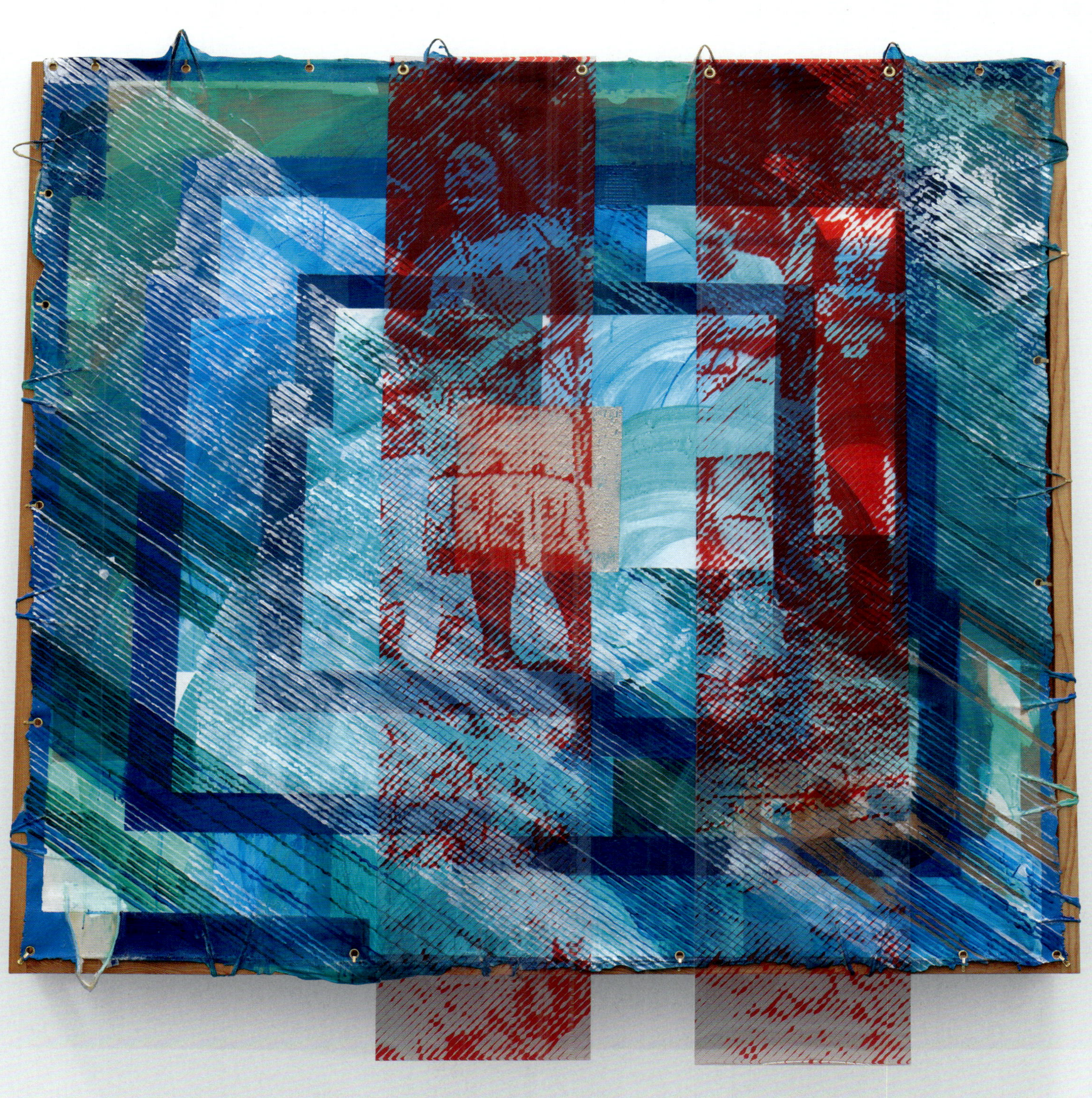

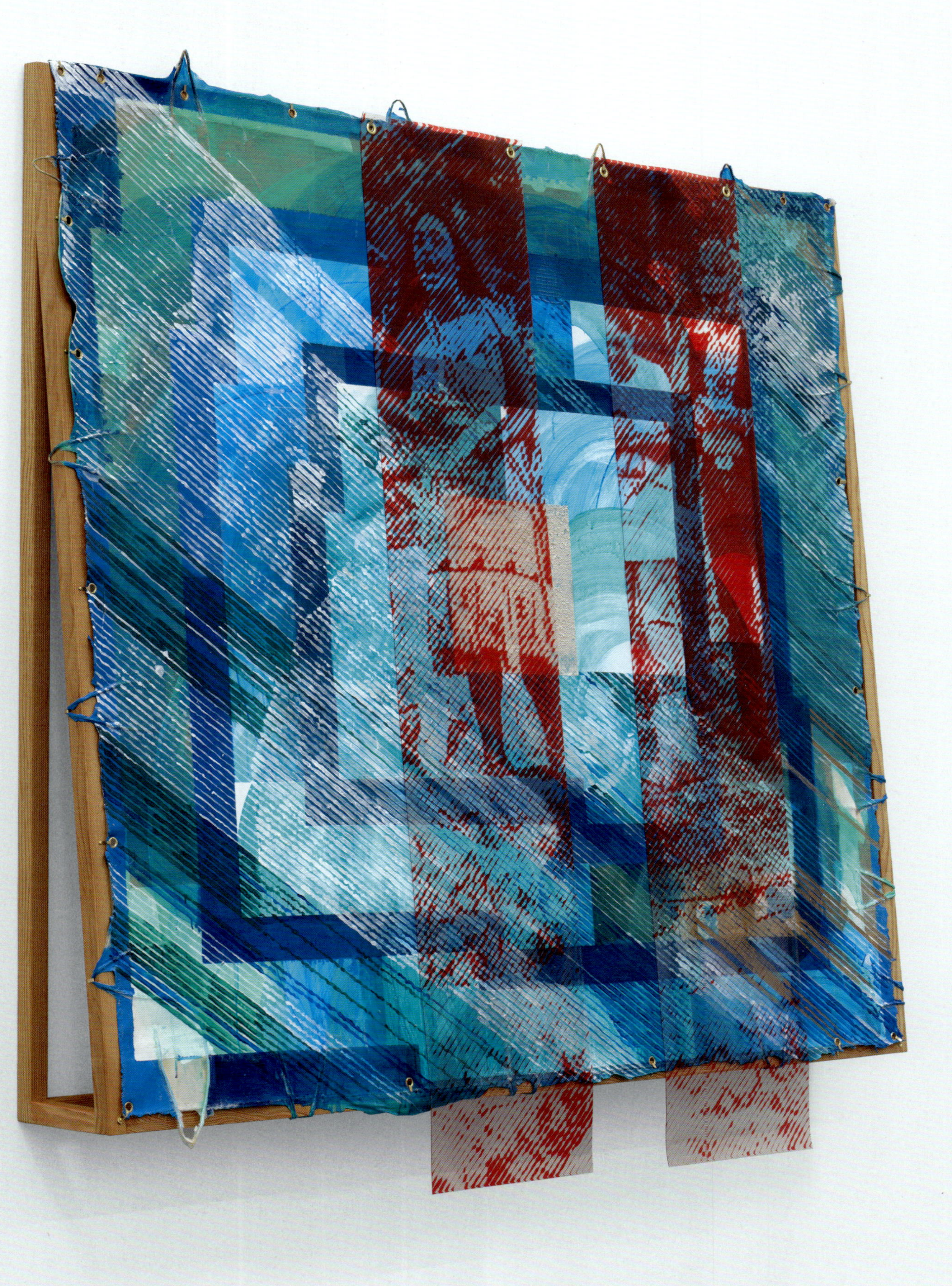

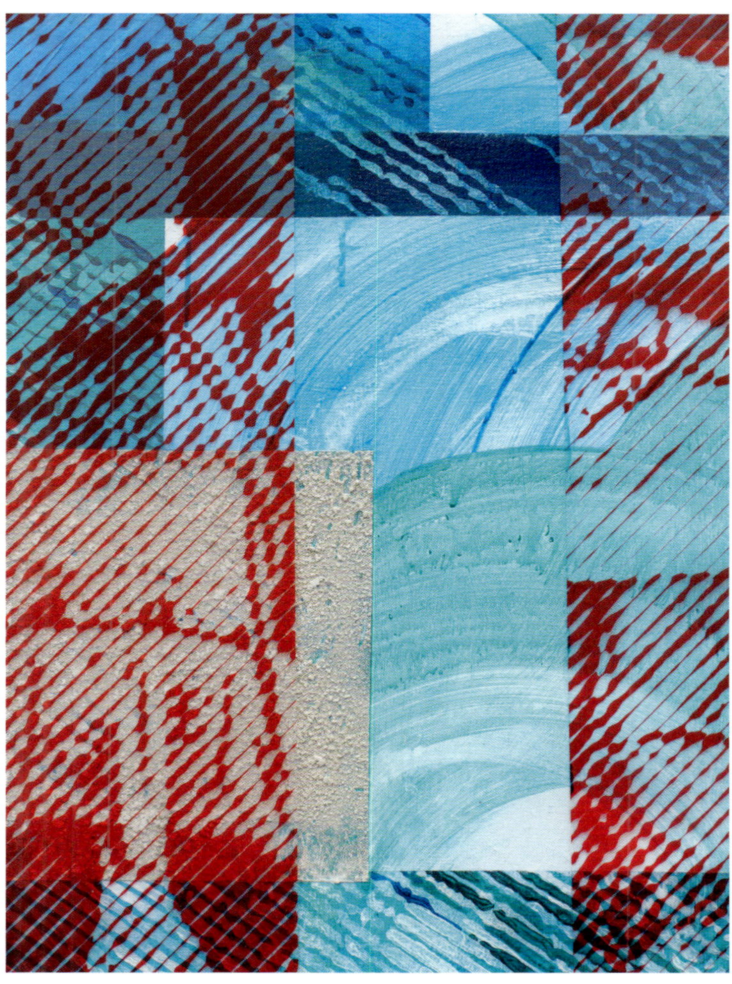

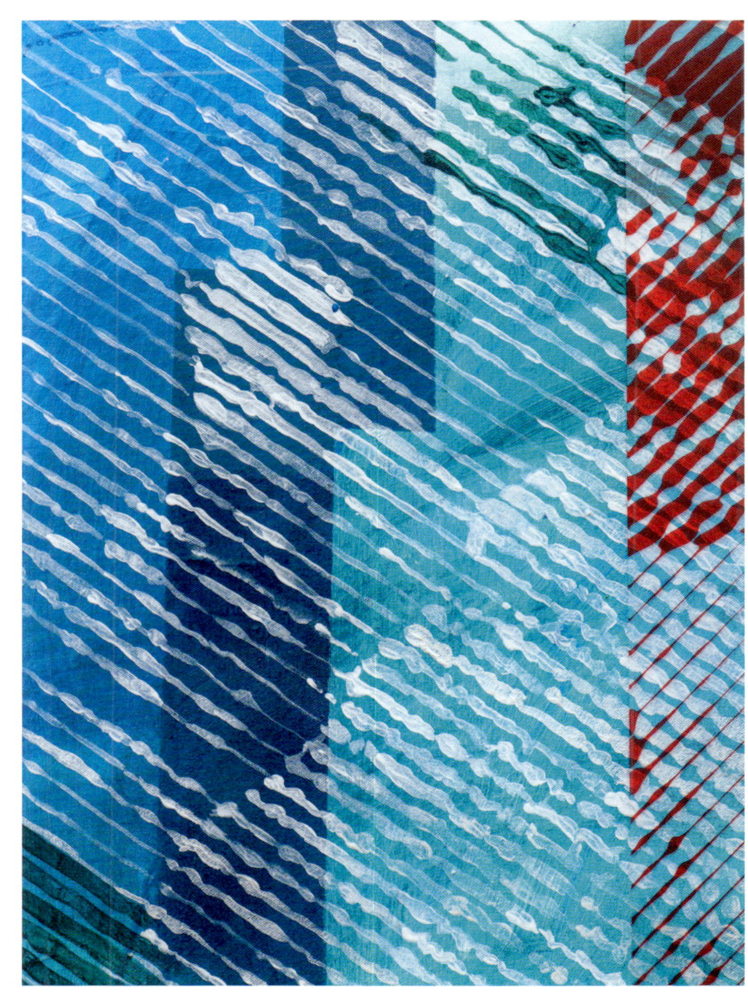

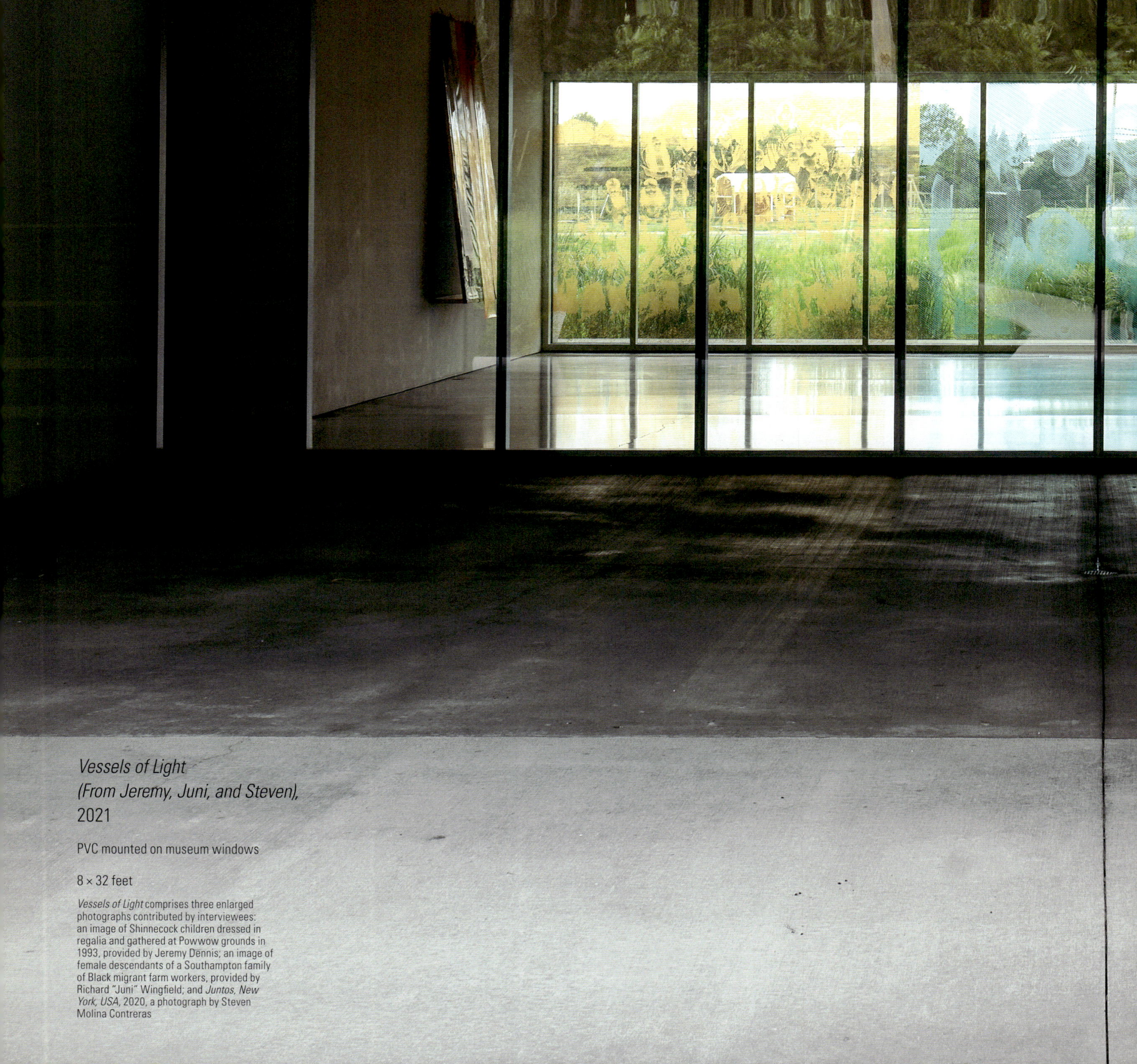

Vessels of Light
(From Jeremy, Juni, and Steven),
2021

PVC mounted on museum windows

8 × 32 feet

Vessels of Light comprises three enlarged photographs contributed by interviewees: an image of Shinnecock children dressed in regalia and gathered at Powwow grounds in 1993, provided by Jeremy Dennis; an image of female descendants of a Southampton family of Black migrant farm workers, provided by Richard "Juni" Wingfield; and *Juntos, New York, USA,* 2020, a photograph by Steven Molina Contreras

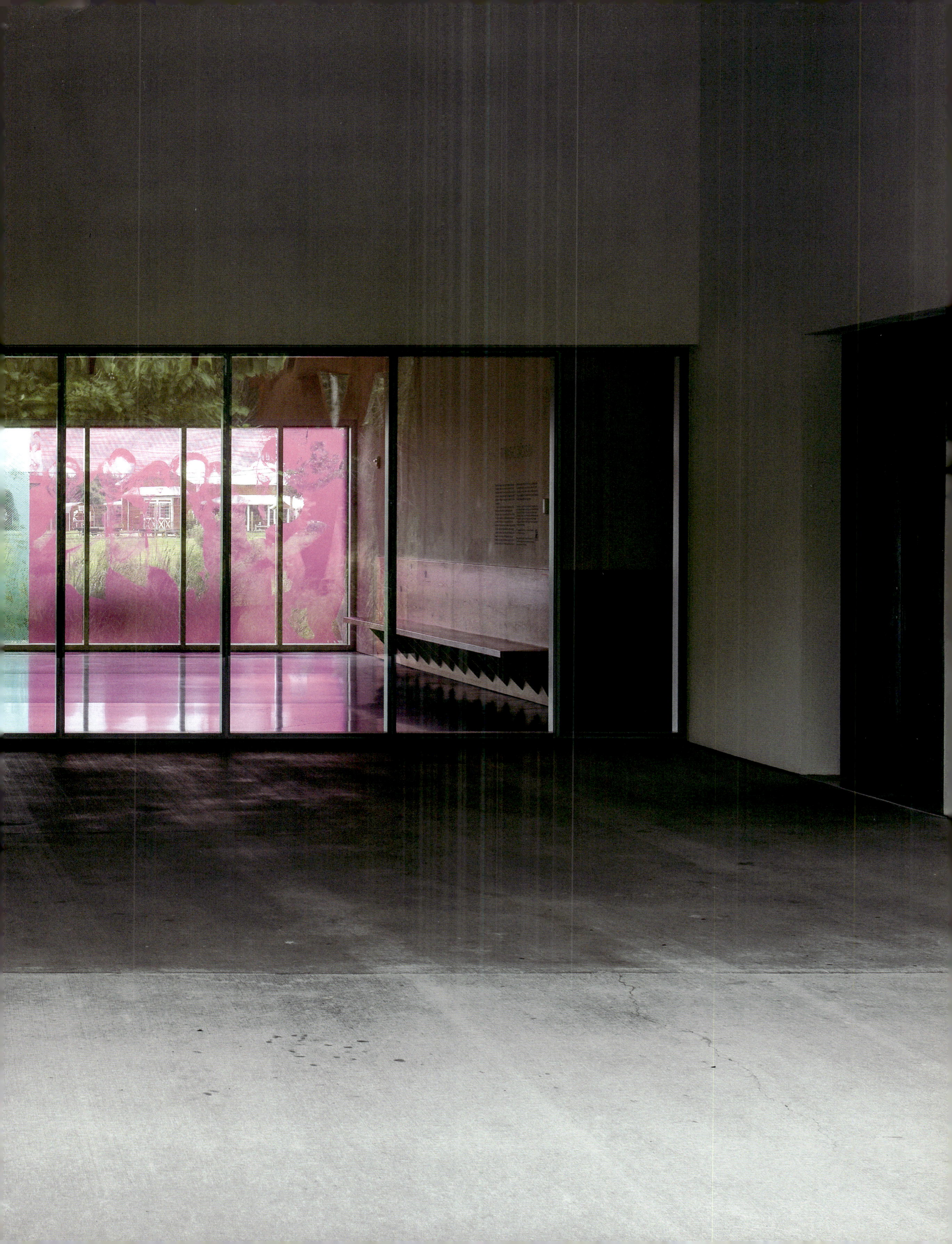

TOMASHI JACKSON

Born in Houston, 1980
Lives and works in New York City

EDUCATION

2019 Skowhegan School of Painting & Sculpture, Madison, ME

2016 MFA, Yale School of Art, New Haven, CT

2012 MS, Massachusetts Institute of Technology School of Architecture + Planning, Cambridge, MA

2010 BFA, The Cooper Union for the Advancement of Science and Art, New York

SOLO EXHIBITIONS

2021 *Tomashi Jackson: The Land Claim*, Parrish Art Museum, Water Mill, NY

Brown II, Radcliffe Institute for Advanced Study, Harvard University, Cambridge, MA

2020 *Love Rollercoaster*, Wexner Center for the Arts, Columbus, OH

Forever My Lady, Night Gallery, Los Angeles

2019 *Time Out of Mind*, Tilton Gallery, New York

2018 *Interstate Love Song*, Zuckerman Museum of Art, Kennesaw State University, Kennesaw, GA

2016 *The Subliminal is Now*, Tilton Gallery, New York

2014 *Love Economy: Emerging Visions of the African American Experience*, Michigan State University, Residential College in the Arts and Humanities, East Lansing

GROUP EXHIBITIONS

2021 *New Light: Encounters and Connections*, Museum of Fine Arts, Boston, MA

Now Is the Time: Recent Acquisitions to the Contemporary Collection, Baltimore Museum of Art

Off the Record, Solomon R. Guggenheim Museum, New York

Light, Miles McEnery Gallery, New York (curated by Rico Gatson)

2021 Texas Biennial: A New Landscape, A Possible Horizon, San Antonio and Houston

2020 *States of Mind: Art and American Democracy*, Moody Center for the Arts, Rice University, Houston

Majeure Force, Night Gallery, Los Angeles

Young, Gifted, and Black: The Lumpkin-Boccuzzi Family Collection of Contemporary Art, Lehman College Art Gallery, The Bronx, New York

Slowed and Throwed: Records of the City Through Mutated Lenses, Contemporary Arts Museum Houston; traveled to Artpace, San Antonio

2019 *Great Force*, Institute for Contemporary Art, Virginia Commonwealth University, Richmond

Rosebud, Matthew Marks Gallery, Los Angeles

cart, horse, cart, Lehmann Maupin, New York (curated by Michael Goodson)

Hold On, Hold Me, Charles Moffett, New York (curated by Kenny Rivero)

Whitney Biennial, Whitney Museum of American Art, New York (curated by Rujeko Hockley and Jane Panetta)

Hinge Pictures: Eight Women Artists Occupy the Third Dimension, Contemporary Arts Center New Orleans

2018 *The Strangeness Will Wear Off*, David Castillo Gallery, Miami

New Suns, Galeria Páramo, Guadalajara, Mexico

Nine Moments for Now, The Ethelbert Cooper Gallery of African & American Art, The Hutchins Center for African & African American Research, Harvard University, Cambridge, MA

Take Up Space, Pizzuti Collection of the Columbus Museum of Art, Columbus, OH

What We Make, Richard M. Ross Art Museum, Ohio Wesleyan University, Delaware, OH

Cosmic Traffic Jam, Zevitas Marcus, Los Angeles

Form Shapes Language, Morán Morán, Los Angeles

Surface of a Sphere, Klowden Mann, Los Angeles

Give and Take: Highlighting Recent Acquisitions, Museum of Contemporary Art, Los Angeles

Re:Framed, Re: Art Show, Brooklyn, NY (curated by Jane Cavalier and Nicole Kaack)

The Legacy of the Cool: A Tribute to Barkley L. Hendricks, Massachusetts College of Art and Design, Boston

2017 *On Documentary Abstraction*, ArtCenter/South Florida, Miami Beach

Souvenirs: New New York Icons, Storefront for Art and Architecture, New York

Immigrancy, Samson Projects, Boston

Say It Loud: Art, History, Rebellion, The Charles H. Wright Museum of African American History, Detroit

In the Abstract, MASS MoCA, North Adams, MA

2016 *Double Dip*, Yale School of Art, New Haven, CT

2015 "Tools for Remediation (Red76 Artist Collective)," *Hippie Modernism: The Struggle for Utopia*, Walker Art Center, Minneapolis

Art in Odd Places 2015: RECALL, Ideas City, New Museum, New York

RESPOND, Smack Mellon, Brooklyn, NY

2014 History Design Studio, The Hutchins Center for African & African American Research, Harvard University, Cambridge, MA

Living as Form, Carpenter Center for Visual Arts, Harvard University, Cambridge, MA

The Measure of All Things, Claire Trevor School of the Arts, University of California, Irvine

2013 *Exile*, El Rincón Social, Houston

2012 *Bring Your Own Beamer*, Knockdown Center, Queens, NY

Art in Odd Places 2012: MODEL, New York

Bruceforma, Performance Dome, MoMA PS1, Long Island City, NY

2011 *Experience Economies 4: A Chamber Play*, Harvard University, Cambridge, MA

2010 The Brucennial: Bruceforma 2, Bruce High Quality Foundation, New York, NY

Going Under, The Cooper Union, New York

2009 *Liberating Landscapes*, Togonon Gallery, San Francisco

Fever Grass (Benjamin Menschel Fellowship Exhibition), The Cooper Union, New York

2008 *Drawing Atmosphere*, Super Front Architectural Exhibition Space, Brooklyn, NY

Publication-Schmublication, Broadway Gallery, New York

2007 *For All We Know*, The Cooper Union, New York

2001 *Soul on Rice: A Two-Woman Exhibition*, Togonon Gallery, San Francisco

PROFESSIONAL EXPERIENCE AND RESIDENCIES

2021 Inga Maren Otto Fellow and artist in residence, The Watermill Center, Water Mill, NY

Visiting lecturer, Harvard University, Cambridge, MA

2019 ARCAthens Visual Art Fellow, Athens, Greece

Adjunct professor of sculpture, The Cooper Union School of Art, New York

2018 Adjunct professor of painting, Rhode Island School of Design, Providence

Adjunct professor of drawing, The Cooper Union School of Art, New York

2017 Adjunct professor of painting, Rhode Island School of Design, Providence

Assistant professor, Studio for Interrelated Media, Massachusetts College of Art and Design, Boston

2016 Adjunct professor of drawing, Massachusetts College of Art and Design, Boston

Visiting artist and guest critic, New York University, New York

Game Recognize Game: Artists and Athletes Speaker Series, Yale University, New Haven, CT

2015–2016 Guest critic, Massachusetts College of Art and Design, Boston

Appointed teacher's assistant, Yale School of Art, New Haven, CT

2011–2013 Video editor for Otto Piene and Elizabeth Goldring, Boston

2011 Organizer, *The Uncertainty Principle* by Bernard Burke, live play reading, Massachusetts Institute of Technology, Cambridge, MA

Organizer, TalkDraw@MIT, Massachusetts Institute of Technology, Cambridge, MA

Artist in residence, The Buckley School, Sherman Oaks, CA

2009 Curator, *Fever Grass* (Benjamin Menschel Fellowship Exhibition), The Cooper Union, New York

2008 Curator, *Drawing Atmosphere*, Super Front Architectural Exhibition Space, Brooklyn, NY

Everything There and Not There, Broadway Gallery, New York

Curator, *Publication-Schmublication*, Broadway Gallery, New York

Lead facilitator, Harlem School for the Arts, New York

FELLOWSHIPS, GRANTS, AND AWARDS

2020 Joan Mitchell Foundation Painters & Sculptors Grant

2019 The Andy Warhol Foundation for the Visual Arts Grant for Support for a Single Exhibition at the Parrish Art Museum, Southampton, NY, summer 2020

2016 Toby Devan Lewis Prize 2016, Yale School of Art, New Haven, CT

2015–2016 Blair Dickinson Memorial Scholarship, Yale University School of Art, New Haven, CT

2015 Alice Kimball English Traveling Fellowship, Yale University School of Art, New Haven, CT

JUNCTURE: Explorations in Art and Human Rights Law Fellowship, Orville H. Schell, Jr. Center for International Human Rights, Yale Law School, New Haven, CT

2012 Graduate Student Life Grant, Office of the Dean of Graduate Education, Massachusetts Institute of Technology, Cambridge, MA

2011 Diversity Fellowship, Office of the Dean of Graduate Education, Massachusetts Institute of Technology, Cambridge, MA

Project Grant, Council for the Arts, Massachusetts Institute of Technology, Cambridge, MA

2010–2011 Presidential Tuition Fellowship, Massachusetts Institute of Technology, Cambridge, MA

2010 Richard Lewis Bloch Memorial Prize, The Cooper Union, New York

2008 Benjamin Menschel Fellowship for Creative Inquiry, The Cooper Union, New York

2005 Full-tuition scholarship, The Cooper Union, New York

PUBLIC COLLECTIONS

The Solomon R. Guggenheim Museum, New York

Museum of Contemporary Art, Los Angeles

Pizzuti Collection of the Columbus Museum of Art, Columbus, OH

Whitney Museum of American Art, New York

Baltimore Museum of Art

Museum of Fine Arts, Boston

The Studio Museum in Harlem, New York

PUBLICATIONS

Sargent, Antwaun, ed. *Young, Gifted and Black: A New Generation of Artists.* Distributed Art Publishers, 2020.

Sarra, Janis, and Cheryl L. Wade. *Predatory Lending and the Destruction of the African-American Dream.* Cambridge University Press, 2020. Jacket art by Tomashi Jackson.

Jackson, Tomashi, and Jennifer Roberts. *Brown II.* Edited by Rachel Vogel. Radcliffe Institute for Advanced Study, Harvard University, 2020.